Ch'ang Hon Taekwon-do Hae Sul

Real Applications To The ITF Patterns

CheckPoint
Press

Ch'ang Hon Taekwon-do Hae Sul

Real Applications To The ITF Patterns

By Stuart Paul Anslow

창
헌
류
태
권
도
해
설

2nd Edition

蒼
軒
流
跆
拳
道
解
說

Warning

This book contains dangerous techniques which can result in serious injury or death. Neither the author nor publishers can accept any responsibility for any prosecution or proceedings brought or instituted against any person or body as a result of the use or misuse of information or techniques described or detailed within this book or any injury, loss or damage caused thereby. Some of the techniques and training methods described in this book require high levels of skill, control and fitness and should only be practiced by those in good health and under the supervision of a qualified instructor.

Ch'ang Hon Taekwon-do Hae Sul

Real Applications To The ITF Patterns

By Stuart Paul Anslow

2nd Edition

Photographs by David Lane

Cover Layout and Chapter Graphics by Dennis Potipako

Interior Layout by Stuart Anslow

Edited by Gill Nightingale

British Library Cataloguing In Publication Data

A Record of this Publication is available

from the British Library

ISBN 978-1-906628-04-8

2nd Edition Published 2009 by

CheckPoint Press, Dooagh, Achill Island, Co.Mayo, Republic of Ireland

Tel: 00353 9843779   www.checkpointpress.com

Disclaimer: Various pictures and information related to the *'Pattern Introduction'* sections of this book been researched and sourced via the world wide web. Though every effort has been made to obtain the necessary permissions with reference to copyright material, both illustrative and quoted; should there be any omissions in this respect we apologise and shall be pleased to make the appropriate acknowledgements or remove the material in any future editions.

'For Chloe, Callum, Logan and Jorja
My Ki'

'Two roads diverged in a wood, and I took the one less travelled,
And that has made all the difference'

Acknowledgements

If I saw this far, it is because I stood upon the shoulders of giants

- Isaac Newton

Writing a book of this magnitude doesn't just happen, and these pages are dedicated to those who helped me along the path to where I am today, as well as those that helped with the book itself.

My appreciation and admiration goes out to my first (and only) instructors in Taekwon-do, Sabum David Bryan, 6th degree and Sabum John Pepper, 2nd degree (now retired from teaching). Both these instructors I hold in the highest regard and no matter what grade I become in the future, they are and always will be my instructors and my seniors. They laid the foundation to both myself and in a way, this book and I am forever grateful for their patient and guidance as I travelled my path.

I would also like to express my appreciation and thanks to my original training partner, John O'Conner, whom I have had full on sparring sessions with too many times to be under any misapprehensions that overly showy techniques work for real… he takes no prisoners when sparring, and is enough to open chinks in anyone's armour. John and I graded 1st and 2nd degree together and he has always supported any moves I have made.

Many thanks as well goes to my good friend, Derrick Clarke, whom despite being an accountant (LOL) is a formidable Taekwon-do exponent and has supported me since his early days at our original club and continues to do so, for which I am eternally grateful.

This book and my own knowledge has been enhanced immensely via my many conversations with my friend and fellow Taekwon-do instructor Yi, Yun Wook. For many years now we have exchanged information on all facets of Taekwon-do and though he always claims it's a two way street, I feel I am more indebted to him than he should be of me. Wook wrote the '*Ki*' chapter in this book especially for me, and many other details in this book have directly or indirectly come from him. Thank you my friend.

My appreciation and thanks goes to David Lane, one of my students, who aside from his dedication to Taekwon-do, agreed to take the hundreds of photographs contained within this book, as well as appearing in some himself. Thank you as well to Dennis Potipako for helping with the cover design and the funky images that accompany the chapters.

Of course I must thank all the students of Rayners Lane Taekwon-do Academy who gamely agreed to take part in the photo shoots for the book. For the record they are: Vikram Gautam (Rayners Lane Taekwon-do Academy's assistant instructor), Farhad Ahmad, Parvez Sultan, Dev Patel, Tomasz Kubicki, Lyndsey Sainsbury, Colin Avis, Fayaz Latifi, Lloyd Lewis, David Lane,

Priya Shah, Paaras Tank, Sonal Lakhman, Kanai Brand, Ben Clarke, Sharad Nakarja, Kate Barry, Vijay Sood, Abdi Yassin, Abhijay Sood, Saphaa Simab, Zuhayr Chagpar, Dennis Potipako, Saphwat Simab, Richard Simon, Marek Handzel, Joseph Lewis, Jammal Yassin, Qadir Marikar, Vikram Bakshi, Omid Sekanderzada and Simon Courtenage. Many of whom allowed the applications to be performed on them for real in order to attain the reality you can see in the photographs.

Many thanks also to Karl Webb for the linage tree found in Chapter 1, Andy Wright for his assistance with information regarding Shotokan katas, Iain Abernethy for his help and advice on both Karate and publishing matters, Rick Clark for checking the Pressure Point reference section, Manuel Adrogue for pointing me in the direction of some great resources and Ron Hartman for his invaluable resources with regards to the introductory text of the patterns.

Last but by no means least my thanks and appreciation goes to my partner Gill Nightingale, who fully supported my endeavours and put up with my many extra hours away from home, doing the photo shoots for the book and many lonely nights whilst I tapped away at the computer, thank you for proof reading and helping to edit the final version.

'One does not need buildings, money, power or status to practise the art of peace, heaven is right now where you are standing and that is the place to train.'
– Morihei Ueshiba

Foreword by Yi, Yun Wook

I have met many practitioners of various martial arts since I started Taekwon-do some 30+ years ago. I was trained by some of the best of the military Taekwon-do drill instructors under the direct auspices of General Choi, Hong Hi, the founder of Taekwon-do. I realized what Taekwon-do excellence was from these instructors: Solid basic foundations from the beginning. They were found in force flowing in the basic moves; in the tuls (patterns); in choreographed three-step up to multiple attacker free sparring; in hosinsul (self-defense); and destruction techniques. The standardized Taekwon-do curriculum of basics, patterns, sparring, hosinsul, and destruction all carried equal weight. The standardized curriculum were executed by applying the distinct theory of power only Ch'ang Hon Taekwon-do offered.

Destruction: Two x 5 cm (2 inches) thick concrete edgings without spacers

Over the years, things have changed. People opted for getting the next belt with less effort. Riding on the same bandwagon, unscrupulous *"masters"* often used quick sales pitch to make profits for this popular martial art called Taekwon-do. The quality instructors decreased as instructors ready-for-profit would forego many basic moves essential for the strong foundation of Taekwon-do. More students flocked to the lesser quality instructors for ease of effort. Excellence in Taekwon-do waned as only *"tag kicking"* became the rage in the sports arena and less skilled unscrupulous instructors joined in the foray of self-marketing.

The philosophy of these *"masters"* of *"why bother teach unnecessary moves that gets in the way of quick profits?"* further allowed essential basic techniques to disappear at a horrendous rate. Some *"masters"* even made *"absolutely no-contact rules"* in Taekwon-do (less insurance, more students, and quick promotion fees). In traditional Taekwon-do, there are at least 7 basic elbow strikes TIMES several angles based on 3 dimensional space and your target. You trained your elbows over and over on different angles and targets, with training equipment and partners. The same training is applied to all the other techniques in Taekwon-Do. The techniques eventually became part of your survival instinct; the true essence of the martial art.

The effectiveness of this type of training proved itself during the Vietnam War. Even 3rd degree black belts and higher ranks in watered down Taekwon-do nowadays would not know how and when to apply what elbow strikes. Or worse, come to realize *"that many"* elbow strikes or target practice training regimen for each different elbow strike, even existed. Another disconcerting point in present day Taekwon-do is lack of respect towards other martial arts. There is no one superior martial art. They all complement each other. True practitioners of any martial art respect other martial arts. False *"Taekwon-do masters"* set out to disrespect other arts and eventually brought disrespect to Taekwon-do itself.

Stuart Anslow, has maintained the tradition of excellence with his standardized Taekwon-do curriculum. His persistence, perseverance, and passion in Taekwon-do well exceeds even the spirit of some of the pioneer Korean Taekwon-do masters I have known. Moreover, he has the insatiable curiosity to learn as a student. He wants nothing less than excellence when teaching

Taekwon-do. He practices what he preaches. His performance in tournaments (how many instructors nowadays actually attend tournaments to compete against others along with their students?), his students performance in tournaments, his website, and his discussions with me over the years well attest to this fact.

This excellent book, one of its kind, reveals what is hidden in Ch'ang Hon tuls and is an epitome of Mr. Anslow's culmination of perfection and excellence over the years. Many techniques and applications in Ch'ang Hon tuls faded away as Taekwon-do transitioned from a military martial art into a civilian martial art. The only ones who still knew the actual applications were spread out among the first generation Taekwon-do Grandmasters who were under General Choi.

This book is a compilation of Mr. Anslow's quest to find the lost techniques. The techniques and applications he has in this book are what Mr. Anslow's research found (along with his own studies), and sourced together what numerous 1st generation Korean Taekwon-do Grandmasters originally taught, but have since stopped teaching - the true applications. They are the *"lost techniques"* from the first generation Taekwon-do Grandmasters. This book in essence brings back the *"lost legacy"* of Gen. Choi's Ch'ang Hon Taekwon-do.

I know of neither a Western nor a Korean author who has gone this far to publish a book on Ch'ang Hon Taekwon-do tul/pattern analysis with such passion in Taekwon-do as Mr. Stuart Anslow. I am already looking forward to Volume 2 with great anticipation.

- 李演郁 (*Yi, Yun Wook*)

Mr. Yi, Yun Wook is a Taekwon-do Instructor with over 30 years experience whom first received martial art lessons from his father; a retired General and Korean War veteran, who was a graduate of the Korean Military Academy and studied Judo, Shito-Ryu Karate, Okinawan Karate and Tang Soo Do, he was also a Taekwon-do instructor in the military when it was being formulated and finally named "Taekwon-do".

Mr. Yi, Yun Wook has trained under some of the most awesome and legendary instructors in Taekwon-do (listed in order of training):

- Grandmaster Lim, Won Sup of Sweden, former military Taekwon-do instructor during the Vietnam War and member of the elite instructor group to North Korea led by General Choi. Head of AMEA.[1]

- Master Nhumey Tropp of Seattle, Washington, USA trained by Grandmaster C. K. Choi, 1st generation Taekwon-do Grandmaster.[2]

- Grandmaster J. H. Kim of Boston, Massachusetts, USA trained by General Choi, founder of Taekwon-do.[3]

- Grandmaster Lee, Myung Woo former military Taekwon-do instructor during the Vietnam War, now of Master Lee's Black Belt Academy in Mill Creek, Washington, USA.

- Grandmaster Hee IL Cho of Honolulu, Hawaii, USA. Member of the 1st graduating class of military Taekwon-do instructors by General Choi to be sent overseas. Head of AIMAA.[4]

---

[1] http://www.amea.nu/maineng.htm

[2] http://www.seattlemartialarts.com

[3] http://www.tkd-boston.com

[4] http://www.aimaa.com

Foreword by Iain Abernethy

In recent years we have seen an ever growing number of martial artists re-evaluating all aspects of their training. Whereas once people would practise without ever questioning or testing the information received, today's martial artist wants to fully understand their art. They want to know why the techniques are performed as they are, they want to understand how to correctly apply the techniques, they want to understand the origins and development of their art, and they want to know how to brining it all together to make the art work.

This new questioning approach to the martial arts has brought innumerable benefits to all the martial arts and their practitioners. For practitioners of traditional systems, a key benefit has been the growing number of people revaluating the role of Kata, forms and patterns. In many modern schools the forms are used as physical exercise, art for art's sake, an internal quest for perfection, or even as a "refuge" for those who wish to avoid the martial side of the arts. But is that all they have to offer? Surely, as a key part of the martial arts, they must have a combative function?

As a karateka, it always seemed obvious to me that there must be a reason why the formulators and developers of karate insisted that kata were the key to the art. The formulators of karate were fighting men who would have had little time for activities that didn't directly enhance fighting skill. It is my view that the kata are wholly about recording combative methods and all other "uses" for kata – worthwhile as some of them may be – are modern "spin offs" and not what the kata were created for.

My own training and research led me to the conclusion that it is within the kata that the true martial art is found. Study of the kata reveals the close-range strikes, chokes, strangles, throws, grappling, limb-control, locks and a whole host of combative methods that make karate a holistic and pragmatic art. Without an understanding of kata, all the modern martial artist has left is a hollow shell of the original art and the techniques of modern sport. Many others have shared my experience and interest in the combative applications of the kata is growing all the time. People are simply no longer content to practise a "partial art".

I've written four books on kata application and made around 20 DVDs on the subject. One of the great things about producing such material is that they have brought me into contact with many other martial artists who have also written, or are writing, books to share their approaches to kata application. For me, it's really exciting to see all this great information being openly shared and made so widely available!

Due to the rise in a questioning approach to the martial arts, and the increasing availability of information, there has never been a better time for those who practise kata to understand just what they were created for and how the information recorded in them can be extracted and used in combat.

My own martial background is firmly grounded in traditional karate. To the uninitiated, karate is considered to be a single martial art with a uniform way of doing things. The reality, however, is that "karate" is a coverall term for a wide range of combative systems originating from Okinawa. Whilst the traditional karate systems have a great deal in common, they also have many differences.

One of the key differences between the many karate systems is the kata that they use and the way in which those kata are performed. Thankfully, there are many experienced karateka, from a wide range of the styles, exploring kata application. This has meant that there is a good amount of quality information available on almost all karate systems, karate kata and their many variations. However, sadly there is still relatively little information available on the application of the Taekwon-do patterns. Taekwon-do practitioners who have an interest in the application of the patterns sometimes therefore find themselves having to adapt the karate applications to fit their forms. This is obviously not ideal.

Karate and Taekwon-do have some common ground (the Shotokan karate system being one of Taekwon-do's roots) and therefore the information available on the karate kata will have some relevance to the motions in the Taekwon-do forms. However, Taekwon-do has its own unique forms, and its own unique way for performing the movements that make up those forms. It is for that reason that books such as this one are so very important. Books like this one have a great deal to offer Taekwon-do practitioners as they will allow them to access parts of their art which would otherwise remain locked away within the patterns. Stuart Anslow is to be congratulated for sharing his approach to Taekwon-do patterns in this way. By doing so, he is doing a great service to Taekwon-do practitioners and the art itself.

Reading through the pages of this book makes it abundantly clear just how much thought, time and effort Stuart Anslow has put into examining the ITF patterns. Not only does this book detail applications for the motions within these patterns, it also explores the background to each form and, perhaps most importantly, it also details the thought process that gave rise to the applications shown. Stuart has a clear and engaging writing style and the book is beautifully presented. I feel certain that this book will have Taekwon-do practitioners looking at their patterns from a new angle and with renewed enthusiasm. *Ch'ang Hon Taekwon-do Hae Sul* should be in the library of all practitioners of ITF Taekwon-do. Read on, learn and enjoy!

Iain Abernethy 2006

5th Dan Karate

(British Combat Association and Karate England)

About The Author

Stuart Anslow received his black belt in the art of Taekwon-do in 1994 and is now a 4th degree.

He is Chief Instructor of the renowned Rayners Lane Taekwon-do Academy, which was established in 1999 and is based in Middlesex, UK.

During his martial arts career, Stuart has won many accolades in the sporting arena, including national and world titles. His Academy is one of the most successful in the country winning numerous gold medals at every martial arts championship his students enter, a testament to his abilities as an instructor.

In 2000, Stuart won a gold and silver medal at Grandmaster Hee Il Cho's, 1st AIMAA Open World Championships in Dublin, Ireland and in 2004 he returned with 14 of his students to the 2nd AIMAA Open World Championships where they brought home 26 medals between them, 7 of them becoming World Champions in their own right, 2 became double world gold medallists, all from a single school of Taekwon-do.

In 2002, Stuart founded the International Alliance of Martial Arts Schools (IAOMAS) which drew martial artists from around the world together, growing from a few schools to over 400 in under a year. This non-profit organization is an online student and instructor support group that gives travelling students the ability to train at over 600 affiliated schools worldwide and is truly unique in the way it operates.

Stuart is a regular writer for the UK martial arts press, having written many articles for *'Taekwon-do and Korean Martial Arts'*, *'Combat'*, *'Martial Arts Illustrated'* and *'Fighters'* magazines, as well as taking part in interviews for some of them. His numerous articles cover the many related subjects of martial arts from training to motivation, but his main love is Taekwon-do. In 2001 he published an article broaching a similar subject matter, titled: **Patterns: Are We Missing The Point?** [5] He continues to write interesting articles for the martial arts press and is a regular panel member in *'Combat'* magazines monthly *'Combat Panel'* [6]

As well as his Academy, Stuart is the martial arts instructor for two local schools (one private, one comprehensive), one of which was the first school in the country to teach martial arts as part of its national curriculum.

---

[5] Published in Taekwon-do and Korean Martial Arts Magazine, March 2001

[6] Many of the articles can be found by visiting www.raynerslanetkd.com, the Academy website

In 2002, Stuart received an award from the Hikaru Ryu Dojo, a martial arts academy in Australia, presented by their Chief Instructor and fellow IAOMAS member Colin Wee when he visited Stuart's Academy in the UK. In recognizing Stuart's contribution, Colin stated (referring to IAOMAS) that *"nothing to date has been so foresighted and effective as Stuart's work in establishing this worldwide online martial arts community."*

In October 2003, Stuart was inducted into the world renowned Combat Magazines 'Hall Of Fame 2003' for his work within the field of martial arts on a worldwide level. Combat magazine is the UK and Europe's biggest martial arts publication.

In 2004 he was selected as the Assistant Coach for the Harrow Borough Karate team, to compete at the prestigious London Youth Games held at Crystal Palace and has held this position ever since. During the same year Stuart also received various Honorary awards for his work in the International field of martial arts. From the USA he received a *'Yap Suk Dai Ji Discipleship'* award for his innovative work within IAOMAS and *'T'ang Shou`* society award for promoting martial arts on a worldwide scale.

Chloe Callum

Logan Jorja

In 2006 he was presented with a *'Certificate Of Appreciation'* from the members of IAOMAS Canada which read *'In recognition of your un-dying contribution to the evolution of martial arts and your inspirational and innovative formation of the International Alliance Of Martial Art Schools`*. Though just a humble instructor or student as he refers to himself, he continues to inspire others.

Stuart is well known in the UK and internationally and apart from being a full time instructor of Taekwon-do, teaching at two local schools and running Self Protection courses for groups associated with his local Council, he is the father of four beautiful children, one with Downs Syndrome, whom he supports and cherishes to the best of his ability, despite his hectic work schedule.

Though a full time instructor, his reputation is gained not only by his own career but also by his uncompromising approach to teaching and the standards within his Academy and that of his students. The students quality are testament of his *'no short cuts'* approach to how martial arts in general and Taekwon-do in particular, should be taught. His classes flourish with quality students despite much local competition from schools with a more *relaxed* approach to teaching and grading's. Many of his students feature in the photographs within this book.

Table Of Contents

Introduction

It is estimated that over 50 million people worldwide practice Taekwon-do. All systems of Taekwon-do contain patterns of one sort or another, whether they are called tul, hyung, forms, poomse or kata they all follow the same format; a myriad of blocks, kicks and strikes and this is the way it has remained since the beginning, *until now!*

This book details complete applications to the Ch'ang Hon[7] pattern set as taught by the International Taekwon-do Federation(s) and various Taekwon-do Association's around the world today. The *'Ch'ang Hon'* or *'Blue Cottage'* forms were the first of the Korean forms in Taekwon-do and are still practiced today. They remain virtually the same way as when they were first introduced back in the 1950's even though they have undergone a significant number of changes since their inception.

Taekwon-do was a martial art designed, developed and first taught to an active modern military force, proved and tested in combat, in the harshest arena in the world; the battlefield, where the cost of knowing what works and what didn't really was the difference between life and death. It is one of the few arts that truly and rightfully fits the term martial.[8]

However, since its illustrious beginnings in the 1940's to its introduction to the world in 1955, to this present day, things have changed. Taekwon-do has gone from being an awesomely effective martial art (so feared by the Viet Cong that soldiers were told to avoid engaging in combat, even when Korean soldiers were unarmed, due to their knowledge of Taekwon-do[9]), to an art in crisis by fragmentation, McDojangs and politics, though despite several changes, the actual patterns remain largely the same as when first introduced. In a volume of the *'Guinness Book of Records'* from the 1970's Taekwon-do is described as *'Korean Karate for killing'* due to its battlefield reputation. Times have changed, Taekwon-do has changed (though not always deliberately); from a martial art, to a martial way, to a martial sport in some cases, but what of the original?

> (On the night of St. Valentine's Day, a North Vietnamese regiment of 1,500 men struck at the 254 man Korean Company.)
>
> It was knife to knife and hand-to-hand and in that sort of fighting the Koreans, with their deadly (a form of Tae kwon Do), are unbeatable. When the action stopped shortly after dawn, 104 enemy bodies lay within the wire, many of them eviscerated or brained. All told, 253 Reds were killed in the clash, while the Koreans lost only 15 dead and 30 wounded.
>
> —Time— 24 Feb 1967

'A Savage Week'. Time Magazine, 24 February 1967

Patterns today are practiced in similar ways, in a myriad of Taekwon-do schools around the world but for varying reasons. Many students cannot relate their patterns to self defence (Hosinsol practice), preferring to feel that sport based sparring is closer to an actual combat

---

[7] Throughout this book I use the term 'Ch'ang Hon', others use the term 'Ch'ang Hun'. Neither are incorrect as Hon/Hun is 'Huhn' when pronounced in Korean. General Choi used the spelling 'Ch'ang Hŏn' in his 1965 book 'Taekwon-do'

[8] Martial Art is a term made up of two words, Martial and Art. The 'Martial' is so called after 'Mars the God of War' so martial arts can be translated as 'Arts of War' or 'War Arts'. Furthermore, Donn Draeger, a noted scholar and martial historian noted that to be properly termed a martial art, the system had to have been used in battle by an active military force

[9] 'Captured Viet Cong orders now stipulate that contact with the Koreans is to be avoided at all costs unless a Viet Cong victory is 100% certain. Never defy Korean soldiers without discrimination, even when are not armed, for they all well trained with Taekwondo.' - An excerpt from an enemy directive seized. - July 22, 1966

situation. Many maintain they have no practical value above being a historical tie to the traditional side of Taekwon-do; they practice because of tradition, placing no value on the movements at all. Still others that do place value, place it in the wrong context, citing they are for purely technical reasons like developing technique. This is further fuelled by the pattern elements in competition, where aspects like where your hand exactly finishes are much more important than what that hand is actually meant to be doing.

But surely, the 24 patterns of Taekwon-do which were in development for over 40 years must have more meaning than just maintaining tradition, developing technique or as a means to win medals at tournaments. This book looks to explain what is sorely missing in today's practice and performance of the Ch'ang Hon patterns and attempts to recapture one part of the missing element that made Taekwon-do so feared on the battlefield.

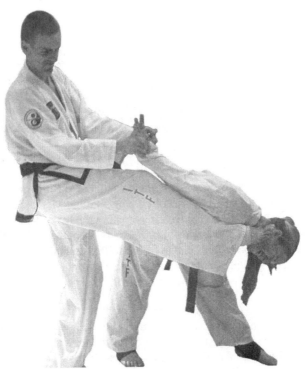

'Action without vision is pointless,
Vision without action is fruitless,
With vision and action you can change the world'

Why Did I Write This Book?

'Only dead fish swim with the stream'

The reasons behind the writing of this book have evolved as time has gone by. Originally I felt much of how Taekwon-do is taught, shown and perceived by others today as lacking in many areas and I wanted to convey what the original intent in these areas of Taekwon-do were. To highlight what parts have been down played or ceased to be taught and what should be included in the standard curriculum of all Taekwon-do schools professing to teach the art and how these areas were, and should, be trained.

For example, 99% of Taekwon-do sparring today is simply sport related, no sweeps, no low kicks and no throws. Visiting students often look shocked when they visit my classes and don't pad up to spar or are grabbed, thrown or swept by one of my senior grades. In many schools one step sparring is performed robot fashion, rather than utilizing reaction and many people do not even know why they practice three, two and one step or seem to ignore or simply not realize, the main reason we practice patterns (tul). Very few schools do any kind of conditioning work and so many schools do not teach throwing that it is widely believed that throws do not exist in Taekwon-do at all, when in fact they do. This book was, at first, simply looking to set the record straight and inform students of such misconceptions that are abound within the Taekwon-do world and hopefully get them to start practicing their art as it was originally intended.

A Taekwon-do throw!

Although I felt my first book idea is needed, there is more call for a book that explains actual applications in the patterns of Taekwon-do, step by step, and this is what I resigned myself to do. This came about from discussions with Taekwon-do students at tournaments and Taekwon-do related internet forums, after seeing the now immortal phrases, *'what's this movement for?'* or *'can someone explain why we do this in this pattern?'* etc, time and time again, relating to various movements contained in a Ch'ang Hon pattern.

I was surprised at first, as many of the questions asked were what I originally thought were the standard applications taught to everyone. I became even more surprised when no one appeared to offer answers, or inevitably answers would start with the words *maybe* or *perhaps*, so I ended up answering myself. However, the worst thing is, these questions were not always from junior graded students, but people teaching this art to others, the instructors.

I finally resolved to write this book when I read that a black belt had just been *enlightened* about a movement that had foxed him for years after attending a patterns course with a Taekwon-do patterns expert! The movement was from Juche, the technique was the fingertip cross-cut, the student was ecstatic as he had finally solved the riddle that had foxed him for so long. He had been told this technique was designed to… knock an opponents glasses off! And this was taught by high grade (modern) master! To say I was shocked was an understatement and my mind was made up, it was time to set the record straight!

As well as listing more realistic applications, I have felt dismayed for quite some time at just how much patterns and indeed patterns training is disregarded as to how it translate to self defence. I have come to the conclusion that the first hurdle was having actual applications that work and that are realistic in their approach. However, even with that knowledge and the step by step layout of how to do them, the student or instructor needed to understand where these applications fit into the actual framework of self defence, by understanding their relevance the student is able to jump the second hurdle – that of understanding their role. The techniques and applications only retain their value if they can be utilized as they are meant to be, so the final hurdle was how to train them effectively, so that when called upon they can not only be used, but be effective in their use in the relevant environment, which is of course self defence of ones self, so I have also listed ways to train the patterns to accomplish this.

However, this idea evolved further still. Because I wanted to include a study of why applications had changed or why they were designed the way they were. I did some research and this led me to form other opinions, conclusions and realizations which I will relay in the course of this book as well as offering some useful alternatives to enhance everyone's understanding of Taekwon-do. Finally, I originally had small introduction sections to each patterns definition. I felt these were a little too brief and so did further research into this area finally turning it to quite an in-depth look at the historical characters behind the pattern names, which I feel, like me, many will find fascinating.

The purpose of this book is to:

1. Look at Taekwon-do's development of the patterns and how and why they evolved the way that they have.

2. Detail applications that make much more sense than many of the standard explanations given, that were originally in the art. We find these by looking into Taekwon-do's history, how its patterns were formulated as well as Taekwon-do's DNA (its genetic make up).

3. Detail alternative applications to techniques by comparing similar movements in martial arts that were part of Taekwon-do's initial development.

4. Discuss some of the original applications that still continue to confuse or confound many students worldwide and clear up some of the common misconceptions to pattern movements and applications.

5. Dispel some of the myths that continually surround Taekwon-do.

6. Learn how to utilize patterns training and make the transition from technical training, to realistic and effective self defence techniques.

7. Detail a deeper insight into the historical figures which the patterns are named after.

8. Further our knowledge and depth of Taekwon-do and martial arts in general.

9. Bring Taekwon-do back to the art it was meant to be.

CHAPTER 1

Where's The Applications

'If all you have is a hammer, everything looks like a nail'

I fervently believe that the Taekwon-do world is literally crying out for detailed applications on their patterns. For many years thousands of students have been taught how to block, where to block, how to strike, where to strike etc. but there was always this niggling feeling that there was more to them. Surely a 9th kup (white belt) wasn't meant to have the same applications in their patterns as a 5th degree black belt? – this made no sense.

The Taekwon-do world has a detailed manual of Taekwon-do technique, revised and reprinted time after time and now even available on DVD. In its earlier forms it was often referred to as the bible of Taekwon-do, now it's the Encylopedia, but despite its 15 volumes it concerns itself more with how to do the movement rather than what the actual movement is for. There are literally hundreds of books concerning Taekwon-do patterns but none seem to go any deeper than a block is a block and a punch is a punch. To my mind, for Taekwon-do this is the first *real* book on the subject.

The Encyclopedia Of Taekwon-do, was written by its founder, General Choi Hong Hi and is one of the books I have use for technical analysis. These books carefully list each movement of each pattern, as well as how to perform single techniques like the various kicks used in Taekwon-do plus many other areas relating to the art. The full volume, which is 15 books long, (rather than the Condensed Encyclopedia of Taekwon-do) was written in the 1980s, but General Choi published books on Taekwon-do much earlier on, I have one simply called 'Taekwon-do' which was published by the Daeha Publication Company of Seoul Korea in 1965.

A real application of the 9 Shape block

From this fifteen volume encyclopedia, eight of those volumes are concerned with just the Ch'ang Hon patterns alone. Each of these eight volumes cover around 3 patterns and show various applications to the movements contained within the patterns. However, after a while they seem very basic and many applications appear to be the same for different movements, for example low section outer forearm block taught to a 9th kup (white belt, yellow tag) has the same application to the more advanced 9–shape block, as learnt at black belt levels.[10]

When questioned about this aspect, many senior black belts will say its because to list all the movements applications would take another 15 volumes! Others say that Taekwon-do was so scientifically advanced that it wasn't pertinent at the time to list all the applications, as too much was needed to simply ensure students were doing the techniques technically correct.

Neither of these arguments hold much weight. Firstly, General Choi was looking to propagate Taekwon-do on a world wide level and writing an in-depth '*how to*' manual was a good way to ensure that even with an ocean in between them, students from different continents were performing the same Taekwon-do. He also found the time to write other books, such as his

---

[10] Volume 8, page 123 (Chon-Ji) and Volume 11, page 209 (Ge-Baek) of the Encyclopedia Of Taekwon-do show a low section outer forearm block and a 9 shaped block both blocking a front kick.

autobiography and ones on moral culture, so why not simply have a '*Taekwon-do Applications*' manual as well if they couldn't fit in the original book. He also had a vast array of highly knowledgeable and highly skilled instructors that could have easily done the same thing, but didn't!

He proved Taekwon-do can be taught as quick as any other martial art by its rapid development in the military and once formulated properly, Taekwon-do was easily taught to the dedicated student. His books also lists details which must have been very time consuming, such as the 30 pages with charts to show the relation of attacking tools and vital spots.[11] Taekwon-do had been developed with lots of thought, the encyclopedias are immense; this is not the sort of book you leave unwritten chapters for, to be filled in later. Size, space or time were not issues, neither were ensuring everything was totally correct before moving into another related area.

Much care and attention was taken ensuring each movement was photographed properly for the encyclopedias, with numerous before, in-between and after shots attached to the main shot to show how to move from one motion to another. Applications of the movements are shown in photographs as well – but why do they seem to repeat for advanced level techniques?

Though they are not listed in the pattern sections of General Choi's or other Taekwon-do pattern books, many of the techniques lead the student to the feeling that there are more in-depth applications possibility contained or hidden within the patterns, applications that they'd like to see and learn. After all, Taekwon-do has throws, locks, strikes to vital points, even pressure point applications, many of which are demonstrated during Hosinsol (Self Defence) practice, but why are not more of these applications detailed in the patterns?

In 2004 I personally interviewed one of General Choi's first generation instructors, Master Kong Young Ill, 9th degree, whose answers to some of my probing questions further cements this claim. For example, I asked Master Kong "*Has Taekwon-do many hidden applications, like those in the Karate world feel are hidden in kata's?*" to which he replied "*I do not believe there are hidden techniques. Taekwon-do is a very precise martial art and every action is explainable by any good instructor.*" I also asked why the 'W' block found in Toi-Gye was repeated so many times, Master Kong simply said "*General Choi says so!*" (and laughed).

One other question I put to Master Kong was: "*Some instructors teach different applications for the same technique, for example, the twisting hands motion in Yoo-Sin I have learnt as a trapping technique and also as a wrist lock technique, which is correct?*" to which Master Kong replied "*In this particular pattern, it was never made clear to me by General Choi exactly what the application of this move is (within the pattern). However, this certainly does not mean that it can not be used for many other applications.*"[12]

---

[11] Encyclopedia Of Taekwon-do ,Volume 2, pages 100 to 129

[12] The full interview with Master Kong was printed in 'Taekwon-do and Korean Arts Magazine', November 2004 and 'Combat' Magazine, January 2005. The full interview can still be read by visiting http://www.raynerslanetkd.com/ARTICLES_MasterKong.html

It seems a bit strange to me, that these high quality instructors were sent forth to spread Taekwon-do around the world but were not told the finer or inner details, or the meat in the sandwich as I've heard it termed. Believe me, Master Kong is a credit to Taekwon-do, he is highly regarded and was a member of the International Taekwon-do demonstration team, that travelled round the world displaying Taekwon-do (1963 – 1980). After the demonstrations, there were open invitations to the public to fight any demonstration team member. Grand Master Kong fought martial artists of all kinds in 127 countries and never lost a fight[13]– he is a great Taekwon-do exponent as are all the original pioneers of Taekwon-do, that is beyond dispute.

Though it is hard to believe, and I may even be labelled as a heretic, if we look at the history of Taekwon-do, the answer is actually quite simple - its because General Choi didn't know them! He knew the movements, but not the fine details, but before you slam my book down in disgust, let me explain further.

Gichen Funakoshi

1868 - 1957

Founder of Shotokan

The reason for this is that Taekwon-do was in part at least, derived from the Generals training in Shotokan Karate, the patterns section of the style obviously has large influences from the Karate Kata that he learned. He learned his Karate from an instructor that learned from Funakoshi (or even Funakoshi himself as detailed later on in this chapter), and Funakoshi is known to have not been taught in-depth kata applications of his system by his own instructor Itosu. We know this as one of Funakoshi's fellow students, Choki Motobu, publicly derided Funakoshi for not knowing proper explanations to his katas movements when Funakoshi was introducing Karate to Japan.[14]

So like his instructor, like Funakoshi, he knew the basic outline, but not the details (of the pattern motions). Think of it as having a '*paint by numbers*' picture, with no numbers on it! It was left to General Choi to colour the picture in as he chose, the same as it was with the Karate masters who trained onwards from Itosu, including Funakoshi, not knowing exactly what colour was supposed to go where, though it was a beautiful picture nonetheless.

This is why some explanations of movements seem vague or inappropriate, as these masters where left with educated guesses only and not detailed information. All knew what were the considered applications at the time (which still exist to this day), these were what students learn in the dojangs around the world; that a low

Just a metaphor, but what colours would you have added?

13 http://www.ictf.info/biographies.html - Biography of Grand Master Kong, Young Il, 9th Dan

14 Ancient Okinawan Martial Arts, McCarthy, 1999, page 126

block is purely to stop a front kick, a knife-hand stops a punch etc, often these techniques seem slightly inappropriate, especially at higher levels. Many of the movements of the kata listed in General Choi's 1965 book *'Taekwon-do'* are either exactly the same, or very similar to how they are in the Ch'ang Hon tuls, as well as the order that certain combinations of techniques run and specific movements remaining as vague in application now, as they were then![15]

These thoughts are further confirmed by the many thousands of students who have attended seminars with the General where questions on applications were given different answers on different occasions or simply ignored. Many of today's instructors give the answer to this as *'does everything have to have a reason'?* When it comes to something as deeply designed, taught and as far as the technical aspects are concerned, published, then I feel the student of Taekwon-do deserves a better answer than that. This book addresses the answers we are seeking.

The Purpose Of This Book

This book doesn't concern itself with Taekwon-do the whole art, just the area of patterns. We already know it's a great art, with many different facets and that patterns are only one of those facets, one of the parts that make the whole, despite the fact that many of these other parts are no longer taught appropriately either.

What we are looking at are only the patterns and Master Kongs comments certainly imply that the knowledge passed on in patterns certainly wasn't as in-depth or much more than basic (block/strike) applications. This takes nothing away from Master Kong or any other Taekwon-do exponent, nor does it take anything away from General Choi or the art he unleashed on the world. It only tells us applications in patterns most of us *feel* are there, were not taught or passed on and this is because they were not taught to General Choi and other applications were found to replace the missing elements.

It should be remembered that patterns have a different role in Taekwon-do than kata do in Karate. In Karate they are seen as the backbone or the heart and soul of the art, whereas in Taekwon-do they are seen as part of the whole, but no more important than the other facets of basics, fundamentals, sparring, destruction, hosinsol etc. It could, in theory at least, be concluded that the reason for  this was because of the lack of in-depth applications taught to General Choi that he had assumed similar, so felt the need for the other areas to be trained sufficiently to compensate (perhaps the

---

reason for separate hosinsol practise) and its all these together that make Taekwon-do…
Taekwon-do.

The Encyclopedia Of Taekwon-do

If the encyclopedia doesn't give the whole or deeper story is it a waste of time? Certainly not, the encyclopedia is an in-depth reference to the art. Apart from the step by step pattern guides, it covers many other areas including all the different types of sparring, basics, fundamentals, conditioning, training aids, moral culture, vital points and other areas related to Taekwon-do.

With regards to the pattern applications themselves that are contained within the encyclopedias, I prefer to think of them as showing the student basic applications that they can visualize, whether good or bad. This enables them to perform the complete technique and as we shall see later, this is vitally important for more advanced or in-depth applications. Whether this was the original intention or purely my own romanticized version is open for debate, but it is a useful way to utilize this part of the encyclopedias above simply learning just the steps. It gives each student an instant, easily seen, remembered and visualized application to utilize during patterns practice, whilst ensuring they perform each technique in its entirety. Besides which, not all the applications are bad applications, its just there's so much more to them than shown in it.

As part of my research into the patterns, I delved into some of the lesser known or even unknown true applications of techniques found within the patterns, such as the infamous San Makgi *(W Block)*. I was simply going to list them, but have decided to include them within the text of the relevant chapter, not all is as it may seem!

Food For Thought

If you are reading this as a 2nd degree black belt or above, think of when you passed your 2nd degree. Take away your martial arts book collection, stop your internet for referencing, just rely on what you were taught in your standard Taekwon-do school (oh, and erase any questions you may have asked as this wasn't the done thing in martial arts years ago!). Now ask yourself, did or do you feel capable if asked, of forging a martial art not for the general public, not for a single school but for an entire countries military force, perhaps your own countries?

Think of how big a task that was 60 plus years ago. The fact is, General Choi did an amazing job considering the tools he had available at the time, he filled in his metaphorical *'paint by numbers'* picture very, very well. His art has spread globally to millions of eager students, and the questions without answers, the sections of the picture without numbers, have been filled one way or another. But years on, with the knowledge we have available today, maybe we can now see that not all the colours were the right ones. They looked okay back then, but now we can see things more vividly than ever, maybe that blue should have been a purple and the green looks more like it should have been red!

What *colours* would you have added to this technique?

This?...

Or this?

General Choi was the Picasso of his day within martial arts, highly revered, but as the times change, the paintings are still great, masterpieces in fact, but like Picasso's work, some can look a little odd and may even look a little better with different colours in certain places.

As mentioned previously, some movements remain vague as to how or why they are performed and are seemly exported directly from General Choi's learning of the Shotokan katas. Examples such as: Placing the hands on the hips in what looks like Twin Side Elbow Thrust (Toi-Gye), the slow Palm Pressing Blocks (Joong-Gun), Angle Punch going past the centre line (Joong-Gun), the fast then slow movements of the Twin Knife-hand Strikes at the start of Kwang-Gae and many more examples of movements that different instructors offer different reasons for – with no exact reasoning as to why they are performed that way or a decent application to support them! Ready Stances seem to follow a similar trend[16]

Finally, if all that I've mentioned previously doesn't convince you that there's much more to patterns than what is presently offered or depicted in the numerous books, I offer you this simple thought.

If we are shown 5 blocks to stop an incoming punch, lets call them #A to #E and they all do the job to some degree but #A is slightly better than #B, #B slightly better than #C and so on to #E. That means #A is *much* better than #E, so why continue to teach #E at all if #A and #B are so much better? It simply doesn't make sense to teach something that is much less effective than something else, when we are trying to teach the most effective and efficient way of doing something, in this case blocking a punch! So there must be another reason for teaching all these blocks and that reason is because they are not blocks, well at least their primary purpose isn't.

Granted, they *can* all be blocks, but many actual blocks are often better employed as something else, leaving the student to train the techniques that are actually intended to stop a punch, rather than those that are not. Whilst the training of certain techniques for their other specific uses such as locking techniques, is a better use of training time, than wasting time training it to do

16 See Chapter 7

something when there is a better technique already for that purpose! There are of course variations to this theme, usually based on distance or angles, but in the main, most blocks have different purposes or intent as far as applications go.

The Shotokan Connection

Classic Shotokan [19]

Shotokan Karate had a major influence on the development of Taekwon-do, General Choi was taught by the an unnamed Karate instructor[17] in the system taught by the legendary Funakoshi himself, and gained a 2nd degree rank in Shotokan. Back then, 2nd degree (dan) was a fairly high level to obtain and therefore a good foundation for when General Choi returned to Korea to start the development of Taekwon-do. By his own words[18], General Choi was adept at Shotokan.

As mentioned previously, in Karate circles, it is known that Funakoshi, despite having a good knowledge of the systems outline, was not taught in-depth applications to many of Shotokans movements, so it stands to reason these weren't passed on to any instructors Funakoshi taught, and therefore could not be passed on to General Choi. After all, you cannot pass on what you don't know.

---

[17] In his autobiography, General Choi states that Mr Kim took him to the University of Doshisha (Japan) where he witnessed Karate being practiced and decided to start but never mentions the actual instructors name. He also mentions that Mr Kim was 'a well trained Karate apprentice' but doesn't actually say that he was his instructor. However, in a Taekwondo Times magazine interview (January, 2000), General Choi states he learnt directly under Funakoshi. But learning the kata Ro-Hai seems to throw some doubt on this – see Appendx iii

[18] Many accounts of General Choi's skills in Karate are recounted in his autobiography 'Taekwon-do And I'

[19] Photo courtesy by Sensei Andy Wright, 5th Dan

So when General Choi set about developing a martial art for Korea, of unifying existing arts (like Kwon Bop), the existing schools (kwans) and adding a Korean identity, he had some tools passed forward through his Shotokan training, but not the total in-depth knowledge of how they worked.

Never the less, Taekwon-do was born and from 1955 it exploded world wide, with small improvements or alterations being made along the way.

The Kwon Bop Connection

Chinese influences obviously spread far and wide and were not resigned to simply landing in Okinawa (where Karate was born). Kwon Bop was a development of the Chinese systems, but in Korea. Though its heritage is Chinese and it contains the Buddhist influence from China it found its way into Korea's Royal Courts. Kwon Bop's name is derived from the kanji (Hanja in Korean) meaning *'Law of the Fist'* or *'Kempo'* (*'Chuan Fa'* in Chinese) and can be considered the Korean version of Karate development. It developed down similar lines to Okinawa but with a different emphasis. As such it included many circular techniques not found in Shotokan today but still found in Chinese styles and Karate styles that didn't develop directly through Itosu like Shotokan did. It spawned many different arts with different names (such as Soo Bahk Do, Kwon Bop, Kong Soo Do, Tae Soo Do and Kang Soo Do), but all were in essence derived the same way.

All countries developed martial arts during their warring histories, Korea had many of its own unique arts as well as Kwon bop, such as T'ang-su and Taek Kyon (often refered to as Subak), plus its history of Hwarang-do which dates back over 5,000 years to the formation of the Kochosun kingdom (from where Hwarang-do developed). When Taekwon-do was finally formed and named, the need for a uniquely Korean martial art meant all these arts were incorporated and in one way or another possibly had influences on the final development of what we now refer to as Taekwon-do. And this is another of the elements that make Taekwon-do unique in that in one form or another it has influences from both Japanese and Chinese martial arts which were indoctrinated into Korean systems either 'as is' or modified to suit.

It should be noted, some Korean arts are still taught as they were or via direct lineage, but as this is about Taekwon-do, it is enough to say they played a part in its development.

The Taek-Kyon Connection

Though its actual roots are unknown, Taek-Kyon (meaning foot techniques) was originally simply a recreational activity (what we might term a sport). In the course of Korean history, it was turned into a more formidable martial art for the benefits of self defence and health to the nation, which included not only the common folk of the time but also the military and royalty of Korea. Taek-Kyon had periods where it flourished but eventually phased out with the introduction of firearms into warfare where it ended up being practiced by just the common people until the Japanese invasion in 1910, which banned all martial arts practice. It is however interesting to note that it was, and is, seen as a distinctly Korean art and is thought to have influenced arts in China, rather than the usual reversed story of Chinese arts influences others.

Whatever the case, during Korea's history Taek-Kyon was considered uniquely Korean and this was one of its main connection to Taekwon-do and one which led to the eventual name we use to day (notice the similarities!)

Taek Kyon

In 1945 when Korea was liberated from the Japanese, many Taek-Kyon schools re-emerged, one which was taught by General Choi (then a Second Lieutenant). General Choi learnt Taek-Kyon from his calligraphy teacher Han II Dong[20] who considered it good training to build a then young Choi, Hong Hi's frail body, this was Taek-Kyon's second connection to Taekwon-do.

President Syngman Rhee
1875-1965

Korea officially formed its armed forces in 1945, its modern military. In 1952 during the Korean war, President Syngman Rhee saw a demonstration by the military Korean martial arts masters. He was so impressed he ordered that it be taught to all military personnel and this propelled Korean martial arts forward like a rocket. General Choi is known to have been teaching martial arts to his 29th Infantry Division on Cheju Island in 1953, his school, known as Oh Do Kwan (Gym Of My Way) was seen as the catalyst for the formation of Taekwon-do. General Choi was teaching the soldiers his Taek-Kyon and Karate, and at the same time formulating Taekwon-do, though it had yet to be named.

The Tae Soo Do Connection

In 1955 it was decided to merge all the various Korean arts into a single art, with a national identity. The name *'Tae Soo Do'* was accepted by the many kwans (schools) of the era. However *'Tae Soo Do'* meant *'Way of the Chinese hand'* so, as his influence grew, General Choi suggested the name *'Taekwon-do'* as it sounded similar to Taek-Kyon, Korea's unique martial art, and thus added to the national identity of Korea. It also describes the art more accurately as it denoted both the hand and foot techniques found in the art, unlike Taek-Kyon which simply meant Foot Techniques.

---

[20] As mentioned in General Choi's autobiography, *'Taekwon-do And I'*

The Birth Of Taekwon-do

Though this is not a book covering all aspects of Taekwon-do, it goes some way to help us understand or evaluate the patterns if we realise what could have influenced Taekwon-do and how it differs from Karate and other martial arts. As we know, Taekwon-do was born officially on the 11th of April 1955. However, despite the naming of the art by a sole person (it was General Choi who suggested Taekwon-do), the

Photograph from the meeting when they named Taekwon-do, many martial arts masters were present. General Choi can be seen at the head of the table. circa 1955

formulation of a uniquely Korean martial art was founded from many different arts, styles and influences and given my research, there is a strong possibility that parts of these arts were infused to some degree in the creation of Taekwon-do.

Though he states that Karate and Taek-Kyon were used simply as reference studies, it stands to reason Taek-Kyon's influence is much further reaching due to Taekwon-do dynamic kicks, and it is easy to see Karate's influences.

As a personal note, I have read interviews with the General in Combat magazine (a UK martial arts publication) from the 70's, 80's and early 90's, with this opinion changing each time. Though I no longer have the magazines I remember in the 70s interview, when asked about Karate's influence General Choi said something along the lines of "*Without Karate there would of been no Taekwon-do*", in the 80's interview his opinion changed slightly to what he stated in the encyclopedias, along the lines of "*Karate was simply a reference tool that helped*" and in the 90's interview he said something like "*Karate had only a minor or no impact on Taekwon-do*" or even "*Karate has nothing to do with Taekwon-do*" (I cannot remember exactly now).

No matter what one's opinion may be, we only have to look at the Shotokan katas to see their heavy influence on Taekwon-do. In the photographs below and on the next page we can clearly see parts of the kata Pinan Shodan being performed by Gichin Funakoshi that anyone of 6th kup or above should recognize as these combinations are the same as in Won-Hyo tul.

What sets Taekwon-do apart from both Karate and Taek-Kyon, is that General Choi added many scientific principles to his emerging art, particularly theories from Newton's Laws of Physics. Korean cultural heritage was added in various guises, from the pattern names to the uniforms we wear (doboks) as well as military tactics. General Choi's personal influence may also be noted as well in some of the *'ready postures'* of the patterns. Taekwon-do also did away with the mainly linear motions of Karate and re-introduced many circular motions for their added power elements, though even these were revised. The *'Do'* or *'Way'* was more emphasized, especially in regards to what is known as *'Moral Culture'*. Taekwon-do out-grew its roots eventually and became unique in its own right.

Taekwon-do On The Battlefield

As mentioned in the introduction to this book, Taekwon-do is a proven, battlefield tested, Korean martial art. This is no more evident that the use of Taekwon-do at the battle of Tra Binh Dong in Vietnam[21] in 1967. In an article by LtCol James F. Durand of *'The Battle of Tra Binh Dong and the Korean Origins of the U.S. Marine Corps Martial Arts Program'[22]*, in the section *'Lessons Learned and Epilogue'*, Taekwon-do and its use in the battle was discussed and the article had this to say:

> The battle of Tra Binh Dong is studied by military professionals throughout Korea, and its lessons are taught to all Marines. The ROK Marine Corps (ROKMC) cites four factors as critical to the 11th Company's victory: the distinguished combat leadership of the company and platoon commanders, the hard fighting by all Marines in the unit, the effective use of fire support, and the boldness of the counterattack.

> The role of martial arts training in the battle has been a topic of discussion for nearly four decades. At the press conference following the battle, Capt Jung was adamant in his opinion that tae kwon do contributed greatly to the combat abilities and fighting spirit of the Korean Marines, both enlisted and officers. In a graphic description, *Time* noted that martial arts training was critical to the victory:

---

[21] A step by step description of this dramatic and heroic battle can be found in Appendix vii

[22] Reprinted by permission of the *Marine Corps Gazette*

It was knife to knife and hand-to-hand—and in that sort of fighting the Koreans, with their deadly tae kwon do (a form of karate), are unbeatable. When the action stopped shortly after dawn, 104 enemy bodies lay within the wire, many of them eviscerated or brained[23]

Asked to provide their opinions for this article, both Taeguk Medal recipients stated that martial arts training significantly contributed to the Marines' victory. LtCol Jung, now retired and living in Seoul, emphasized two areas in which tae kwon do influenced his Marines:

First, the enemy suddenly overwhelmed our trenches and continuously piled up to the degree that we were unable to use rifles and bayonets as weapons. There were many instances in which we were pushing and pulling each other inside the trenches. At that time, Tae Kwon Do became the Korean Marines' weapon and by hitting the enemy in his vital parts, we brought him under our control.

Second, it can be seen that the courage to be unafraid when facing your enemy was trained through Tae Kwon Do. Although we didn't have a path of retreat and had to stay in our position, the fortitude to fight bravely while exposed to the enemy led to victory at the Battle of Tra Binh Dong[24].

Retired MajGen Shin Won Bae, who later commanded the Blue Dragon unit (now the 2d ROK Marine Division) provided similar insights, noting:

Even though tactics call for fixing bayonets to rifles during close quarters to neutralize the enemy, our weapon at the time, the M–1 rifle, was not a weapon that could be wielded quickly. In urgent situations, the Marine in the front would fiercely strike the enemy's face and vital parts using Tae Kwon Do, causing him to momentarily lose his will to fight. Then a second Marine would finish off the enemy with the rifle. Additionally, striking the enemy with an entrenching tool was highly effective in destroying the will to fight among the enemy's lead elements. While Tae Kwon Do demonstrated its practical effectiveness on the battlefield, more importantly, martial arts training instilled the confidence to defeat the enemy in each Marine. I think this is the greater significance of Tae Kwon Do training[25].

Yet LtCol Jung is careful to emphasize the importance of fire support in the battle, noting that the artillery and mortar fires prevented the North Vietnamese from sending reinforcements to the troops engaged with the Korean Marines.

As if to underscore the strength of the ROKMC Martial Arts Program, the Korean Marine team won the National Tae Kwon Do Championship in November 1967, the same year as the battle of Tra Binh Dong. The following year ROKMC headquarters began to include tae kwon do with marksmanship qualification and physical fitness testing as measures of combat readiness. (Tae kwon do is now part of the ROKMC physical fitness test.)

For American Marines, the early history of the Korean martial arts program and the battle of Tra Binh Dong provide four important lessons. First, developing and instituting the program took time and required the dedicated efforts of senior leaders and commanders. It took over a

---

[23] 'A Savage Week', Time Magazine, 24 February 1967

[24] Personal letter from Lt Col Jung Kyung Jin, ROKMC(Ret) to Lt Col James F. Durand

[25] Personal letter from Major Gen Shin Won Bae, ROKMC(Ret)

decade from the first demonstrations to the adoption of training objectives and standards. Second, because many of the program's initial benefits were psychological, they were difficult to measure. Indeed, it is impossible to quantify how the confidence and fighting ability of soldiers and Marines were improved through tae kwon do or the number of times North Vietnamese or Viet Cong units bypassed Korean units. Third, martial arts training proved critical in close combat. The ability of the Korean Marines to prevail against overwhelming odds in hand-to-hand fighting in the battle of Tra Binh Dong is a testament to the benefits of tae kwon do training. Lastly, martial arts training is one of many necessary combat skills. Timely and accurate fire support, exceptional combat leadership, and countless individual acts of courage all contributed to the 11th Company's victory.

Fifty years after MG Choi began to advocate martial arts training for Korean soldiers, tae kwon do has grown far beyond its military roots. It is the national martial art of Korea, practiced by millions throughout the world, and has been an Olympic medal sport since 2000. In turn, the growth of tae kwon do as a sport has further strengthened the Korean military's martial arts program. Most men entering the military have already received significant training in some form of martial arts. Because of its focus on developing the physical skills, combative fitness, and mental discipline for combat, it is unlikely that the MCMAP will spur a similar revolution in sport. However, the MCMAP has been an unqualified success in improving the fighting abilities and warrior ethos of all Marines. Commenting on its applicability to today's conflicts, GEN Shin notes, *"For the U.S. Marine Corps, which will encounter battlefields in various countries in the war against terrorism, Tae Kwon Do training on a regular basis is advisable."* Whether at bases in their home countries or deployed overseas, American and Korean Marines continue to train in martial arts, working to uphold the ideal that Marines are the most respected and feared adversary on the battlefield.

Formulation Of The Ch'ang Hon Tul

Contrary to popular belief, all 24 Taekwon-do patterns were not already formulated when Taekwon-do was introduced to the world in 1955. In his 1965 book simply called 'Taekwon-do', General Choi lists the following patterns: *Ch'on-Ji, Tan-Gun, To-San, Wŏn-Hyo, Yul-Kok, Chung-Gŭn, Toi-Gye, Hwa-Rang, Ch'ung-Moo, Gwang-Gae, P'o-Ŭn, Kae-Baek, Yu-Sin, Ch'ung-Jang, Ul-Ji, Sam-Il, Ch'oi-Yong, Ko-Dang, Se-Jong, and T'ong-Il.*[26]

The introduction to these patterns says: *Ch'ang Hon or 'Blue Cottage' is the authors pseudonym. The hallmark of this school is the combination of fast and slow, light and forceful movements together with extensive foot-work. The name, the number of movements as well as the diagrammatic representation of each pattern have a specific significance which symbolizes its namesake or relevance to same*[27] *historical event.*

---

[26] The spelling was probably changed to make the names phonetically more universal. When this change actually occurred, I have not been able to verify.

[27] This is not a typing error, but how its actually written.

In the same book, he lists the following Karate Katas: *Hei-an, Bat-Sai, En-Bi, Ro-Hai, Kouh-Shang-Kouh, Tet-Ki, Jit-Te, Han-Getsu and Ji-on*[28]

The introduction to these kata describe the Sho-Rin and Sho-Rei systems that they come from. With Sho-Rin being characterized as light and speedy and suitable for a light person and the Sho-Rei as slow and forceful for muscle development and favoured by a student of heavier frame. Notice how the Ch'ang Hon patterns are a mixture (in definition) of both, hence General Choi took what he thought was good about both and combined them in the Ch'ang Hon Tul.

It is a popular misconception that the Ch'ang Hon patterns were created in order, from Chon-Ji onwards. The first official Ch'ang Hon patterns devised were actually *Ul-Ji* (4th degree), *Choong-Moo* (1st kup) and *Hwa-Rang* (2nd kup).

Other patterns were developed to a total of 20 and around the 1970's General Choi added the remaining four patterns: *Eui-Am, Moon-Moo, Yong-Gae and So-San* which brought the total of patterns in the Ch'ang Hon system to twenty four, as it remains today.

The printing of the Karate katas in his books was discontinued, which made this the point where Taekwon-do really broke away from its roots, as until this time, many instructors under the General remained learning both sets.

Officially, in the 1980's General Choi considered his patterns missed some important techniques, which he instituted into the set by replacing Ko-Dang tul with Juche tul.[29]

The order of the patterns have changed over time, with some instructors teaching patterns at different levels to what is set today. This is because this is the way that they learned them. This can also be noticed when you read renowned Taekwon-do Master, Hee Il Cho's pattern books, which only go up to twenty patterns in total, as he left the General before the final four patterns were added and the books have never been updated. It is also interesting to note that originally, all the patterns were named after famous Korean historical figures except the first and last. The first pattern, '*Chon-Ji*' represents the creation of the world, therefore the creation of Korea and the last pattern, '*Tong-Ill*' represents the reunification of North and South Korea, the beginning

---

[28] See Appendix iii

[29] Another reason often mentioned for the change from Ko-Dang to Juche was the General Choi was trying to achieve either funding or support (or both) from the North Korean government so this was changed to appease them. The meaning of this patterns can be interpreted pretty much to the North Korean communist ideal, though as the cold war was on, and with the dispute between North and the South Korea the *official* line was much more acceptable. This pattern has also been renamed (in 2005) due to its North Korean connection, by one Taekwon-do organisation.

and the end so to speak. With the replacement to '*Juche*' however, this changes the equation slightly, but I feel the names of the first and last patterns in the set were highly significant to General Choi and the Korean heritage and ideals.

In an interview conducted in 1999 General Choi was asked how long it took to research his patterns, to which he replied "*I began my research in March 1946 into what was to be named Taekwon-do on April 11, 1955. My research ended in 1983. The patterns represent my study of the Art in this period.*"[30]

General Choi passed away on 15th June, 2002, leaving an art to be enjoyed, practiced and studied by millions of students around the world – I am simply one of them!

General Choi Hong Hi

1918 - 2002

Founder of Taekwon-do

---

[30] Interview by Maria Heron, (The Times), 1999

Taekwon-do Lineage

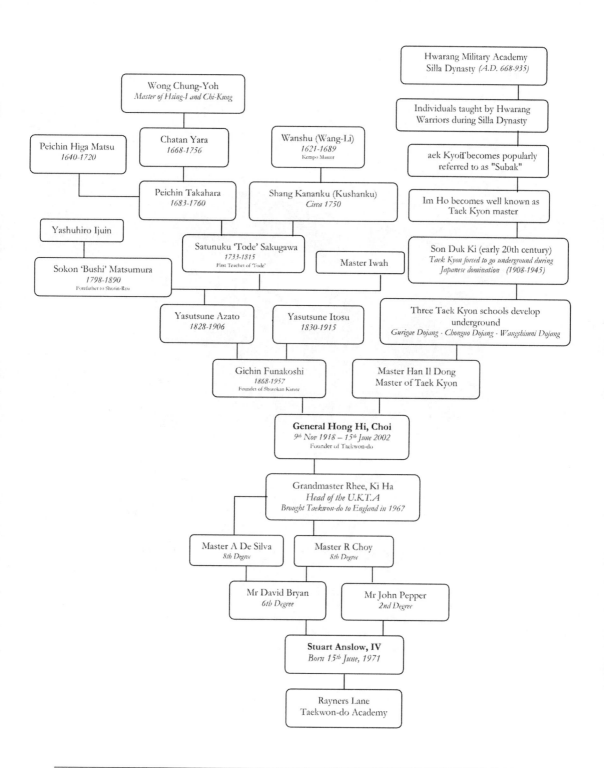

Hwarang Military Academy
Silla Dynasty *(A.D. 668-935)*

Individuals taught by Hwarang
Warriors during Silla Dynasty

aek KyoñTbecomes popularly
referred to as "Subak"

Im Ho becomes well known as
Taek Kyon master

Wong Chung-Yoh
Master of Hsing-I and Chi-Kung

Peichin Higa Matsu
1640-1720

Chatan Yara
1668-1756

Wanshu (Wang-Li)
1621-1689
Kempo Master

Peichin Takahara
1683-1760

Shang Kananku (Kushanku)
Circa 1750

Yashuhiro Ijuin

Satunuku 'Tode' Sakugawa
1733-1815
First Teacher of 'Tode'

Master Iwah

Son Duk Ki (early 20th century)
*Taek Kyon forced to go underground during
Japanese domination   (1908-1945)*

Sokon 'Bushi' Matsumura
1798-1890
Forefather to Shorin-Ryu

Yasutsune Azato
1828-1906

Yasutsune Itosu
1830-1915

Three Taek Kyon schools develop
underground
Gurigae Dojang - Chongno Dojang - Wangshimni Dojang

Gichin Funakoshi
1868-1957
Founder of Shotokan Karate

Master Han Il Dong
Master of Taek Kyon

General Hong Hi, Choi
9th Nov 1918 – 15th June 2002
Founder of Taekwon-do

Grandmaster Rhee, Ki Ha
Head of the U.K.T.A
Brought Taekwon-do to England in 1967

Master A De Silva
8th Degree

Master R Choy
8th Degree

Mr David Bryan
6th Degree

Mr John Pepper
2nd Degree

Stuart Anslow, IV
Born 15th June, 1971

Rayners Lane
Taekwon-do Academy

'Be not afraid of growing slowly, be afraid only of standing still'

CHAPTER 2
Debunking Taekwon-do Myths

'A story gets bigger by the telling'

There are many preconceived notions on what is and what is not part of the Ch'ang Hon system of Taekwon-do. These are brought about by instructors or associations teaching what and how they want, which is not in itself wrong, but it does confuse the student sometimes. Here we explore some of those myths as well as listing what makes Taekwon-do different from other styles, especially its father art, Shotokan Karate.

Taekwon-do Is Mostly Kicks

Taekwon-do is often cited as being mainly a kicking art, but in actual fact is has many more hand techniques than kicks, at a guess I would say the hand techniques out number the leg techniques by around 8 to 1 (I once read there are over 2000 hand techniques, but I've never actually counted them to verify this).

Competition gives rise to Taekwon-do underserved reputation as a kicking only art

W.T.F. (World Taekwon-do Federation) Taekwondo helps proliferate this argument, with its competition format scoring on virtually kicking techniques alone. I.T.F. competition does the same thing although it scores hand techniques more readily, kicks score more as they are considered harder to perform. I.T.F. competitions want to promote this spectacular side of the art as it often looks better than a slug fest using just the hands and shows part of the technical expertise and grace that many Taekwon-do performers have. There is nothing wrong with this and in the main I agree with how I.T.F. based competitions are run, as I too enjoy seeing the kickers perform. However, this _is_ competition and many students and especially those who do not train in Taekwon-do can't dissimilate '_this is competition_' from '_this is Taekwon-do_'. Other connotations about Taekwon-do due to its sport side are abound, mostly from other ill informed martial artists, but if we do nothing to change their views, including via our training methods and they do not delve deeper than what they see in a magazine or on a video, this misrepresentation will persist, as its up to the instructors not the student.

Taekwon-do Is Touch Contact

This is a fallacy born from the semi-contact form of ITF based competition. In ITF competition sparring, contact is suppose to be controlled, though in many of the competitions I have been in as a black belt, the contact levels have varied between medium, to hard, to occasionally full contact. The difference is the rules. The actual rules for ITF competition state '_light contact_' and it is really up to the judge to enforce it. I have never gone into a fight in an ITF based tournament and deliberately gone in with heavy contact. The problem stems from the referees not enforcing rules properly and thus, if an opponent went heavy on me and the referee didn't pull them up, then I had no choice but to give as good as I got.

Those outside of Taekwon-do simply see ITF based competition, with two opponents skilfully controlling their techniques (and it is a skilful opponent that can fight fast and intensely and still control their techniques, as those less skilled rely simply on brute force) and summarize that this represents Taekwon-do as a whole. The fact that in many dojangs, competition sparring is the *only* sparring helps further promote this.

My good friend from Poland, Piotr Bernat, has told me that most Polish competition sparring is heavy and full contact and unlike WTF sparring, allows punches to the head (Competitors wear the same protective equipment as in any standard ITF based tournament) so even in competition, its not strictly true.

Competition aside, in training I have had many heavy contact sessions with fellow black belts. Seniors in my classes spar from light to medium to heavy contact and are also allowed to use take downs, sweeping, low kicks, trips and throws at the same time, depending on the type of training we are doing.

Hosinsol is often performed with techniques at full power, but stopped short to avoid injury. Obviously one cannot strike full contact to a vital point as it would cause major damage to a fellow student, however the strikes are thrown at full speed and intensity and blocks are often utilized at close to full power unless hitting a joint or vital point.

The pattern applications show the full contact state of Taekwon-do. Techniques are designed to maim, kill or destroy an opponent and without full power, this cannot be achieved, hence why patterns practice and more so, patterns practice with visualization, is so essential to maintaining this element.

Taekwon-do Contains No Low Kicks

Another fallacy born from competition only sparring. Students are geared to think they must always kick above the waist. And whilst this is a good criteria for children, beginners and junior grade students, due to their lack of targeting skills and control, it is not such a major issue to a

more skilled student who can chose when to hit hard, where to strike and when to pull a technique for safety. The problem exists and many clubs these days are so competition orientated that they are never allow to blossom into this area which is vital for a full rounded arsenal of techniques. The patterns themselves contain low kicks, so students should be allowed the freedom to train in area's that overlap. Patterns, sparring and hosinsol (self defence) all overlap onto each other forming what is really Taekwon-do, as each on their own are just parts of the whole.

Taekwon-do Doesn't Allow Sweeping

Again, another myth perpetrated by competition and further enforced by schools that only concentrate on competition sparring. Sweeping is as much a part of Taekwon-do as kicking is. Again, even in controlled sparring, sweeping can be practiced by more senior students. Again, the patterns incorporate sweeping techniques, some which are obvious and other which are not so obvious.

Taekwon-do Doesn't Contain Locking Techniques

Taekwon-do contains many locks (and breaks) if we study properly. Early in its development Taekwon-do incorporated elements of another Korean art, Hapkido, including many of its joint locks. However, someone deemed much of them either too long, too complicated or not instant enough so they were discarded and those that were kept centred around being quick to apply or causing a break and not just a lock.[31] Many locking techniques can be found within the patterns.

The author explaining basic joint locking to students

---

[31] Many joint locks simply have to be delivered with more power or followed through to turn them from a joint lock to a joint break

Taekwon-do Doesn't Contain Throws

The encyclopedia of Taekwon-do published by General Choi contains a whole section on throwing and falling. This section contains throws such as hip throws, body drops, even the classic inner thigh throw. If its not being taught to the student, its not because it is not part of Taekwon-do. Deeper inspection of the patterns also reveal many throwing techniques as you will discover.

Taekwon-do Contains Weapons

Contrary to what you may see in some Taekwon-do schools, Taekwon-do contains no weapons. No weapons training and no weapons patterns. These are extra parts brought in from the outside by instructors, some as a means of enhancing their students knowledge in martial arts, but often as a means of hiding their lack of deeper knowledge and often as is the case these days, simply to charge the students more money.

Taekwon-do was an art designed for soldiers and soldiers carry guns. Taekwon-do was there if they couldn't use their gun (rifle or bayonet) for one reason or another, they didn't carry poles and sticks just in case they dropped their rifles. However, Taekwon-do contains what I like to term *'anti-weapons'* techniques and training. These are techniques and applications specifically designed against weapons such as knives, clubs, sticks, poles, bayonet attacks and even against pistols.[32] Many 'anti-weapons' applications are found within the black belt patterns though a student gains an introduction unwittingly as early on as Joong-Gun tul.

Example of *'anti-weapons'* techniques

All the above '*Taekwon-do doesn't contain...*' myths are due to a lack of knowledge in certain areas by instructors or simply because instructors left whomever they were with before gaining a full appreciation of the art. Many modern Taekwon-do books further support this myth by not showing or even mentioning them.

---

[32] The book 'Taekwon-do', published in 1965 by General Choi references self defence '*against pistol*' as Tae Kwŏnch'ong

Taekwon-do Patterns Are Only For ... (*insert here*)

Many students are lead to believe that patterns are simply a form of practice for balance, fitness, poise, technique, smoothness and other reasons, totally disregarding the self defence aspects. Though when asked to recite the definition of *Tul* (Patterns) they happily stand there and say *"Tul is a series of offensive and defensive movements set in a logical sequence against one or move imaginary opponents."*! This is the standard definition of patterns that virtually all students give but still it is ignored! A *series of offensive and defensive movements* sounds like self defence to me! The word *'opponents'* also implies the same!

In the Encyclopedia, General Choi states '*Patterns are various fundamental movements, most of which represent either attack or defence techniques, set to a fixed or logical sequence*'[33]. He further goes on to mention the other benefits of practicing patterns, but before the extra benefits, it is stated that patterns represent self defence techniques, set out logically to aid the students practice, meaning the foremost purpose of patterns, is the practice of self defence. Besides, does anyone really think someone would spend forty plus years developing a system for balance, poise etc and via so many exercises (i.e. the 24 patterns)!

I can see how some may form the conclusion that there is little realistic self defence value in patterns training. The reasons may be as follows:

1. The lack of variety in each movements as to its actual usage
2. The lack of any application beyond blocking and striking (with a few exceptions)
3. The seemingly static stances and pattern movements
4. The basic applications often shown
5. The way patterns don't seem to correlate to sparring
6. The way they are taught in standard classes (as just movements)
7. The emphasis on technical excellence for competitions
8. The opinions of their instructor/group/association, fellow students or other martial artists

This is further enhanced by instructors and organisations, especially in regards to competition and the emphasis placed on technical merit to win gold medals. The spreading of Taekwon-do around the globe also has a part to play in this, as General Choi's first concern was *uniformity* and this is the way pattern seminars have been conducted the world over, with little of no time being given to the self defence value.

---

[33] Encyclopedia of Taekwon-do, Vol 1: Patterns (Tul)

Taekwon-do Patterns Are For Historical Purposes

Aside from the definition of Tul, which clearly states that patterns are a form of self defence, I cannot really believe that General Choi spent over forty years creating something for historical purposes only. In relation to the above, many feel they are unrealistic and these reasons have led to the conclusion by some groups or instructors that the usage and practice of patterns are for no more than historical purposes, allowing them to spend less time on them and more time on getting ready for tournaments etc. As a side note, General Choi was opposed to tournaments as he felt they didn't show Taekwon-do in its proper light and that parts of the art have to be changed or forfeited to ensure the safety of the participants and to a large degree he was right. Pattern performances really only show the shell and from that, no one can tell if the egg inside is good or bad or even if it has yolk at all! The focal point of patterns training today is to excel in tournaments and the same is true with regards to sparring being totally tournament based in many clubs – is it any wonder the more underlying benefits of patterns have been almost phased out!

Personally, I had a good tournament career and feel they are both enjoyable and beneficial to students. They even contain a few elements that overlap fighting or self defence and are beneficial to this area as well, like adrenaline management and confidence. But, competition sparring is not fighting and training patterns solely for competition ensures the student misses out on the real purpose of patterns and doesn't allow the student to develop this area any further than stage 1 of patterns training, as listed in the forthcoming chapters.

Patterns Training Is Dead Training

Some martial arts that place no value on pattern practice also help to propagate this fallacy by pointing out the above and claiming:

- **Patterns training is rigid, static and dead training, as there are no resisting opponents**

Well they are if they are looked at in that way and have no self defence value above learning techniques and how to distribute power into them, but as you will see in the forthcoming chapters, this is not the way it should be, was meant to be, or has to be!

- **When you spar you do not use the movements/techniques as they are in patterns**

Though this is debatable depending on what you term sparring, as it is largely based on the assumption that all Taekwon-do sparring is performed like competition sparring. It also pertains to sparring being confused with fighting or self defence, but as any self protection instructor will tell you, competition based sparring is far removed from either self defence or fighting.

Competition sparring is just that – for competition. Traditional *'all in'* sparring allows greater use of the patterns movements, especially the ones listed in this book, and is more akin to fighting than competition, but is still not the exact environment where patterns are most suited as you will see. This is also discussed in depth in the forthcoming chapters.

Patterns Don't Work

Some 2000 years ago, Cicero, a Roman orator listed the *'6 Mistakes of Man'*. Number 3 was *'Insisting that a thing is impossible because we cannot accomplish it.'* It is therefore feasible that though some may see little or no value in the training of patterns it could simply be because they were unable to make them work for them or more likely, were not willing to invest the time and effort to do so, deciding to *quit* patterns practice to concentrate on areas they felt were more beneficial. This is not to say they were wrong, it was their path, it is however wrong to denounce something just because *you* personally see no benefit in it, even when others do. Others simply *'talk the talk'* of their instructors without ever actually knowing themselves as they have started an art that has this ethos.

History however, speaks for itself, as for every credible instructor that denounces patterns as not working or as dead training, there are hundreds or more acknowledged masters and highly regarded students that went before them, that saw them as the complete opposite, enthused their benefits and trained them to extremes, many of these masters are legends in the history of martial arts but others still live and breathe, putting into practice everyday the benefits of their arts patterns or kata, in fact, one of the senior police trainers in Okinawa is an expert in kata applications and this is how he teaches the officers under him.[34]

I have yet to hear of a highly accomplished patterns or kata master, suddenly denouncing the training of them and if they did, this would carry far more weight in my mind than someone who has never placed a concerted effort into patterns study or effort in training that area in the first place. Only one who has in-depth knowledge of something in the first place can denounce it as useless!

Making Patterns Come Alive

The problem is that often, due possibly to the reasons mentioned above, that the patterns are not studied or taken to the depth of training that they could be. Students reach 1st or 2nd dan and feel they are advanced, whereas 1st degree is just the start of training, meaning the student has a good grasp of the basics. The student then feels that patterns are repetitive, or wonders what's the point of simply learning new sets of movements with no basis and drifts towards competition or sparring and finally feels they are a waste of time and effort, simply doing them because they are a student in a Taekwon-do class, to prepare for tournaments or in order to pass their next dan grade. For some students, this is often short lived as they decide their time could be better served in other areas of training. All this can be rectified by following the training methods detailed in Chapter 5 and a new appreciation of the patterns can be gleamed, as the real benefits of pattern training becomes apparent.

---

[34] As viewed in the National Geographic Channel series *'Deadly Arts'* with Josette Normandeau, now available on DVD

CHAPTER 3
Differences In Taekwon-do

'Where there is no difference, there is only indifference'
Louis Nizer

In this chapter we detail some of the things that are unique to Taekwon-do and the differences in today's Taekwon-do in regards to its roots in Shotokan.

Scientific Applications

General Choi, when formulating and refining Taekwon-do looked at things with a scientific perspective. This is considered to be one of the major differences between Taekwon-do and other martial arts, though many arts, like Ed Parkers Kempo for example, employ some of these principles in one guise or another. However, Taekwon-do employs these principles more *in bulk* and they are often applied to each individual movement, rather than as a general theory and it is often said that Taekwon-do is an art based on '*kinetic energy*' which is the energy of movement. General Choi often employed Newton's principles and these '*laws*' played a large part in how movements were changed to be '*more scientific*' and thus, add more power or speed etc. However, in retrospect, even though this has increased effectiveness to specific parts of the art, it has also done some damage to the effectiveness of the art as well.

Yes, the principles increase power, speed and other attributes but they have also caused three major problems:

1. Most of the principles apply to striking and movement and hamper other applications such as releases, throws and even kicking.

2. Instructors have so much information available on these principles that they often over take the core principle of the martial art; that it should be an effective form of self defence.

3. Because of the above, many believe that every principle listed should be applied into every movement, every time its performed, even if performing a technique in relation to self defence.

I feel that the scientific principles in the main should be incorporated where appropriate, but wavered when not – this way we have the best of both. We can increase the power of our techniques and the dynamics of our art when needed, but it allows us to freely utilize proper applications when necessary rather than instituting applications that wont work just because they are forced to fit the scientific principles.

By the time the student is actually capable of using a technique for self defence, many of the principles should be *ingrained*; not in the students head, but in their body and in their technique, as this is the only way they can actively be utilized with regards to self defence. For example, should a Taekwon-do student need to punch to protect themselves, the dropping motion referred to as sine wave should occur naturally or not at all, it should not be forced if not natural as it will make the student too slow. It is the same as the use of mass and speed, both parts of the theory of power, you either know how to utilize them or you don't.

The same applies to all the principles such as keeping equilibrium, concentrating the strike etc. However, there is one that should always be utilized and one that shouldn't. Correct breath control should be utilized with every movement, as apart from regulating breathing, it helps protect the body against impact and adds power to techniques. The only one that doesn't actually need applying is the reaction hand *principle*, as this is attributed to providing an *equal and opposite reaction* and it does so when performing solo patterns, but when striking an opponent, the *equal and opposite reaction* takes place within the body of the opponent and the pulling back to the hip is no longer needed to provide this. Now you know what the instructor means when they tell you basic technique pulls the reaction hand to the hip but you don't fight like this, though doesn't explain why… this is why! However all this training doesn't go to waste as it is utilized in other ways and as part of many applications as you shall see.

Movement

A classic example of a major difference is the way a Taekwon-do student moves from one stance to the next. In Karate the head is kept level all through the motion (horizontal wave), where as General Choi introduced the original sine wave motion (although it wasn't originally called sine wave – *see appendix vi*), where the body rises up naturally and drops into the movement, thus adding extra momentum and body weight, increasing the overall power of a technique. As sine wave has

taken on different forms in the last decade, many refer to this as natural motion, but properly executed, they are the same thing.

The Theory Of Power

Sine wave wasn't originally listed as one of General Choi's sections of the *'Theory of Power'*, though it was included later (much later). Even without it being referenced early on, it was still taught to a degree (just not by name) and was apparent in any good instructors movements or patterns. Other principles he utilized with regards to Taekwon-do were listed in his books in the section he referred to as the *'Theory of Power'* and included the following:

• Reaction Force

This is basically cause and effect, your blow plus the motion or speed of the attacker increases the power of the attack, so even if you were to throw a light blow at an attacker rushing towards you, your light blow, plus their momentum would equal a blow of much larger force. This is also instigated in the practitioner by use of the reaction arm (hence the name). As an example, all punches contain the reaction hand motion. When practicing a technique within a pattern (solo), we are taught to bring the

opposite hand to hip, thus creating an equal and opposite reaction. However, when we punch an aggressor, we can use the reaction hand to pull them into the punch. If by pulling them there movement creates a force of 50 Newton's and our punch creates a force of 100 newtons, at point of impact there is a total force of 150 newtons returned into the opponent. Consequently, for a blow without using the reaction hand, the reaction force is delivered into the opponent, hence why the reaction hand is only used for basic punches rather than on the street or in a real self defence scenario unless it's a grab or release.

• Concentration

Concentration refers to the focus of force to a small surface area which helps to concentrate the force of the blow and increase its effect. For instance, by focusing your attack on the first two knuckles instead of the whole of the front fist, you increase the force of the attack and thus create more damage. Force is spread out over large surface areas, General Choi uses a good analogy of this with a pair of snow shoes that distribute the weight on the snow or conversely the analogy of using a hose pipe, that by making the hole in a hose smaller the spray is more concentrated and powerful. We use only two of the knuckles on our fist, the blade of our hand or foot etc these are the ways in which a Taekwon-do a student is taught to concentrate their force.

• Equilibrium

Keeping a balanced body throughout each movement is paramount to effective technique. Taekwon-do stances are designed to maintain equilibrium, so weight is evenly distributed when a technique is executed. Some stances work by distributing the weight between both feet, for example: a walking stance, others distribute the weight through the centre of one foot in a stance that has more weight on one leg, for example: rear foot stance. Our centre of gravity should maintain a straight line along the centre of this point.

• Mass

Learning how to employ your body mass into your movements is crucial to powerful techniques. This is obvious when you consider the difference between the damaged caused in a car crash with that in a train crash. For instance, a punch using only the weight of your arms is far less effective than a punch backed by the mass of your whole body. In Taekwon-do, students are taught to increase their own mass or more-so utilize the use of it better by using hip twist, speed, and dropping into stances as mass increases when travelling in a downward motion.

• Breath Control

In Taekwon-do emphasis is placed on proper breathing. This not only keeps you from premature fatigue, but also increases your power by tensing your abdominal muscles and can even stiffen pain when attacked as well as increase power to blows. Taekwon-do students are not only taught to exhale sharply on movements but also to disguise breathing when out of breath, so as not to give our attackers a sign that we are tired, that they may use to their advantage. As a note, audible breathing was introduced into the patterns around the mid 1980's, so wasn't originally part of it.

• Speed

Martial artists agree that speed is a determining factor in effectiveness. The Theory of Power shows that an increase in speed greatly influences the power of ones technique. Power = Mass X Speed^2, so speed is a necessary requirement in the formulation of mass, in fact it is probably the most important aspect, as without it, no matter how heavy you are you cannot hit the target and thus, techniques that can not be performed with speed become redundant.

Non-Listed Scientific Principles

General Choi listed the principles above in the section the *'Theory of Power'* and they were applied to each movement to increase its effect. However, other scientific principles were also adhered to or applied to certain movements and these are not mentioned on the list but are found within Taekwon-do.

These are:

• Interception

This is one of the most overlooked areas with regards to Taekwon-do applications but also one of the most fundamental and it's a simple precedent. When a block is used as a block, it shouldn't impact with the target when its at its full peak of power, but rather it should intercept it. This is the reason that in nearly all the blocking techniques performed in the coloured patterns, that a forward step or forward type motion (a pivot) is used. Intercepting a technique means you make *point of impact* before the attacking technique is allowed to reach full power, meaning it is less powerful when you intercept it, which increase the likehood of your technique damaging the opponent, as your force is stronger.

Basic Blocking

Blocking using the intercept principle

• Torque

Techniques like Reverse Turning kick (*Bandae Dollyo Chagi*) utilize torque. Torque is a way in which rotation is caused and the reverse turning kick is a prime example as it winds up from the head, to the shoulders, to the chest and the waist causing the leg and the foot to rotate round with a terrific amount of force, but all performed in an instant.

• Coiling Of A Spring

A spring winds up, then unleashes itself with a terrific amount of force. The same should be applied to similar motions in Taekwon-do, techniques like back piercing kick (*Dwit Cha Jirugi*) work on this principles and we draw in all our power as we spring, then unleash it *spring like* as we kick.

• Whipping Motions

Most striking applications use this method. Patterns for competition have made students think its okay to hold out their limbs to allow the judges to see their perfect side kick, but in reality this would be a very dangerous practice. The whipping motion is designed to transfer energy from the attacking tool, rather than simply *pushing* the technique into it and relying on mass to do the work. It further allows the student to retract techniques quickly and enables follow up technique more readily. Good examples of this are back fist strikes and the third and sixth movement of Won-Hyo where we drop into fixed stance whilst punching and the sudden stop transfers the energy from our punch into our opponent.

• Muscle Tension

Even within the patterns there are specific muscle tension exercises and blocking techniques to further aid development. Muscle tension works rather like an elastic band that stretches only so far, before it can go no more and suddenly stops. A technique is relaxed until it is fully utilized and then the muscles are tensed. A good example is the circular block found in Won-Hyo. Taekwon-do students are also taught to tense their muscles on impact, this refers not only to the muscles of the arm etc. but also the abdomen to increase overall power by utilizing these larger muscle groups.

• Rhythmical Motion

Taekwon-do patterns are meant to be performed with a rhythmical motion between movements which allows a continual flow of energy from one move to the next. As soon a one technique is completed, another begins. I have heard the reason for this as being based on the Taoist conception of universal continuity and eternal change, though it is an equally valid point that its because a student needs to flow almost seamlessly between techniques in order for them to work correctly because as you will see, that is how many combinations of movements work, with many techniques utilizing or capitalizing on the next in many cases.

• Fire and Water Principles

Students are often taught that blocks, after completion, are solid (at least until the next movement). For example, if we were to use a knife-hand block to block for example a grab, the block would hit the impact point and become solid (via muscle tension) in order to deflect or destroy the attacking limb. However, at black belt we are taught to flow, meaning that we utilize the principle of water to continually flow in a circular motion. This is how Taekwon-do can be used against harder objects like sticks. The hand is simply not designed to take the massive impact a direct block from an inanimate object would cause, yes we may break the stick, or we may deflect it by hitting it at an angle rather than straight on (like Chookyo Makgi – Rising Block) but we would probably break our hand or arm. The water principle keeps the incoming energy (of the stick) moving and thus less energy is absorbed directly in the impact between our arm or hand and the stick itself. The knife-hand for example would hit the stick, but keep on flowing in a circular motion, redirecting much of the energy from the attack. The hard blocks learnt as coloured belts can thus be termed part of the *'fire principle'* and the same blocks utilized as described above are part of the *'water principle'*. Like Hosinsol training, these principles were possibly retained from General Choi's exposure to Hapkido, or brought in by one of the instructors with Hapkido experience.

• Ki

Contrary to popular belief, Ki was originally part of Taekwon-do training. If you look at some of the old reference books on patterns you will see sections where kihaps are included, and these are the basic training for Ki. For some reason it was dropped from standard training, though many of the 1st generation masters still included the Ki (or kihap) points. Why was it dropped? Possibly because as Taekwon-do was for soldiers and they needed instant techniques, the cultivation of Ki was seen as pointless when their training time could be put to better use with the physical side of combat training.

However, my first association didn't teach any Ki attributes at all, and their linage was direct to a pioneering master of Taekwon-do, and even though I have since learnt some basic Dan Jun Ki breathing exercises, and knew that Ki *was* a part of early Taekwon-do history, I felt it prudent to seek another opinion on just why Ki is not openly taught or an official part of Taekwon-do.

My good friend and fellow Taekwon-do instructor Yi, Yun Wook[35] agreed and said it was part of original Taekwon-do and offered the following:

Ki is still used in Taekwon-do, the most obvious *ki* movement in Taekwon-do is the *joon bi* position. When executed properly, you exhale as you make your fist towards the centre of your breathing point called "*dan june*". This is a basic movement in harnessing the universal energy to your energy centre in Chinese *ki* exercises. If you reverse engineer it, the only difference is in the hand movements. The original movement was open hand pushing down motion, TKD uses closed fists.

As in martial artists working with their swords or spears as extensions of their *ki*, the striking movements or kicks in Taekwon-do are also extensions of *ki*. It was always there in Taekwon-do. Only the consciousness part of the *ki* was not explained. Trained martial artists can adjust the level of the *ki* going out or coming in. The purpose of level adjustment varies on situations. The concept is similar to a force shield found in science fiction. *Bona fide* Taekwon-do grandmasters always knew this. Ever wonder why some of the Taekwon-do Grandmasters will use their technique on you with full force contact, but does not hurt you?

In soft and circular martial arts such as Aikido, Jujitsu, Hapkido, or Kung Fu; the opponent's *ki* is used to redirect/deflect to defeat the opponent. *Bona fide* Taekwon-do Grandmasters will also use this technique. But *ki* can be also used for healing or reviving purposes[36]. Bona fide Taekwon-do Grandmasters will use reviving techniques using *ki* on their students who need them.

Ki is not openly taught for a number of reasons. One major reason is that General Choi did not want to teach Taekwon-do techniques or concepts that could not be explained with science. Thus *ki* remained as one of the mystical techniques untouched in Taekwon-do. The closest we get to the concept of *ki* openly in Taekwon-do, is "breathing technique" or "breathing exercise" as you execute the techniques. The majority of *bona fide* old Taekwon-do Grandmasters acknowledge the existence of *ki*. The old Grandmasters taught it as breathing techniques and taught advanced *ki* techniques to entrusted senior black belts.

The second major reason is, Taekwon-do has parts of its foundation based on Japanese Karate, especially the Shotokan style. But Shotokans founder Gichin Funakoshi, also did not teach about *ki*. Either he did not know about the *ki* component from the original Chinese arts or knew about it but did not teach *ki*. Either way, it is not formally taught in the regular Shotokan curriculums.

---

[35] Yi, Yun Wook is Taekwon-do instructor, with 30 plus years of Taekwon-do experience. He has trained, as a student, under four 1ˢᵗ generation pioneers of Ch'ang Hon Taekwon-do. His father was training martial arts in Korea at the time Taekwon-do was officially named.

[36] See Appendix v

The third major reason is, that using *ki* with training is a dangerous technique. *Ki* can be used for good or bad intentions. Good positive *ki* can be developed through many years of training and from sincerity of the heart. Bad *ki* comes from using the *ki* with your ego. Boasting how much you know, bullying others without understanding the full sense of *ki* energy is outright dangerous.

Some other reasons why *ki* is not taught openly in Taekwon-do are:

1. It depends upon the instructor: Some know it but prefer not to teach it because it defeats the purpose when price is tagged on something natural. It would be similar to charging people money for breathing.

2. Some modern day instructors are totally ignorant of *ki* because they were never taught in the first place.

3. It was to be taught as self-realization-just as we realize one day we got the side-kick down. The realization of *ki* coming on as if a light bulb is going on is encouraged as a self-discovery.

To read more about Ki and martial arts in general, Yi, Yun Wook has written a piece that can be found in Appendix v.

The *'Ki'* article was written before this book was completed (hence Wook hadn't read the previous chapters) and the second reason that Wook states above, also seems to concur heavily with the pattern applications or real lack of, that are often taught due to Taekwon-do's Shotokan roots. Ki was inherent in Korean martial arts before Taekwon-do was formed and was probably introduced by masters of other arts that merged into Taekwon-do during its formulation.

Original Ki Cultivation Points

For the record, the original Ki cultivation points in the patterns are as follows:

- **Chon-Ji:** At the last forward punch before ending the pattern. You kihap as you move in.

- **Dan-Gun:** At the last right high punch of the three punch series and at the last high block of the three high block series.

- **Do-San:** At the straight fingertip thrust and at the last movement(right knife-hand strike).

- **Won-Hyo:** At the straight fingertip thrust and at the second side kick (right leg).

- **Yul-Gok:** At the second elbow strike and at the jumping X-stance left hand backfist.

- **Joong-Gun:** At the twin upset punch. There is only one here.

- **Toi-Gye:** At the grabbing of the head and the knee strike and last movement (punching).

- **Hwa-Rang:** At the sliding right elbow strike. There is only one here.

- **Choong Moo:** At the one step flying side piercing kick and the last high punch (left hand)

- **Kwang-Gae:** At the twin forefist punch. Only one here.

- **Po-Eun:** At double fisted side punches. One to the left. One to the right.

- **Ge-Baek:** The jumping side kick after the turning kick with the right foot. And at the jump into X-stance with the double forearm block

Technical Differences With Karate

Many techniques that seem to have been exported straight from Karate and into Taekwon-do have undergone some changes for one reason or another. Here we list some of them:

- **Stances have been changed to make them more mobile, but still retain solidness**

For example, what is called front stance in Karate is called walking stance in Taekwon-do. It was shortened for mobility, but not so short that is wasn't solid. This is also true of L-Stance (termed back stance in Karate).

- **Circular techniques re-introduced for power**

Most Karate techniques are linear in motion. For example a front block, what in Taekwon-do is termed inner forearm block, comes from forward position, whereas the Taekwon-do version comes from the side, in a circular motion. See also chambering positions below. Other examples are turning kicks (round house kicks in Karate) and reverse turning kick (back round house kick in Karate)

- **Chambering of most blocks changed**

In line with the re-introduction of circular blocking techniques, the chambering positions have changed. In Karate, though the blocks are linear in motion, they chamber deep under the upper arm or arm pit. In Taekwon-do, the chambering position of blocks is just above the wrist, on the forearm. With the circular route of the block meaning it takes longer to reach the target but gains more power as it travels a wider arc, the more forward start position mean we trim some of that time off but still gain the added power aspect.

- **Knife-Hand Guarding Block changed**

This is a major technique change from the Karate version. The knife-hand guarding block in Taekwon-do chambers with both hands at the rear to increase its power, whereas the Karate version chambers by crossing the hands and shooting one backwards and one forwards. This means any application for the Karate version cannot be used in Taekwon-do.

- **Straight Finger Tip Thrust**

Though originally this technique used to shoot from the hip (like drawing a gun from a holster where your fingers are the gun) as in Karate, now it starts with both hands out to either side, palms up, with the blocking hand travelling in a split second before the striking finger tips.

- **Double Forearm Block changed**

In Karate, the secondary support hand points towards the blocking arm, almost in an 'L' shape, with the fist on or very close to the elbow joint. In Taekwon-do the secondary arm is along side the blocking arm and almost parallel, though slightly back due to the offset of the shoulders.

- **Twin techniques changed (Twin Forearm and Twin Knife-Hand)**

The above twin techniques are different as in Karate the arms are simple thrown up and out, where as in Taekwon-do, they are crossed and the body muscles are tensed before they are shot out utilizing the coiled spring principle.

- **Bending Ready Stance changed – no resting foot**

The bending ready stance in Karate is utilized by resting the foot of the raised leg actually on the other leg. In Taekwon-do, the leg is in a chambered position, not touching the other leg at all, in preparation for a kick, though the foot still covers the knee for protection. As a note, the protection is by way of dispersal of power rather than stopping an actual blow on the foot itself.

- **Side Snap Kick removed**

Side Snap Kick is one of the first kicking techniques a student learns in Karate. In Taekwon-do, though it is still there, a coloured belt will not come across it as it is in none of the coloured belt patterns (it is in the lower grade Shotokan katas such as Heian Nidan) nor is it usually taught as a basic kicking technique in Taekwon-do.

- **Circular Block changed slightly – two impact points**

The circular block in Taekwon-do is taught to have two impact points, where as in Karate it only has one and seems not to go as low as the Taekwon-do version. The Taekwon-do circular block (*Dollimyo Makgi*) also incorporates muscle tension and the knee spring to increase its effectiveness in application.

- **Turning Kick changed**

Turning kick (called a roundhouse kick in Karate) has undergone changes in not only the execution of the kick, but also the attacking tool. In Karate, the roundhouse kick is commonly employed in a straight line and quickly flicks up at the end to hit with the instep. Another version I've seen is similar to Taekwon-do's turning kick and arcs round more, but the body of the kicker is quite far forward, where as in Taekwon-do, the kick starts chambered at the rear and travels round and extends on the last third of the technique.

Though the instep is used as an attacking tool in Taekwon-do, the main emphasis of turning kick is to strike with the ball of the foot. As far as I'm aware, Taekwon-do was the fore-runner of utilizing the ball of the foot as the chief attacking tool for turning kicks, this could be down to the science involved in formulating Taekwon-do techniques (use of concentration of force for example). However, it could just as easily been implemented due to a simple premise… that soldiers wear boots and army boots do not allow for the instep to be straightened out. Perhaps it was a combination of the two! A Taekwon-do kickers body is also straighter on execution of the technique, where as a Karate student tends to finish in a arc shape.

- **Rising blocks start higher up with little or no twist**

The rising blocks in Taekwon-do now contain only minimal twist if any at all, as it was deemed more vital to enable the student to cover their head quickly from a downwards attack, as whatever weapon (hand, stick etc) was being used, it was already close to the head upon deployment, as a quicker response was needed.

- **Palm Hooking Block**

During research for this chapter of the book I asked many Shotokan Karateka if the Sonbadak Golcha Makgi (Palm Hooking Block), as found in Joong-Gun, is found within the kata's of Shotokan. They all replied that though there are similar techniques (knife-hands, hooking punches etc.) the actual block, as it is performed and executed in Taekwon-do is not found in any of the Shotokan kata's at all. So as early as 5th kup level, we find techniques unique to Taekwon-do and later on it is discussed why that is so!

- **Others/Black Belt Tuls**

Taekwon-do's black belt patterns also contain techniques not found in Karate, especially the kicking techniques like those found in patterns such as Juche tul. Techniques such as Reverse

Turning Kick, Back Piercing Kicks, Hook Kicks and Spinning kicks did not exist in Japanese Karate until way after 1970's or 1980's and were exported in from Taekwon-do after pioneers such as Grandmaster Hee Il Cho used them with great success in the Open Karate tournaments of the 70's and 80's. My friend, Yi, Yun Wook tells me that his father has told him that in the late 50's and early 60's Japanese instructors of Karate used to balk at the idea of exposing your back to the enemy in sparring when he trained with Okinawan Karate guys.

Of course, this list is by no means exhaustive as I would need to have studied Karate, or specifically Shotokan Karate for a reasonable time for a 100% comparison. It should also be remember that this comparison is actually between a specific style of Karate and that other systems may actually include some of the above, but General Choi didn't study all systems of Karate, only one – Shotokan, hence the basis for comparison.

CHAPTER 4

Finding The Applications

'The significant problems we face can not be solved at the same level of thinking we were at when we created them'

Albert Einstein

The Meaning Of 'Hae Sul'

If you do not speak Korean, you may be wondering about the title of this book – 'Ch'ang Hon Taekwon-do Hae Sul'; so I will explain how the title came about briefly here.

The name of the system this book addresses is known as the 'Ch'ang Hon' system of Taekwon-do. 'Chang Hon' was the penname of General Choi, Hong Hi and the patterns or tuls of this system are often referred to as the 'Ch'ang Hon tuls'. This distinguishes them from other patterns taught in other systems of Taekwon-do, for example; the Taeguek forms, the Palgwae forms or the black belt patterns of WTF/Kukki Taekwondo.

The teaching of the applications to the Karate techniques contained in the katas is known as 'Bunkai', the Korean equivalent is the word/s 'Boon Hae' or 'Boonhae'. I have come across a couple of definitions of the word 'Bunkai/Boon Hae', these are:

- To divide and explain
- Taking apart and dismantling

Originally the title was going to read 'Ch'ang Hon Taekwon-do Boon Hae' or dividing/dismantling and explanation of the Ch'ang Hon/ITF patterns.

However, 'Boon Hae' is simply a direct translation of 'Bunkai' (if the same characters were used by Koreans) but the Korean meaning for 'Boon Hae' is different from the Japanese meaning of 'Bunkai'. 'Boon Hae' literally means 'to fall or break apart' where as 'Hae Sul' means 'analysis in-depth', in other words a detailed critique or in-depth study of the 'Ch'ang Hon' patterns – which is what this book really is. It is not just a case of taking apart the movements within the patterns and giving them a meaning or interpretation, but an in-depth study of why they are laid out in the way they are, how this came about and a detailed examination of each movement, the techniques and how they inter-connect with regards to the applications themselves. Of course, after reading the book, learning and then teaching or showing the applications, they are or can be termed 'Boon Hae', or the teaching of applications.

창헌류 태권도 해설

On the book cover (and at the bottom of the chapters) you can see Korean Hangul. Of course this is the book title in Korean, however, for those that may be interested, it breaks down like this:

창 헌 류	태 권 도	해 설	- Korean/Hangul
Chang Hon Ryu	**Tae Kwon Do**	**Hae Sul**	- English
蒼 軒 流	跆 拳 道	解 說	- Chinese/Kanji

The Chinese lettering is for other Asian readers who may not be able to read either English or Korean as even though the bulk of the text is in English, the patterns and their applications are universal and so with the book laid out in the way that it is, its context can be beneficial for everyone, irrespective of race.

But why the Ryu (류)? Well, *Ryu* means *style* and in Korean, the term *'Chang Hon Tae Kwon Do'* is not widely used when referring to or describing General Choi's Taekwon-do, it is always *'Chang Hon Ryu Tae Kwon Do'*.

Taekwon-do For Self Defence

Taekwon-do is an primarily an impact based martial art. On the surface the majority of the defence aspects come about from striking. General Choi simply stated that if grabbed, there are three main options:

1. Perform a release motion
2. Perform a break motion (to break the joint)
3. Perform a strike

Of the three, the strike is the simplest to perform and the most direct, so resolutions to many situations can be found with a well placed strike. For example, a person grabs you arm - instead of trying a complicated technique to release or lock the attacker, simply strike them with the opposite hand, if both hands are tied up, use the legs – in many cases, it really is that simple. Modern Self defence instructors emphasize the KISS principle (**K**eep **I**t **S**imple **S**tupid), this is the same as General Choi did back then, so in fact he was ahead of his time.

The scientific principles that General Choi added to make Taekwon-do what it is greatly enhance the effects of striking and other techniques. However, as you will see, there are more than simple block or strike applications contained within the patterns of Taekwon-do, whether they were meant to be there or not.

You can keep practising Taekwon-do patterns techniques the way they have always been shown if you wish, as even this way, properly trained Taekwon-do offers many solutions in Self Defence situations, but Taekwon-do also offers a lot more if you chose to dig a little deeper and find applications in patterns that may not be strictly Taekwon-do (though they may have been originally), but are still derived via the patterns one way or another.

Application Research

At first I was simply going to detail all the applications I had learnt to the various movements contained within the patterns and research why General Choi would have chosen to alter techniques he learnt from his previous training.

As I started to list out the applications, I came across certain movements and became aware that some applications didn't seem to fit. The encyclopedia had an application which was often very basic or simply had little chance of working. Even though I had often been taught different applications to the same movement that made more sense, when I really dug deep, I realised even these needed to be researched somewhat, which is what I did.

So, apart from detailing applications to certain movement that often confuse students, we are also going to add extra depth and dimensions to what we already (or will soon) know. By using a formula, we can find even more applications than I can possibly list in this book, so after you have exhausted these, you can continue and find even more.

For those that I couldn't determine straight away, we can make educated guesses based on research as to what they can be used for if they warrant being different from those in the encyclopedia because they are often repeated or nonsensical, which is often the case I'm afraid.

To find applications not immediately apparent (or even those that we at first thought were) in the Ch'ang Hon patterns of Taekwon-do we have to look at a number of sources, plus a number of influences.

1. The Katas that had a hand in formulating the Taekwon-do Patterns
2. The Military Factor
3. The Time Period
4. Scientific Influences
5. The Korean Identity

Original Kata

The Ch'ang Hon patterns, are derived largely from the Shotokan kata, which in themselves are derived from Okinawan Kata. However, this is not the whole story, as Okinawan kata themselves were derived from Chinese forms of Kung Fu, but underwent a radical change in their history, resulting in two sets of kata, which, though similar in techniques, varied and differed in application. Different Karate masters taught the different sets depending on their instructors and linage.

So we can look to the sources of the Ch'ang Hon tul in two places.

1. Okinawan and/or Japanese katas
2. Chinese Forms

General Choi would have learnt the Okinawan kata which had been modified and adapted and was taught to Funakoshi, but we can also utilise the original Chinese applications as well, which included many more pressure point applications as well as throws, locking and restraint techniques. These give us two basic starting points when looking for other applications and a point for future interpretations to add to our arsenal.

The Military Factor

The military factor would have played a big role in the formation or changing of many techniques or applications. As General Choi was given the task of teaching self defence to the army it stands to reason applications would reflect that, hence the emphasis on '*one blow, one kill*'. General Choi clearly states he added military tactics to Taekwon-do, he is possibly referring Taekwon-do as a whole, but we have to ask how much of an influence this would have had when formulating the patterns.

In the section in the encyclopedia titled "*Composition of Taekwon-do*" he lists the various facets involved in the art to show its military equivalent.

1. Fundamental Movements = Individual soldier's basic training
2. Dallyon = Maintenance of equipment
3. Patterns = Platoon tactics
4. Sparring = Field exercises in simulated combat conditions
5. Self-Defence = Actual Combat

We can see the Generals military perceptions and how they were infused into Taekwon-do as a whole. He refers to Patterns as Platoon tactics, does this refer to the whole pattern or the individual movements? Personally, from studying the patterns I can see no relevance to '*Platoon Tactics*' other than as a group training exercise, though I am no soldier, so someone from a military back ground may well do. Personally, I believe General Choi was simply referring to how to train a lot of

people (a platoon) at one time, rather than a few and how patterns training fits the criteria.

Time Period

We should remember that Taekwon-do was being formulated during and directly after the Korean war. This gave a unique insight of what did and didn't worked, as it was being battlefield tested and was modified to suit. Basically, it was General Choi's Lieutenants who led the way in stating what did and didn't work, although the final approval for what was, and what wasn't left in probably came down to the General still. Inevitably, different Lieutenants (future 1st generation instructors) would have different applications to the same movement, depending on their preference. Many instructors today miss this important point when quoting from the manuals, though it is understandable.

Apparently, there are records from the Vietnam war of what happened when the Viet Cong engaged Korean soldiers in combat. There was a brutal side to this, as I am reliably informed that some Korean soldiers actually tried their techniques out on the captured enemy so, though vicious, they found out the effects of certain strikes on certain places and even experimented to see what techniques would cause quick breaks, internal bleeding, maim or even kill an enemy instantly. The war was indeed brutal in many areas.

We must consider that during the time period of when Taekwon-do was formulated General Choi was a serving military officer, he came from a military academy and thus, his word carried much more weight than a lower officer or soldier, so others may have had the knowledge of certain applications but unless it was *okayed* by the General, it simply wasn't brought up or stated as the *approved* application.

Taekwon-do was firstly formulated for and with, soldiers in mind, to be used on the battlefield (and it has been very successfully on numerous occasions). This can be clearly seen when referring to different versions of Taekwon-do manuals, where anti-bayonet techniques are prevalent in the early editions and, as Taekwon-do became more popular in civilian society, these were phased out. Other areas were possibly also phased out due to military use such as the Ki elements mentioned earlier.

At the time, the 1940s to early 1950s, information was not widely available as it is now, there was no internet, few books and students were taught and rarely questioned what they learnt! Furthermore, a soldier then has no need for complicated restraint techniques as when grabbed, he needs quick results, he simply needs to destroy the enemy as quickly as possible and move on, hence why a strike is often given rather than a complicated release technique.

Taekwon-do evolved, the evolution can be seen from military to civilian teachings, but it evolved before that, from what General Choi learnt to what he felt was needed to teach soldiers. This opens up much scope, from more complicated movements, to other concepts like Ki (chi) etc. They might even have originally been part of Taekwon-do, but later dropped or discarded much like the anti-bayonet techniques were, after all, a soldier needs instant techniques with solid reliability behind them.

Scientific Influences

We must also consider the scientific influences General Choi added to individual techniques or groups of techniques and movements, especially where a movement or technique has been clearly changed to be unique to Taekwon-do. For example how we perform knife-hand guarding blocks. The most well know are of course illustrated in the Encyclopedias under the '*Theory of Power*' section. Reaction force, concentration, equilibrium, mass and speed are the ones stated, but as mentioned previously, Taekwon-do also utilizes momentum, whipping motion principles, the use of torque and natural body mechanics to enhance its movements. Some movements in the patterns have no primary combat applications at all (though often a secondary application can be incorporated quite easily), their role was to increase the understanding of the scientific principles and train the users body in certain way, like body shifting in mid air.

Korean Identity

Finally, we must factor in the 'Korean identity'; General Choi wanted to formulate an art form unique to Korea, which maintained and adhered to its heritage, hence the naming of the Taekwon-do patterns to famous Korean historical figures, its roots to Taek-Kyon etc. With the exception of two (now three with Juche tul), all the Ch'ang Hon patterns are named after famous Korean historical figures. Infused into the patterns are references or accolades to them. Unfortunately, without an in-depth knowledge of Korean history we may miss these subtle gestures altogether.

A good friend of mine, Colin Wee (Chief Instructor, Hikaru Ryu Gendai Budo, in Perth, Western Australia) a fellow patterns analyser, offers the view that the naming of many of the Ch'ang Hon patterns after famous Korean military figures give us an idea of the tactical elements involved in each separate pattern according the unique personality of the individual themselves.

For example he writes:

- **Choong-Gun** (Joong-Gun)

"A Korean patriot who assassinated the first Japanese Governor-General of Korea"

According to Breen, "In 1905, the Japanese army occupied Korea. Ostensibly, they were 'rescuing' Korea from the French and Russian troops which had entered northern Korea during the turmoil in Asia surrounding the Boxer Rebellion in China at the start of the century. However, their ulterior motive was the use of Korea as a stepping stone for their subsequent imperialist expansion into China and Manchuria. Hirobumi Ito, a Japanese elder statesman, forced the Korean Government to sign a 'Protectorate Treaty', inviting Japanese forces to remain. However, this did not reflect the wishes of the Korean populace. Ahn Choong-Gun left Korea for southern Manchuria, where he formed a guerrilla army, raiding across the border to harass the Japanese. The success of this and similar groups provoked a Japanese military response in the Kando region of northern Korea, where many of the raids took place, and eventually the Japanese sold the region to China. It was this action, of selling off part of his country, that drove Choong-Gun to his plan of assassinating the Governor-General. When Choong-Gun shot Ito at a train station in 1909, he did so in the full knowledge that certain capture, torture, and death awaited him. It is said that throughout five months of vicious torture preceding his execution, his spirit never broke" (2001 p11).

Choong-gun is immediately about tenacity, bravery, and commitment. However, aside from the qualities the form alludes to, Choong-gun is about perseverance and self-application in the face of oppression and physical restriction. Choong-gun knew he was going to get captured. He knew he was going to be imprisoned. The form essentially has to reflect such confines, and the fighter needs to reflect on the manner of obstruction whilst in a physical encounter. Striking arms and legs are obstruction, grappling is a form of obstruction, the surroundings can be a form of obstruction. So a study of combative manoeuvres is part of successful preparation.

In the idea of distances, Choong-gun also provokes one to think about the interplay between distance and reach. Distance being the physical separation between you and your opponent, and reach being how much you need to stretch or extend in order to deliver the correct force on your opponent.[37]

As an added note to Colin's interpretation ideas, in 1984 General Choi introduced the practice of calling out the pattern name upon completion of each pattern and for the student to try to add some of the patterns character into their performance, taken from each patterns definition and historical reference to its name, so may be Colins ideas are not that far from the truth at all!

Research Conclusion

If we do not know a direct application of a technique or wish to analyze it because it doesn't really make sense, we can look to see if a movement is in any of the Karate kata and if so, is it different from one we found to be similar? Then we have to ask why is it different? Was it modified/changed to suit army personnel, was a scientific principle added to it to which may alter it or was it simply changed to acknowledge Korea in some way.

When we want more than we have already, we can look to the original kata General Choi learnt and the katas sources, for directly related Taekwon-do applications we should factor in the military aspects, the scientific principles and the Korean heritage.

Many of the pattern applications can be found by simply studying the Hosinsol sections of General Choi's books, this is another way Taekwon-do training differs from other arts; the way parts of the whole are separated and then rejoined! Another example is kicking practice, where many kicks are practised outside the patterns, but are included at higher levels.

Finally, as the student passes from coloured belt to black belt level new concepts come into play. Concepts like minimal movement, flow, fire and water principles and even multiple pressure point effects.

---

[37] Taken from the draft version of the manuscript titled 'Fighting Heaven and Earth: Unlocking the secrets of martial arts through form interpretation' by Colin Wee

Should We Look Deeper?

If General Choi wanted Taekwon-do to be a scientifically *impact* based martial art, should we look for deeper meanings or applications in the patterns? Taekwon-do may have undergone a similar change to that of Karate when it was introduced to the school system in Japan.[38] As Taekwon-do became more mainstream, perhaps less lethal adaptations of techniques were used so as to ensure it looked *'artful'* and not *'thuggish'* and thus gained better acceptance as an *'art for all'*. It is clear certain military techniques were phased out, like the anti-bayonet techniques no longer found in any of the manuals, but perhaps this was more far reaching than most consider.

As the majority of students today are not soldiers, totally destroying the opponents are not always the responses we want in today's society, so if we can utilize our Taekwon-do knowledge to make things more applicable, then why not! On the other side of the coin, it is nice to know our art contains what is needed when required, even if the situation is grave. Though the applications shown throughout this book work on a certain Modus Operandi they can easily be adjusted by the adept student to be less brutal or non-lethal. Referring back to my interview with Master Kong Young Ill, you may recall he said "...*this certainly does not mean that it cannot be used for many other applications* ".

The tools are there, we only have to research and dig a little deeper. In turn, instead of single responses, we now have options. We enhance our art where we can choose to destroy, restrain or simply release and walk away, this is more applicable to a martial art today. An art needs to consider the laws of the land more than the laws of military combat, but still needs to keep its purpose of defence and its heritage and its bottom line of self defence come what may!

Plus of course, we enhance the training of patterns and what an instructor can offer and teach students in their dojangs, after all, a students training, knowledge and skill level *should* be our first priority!

---

[38] It is a common thought in Karate circles that the lethal techniques of Shotokan were removed to make it more acceptable to the general public of Japan and suitable for teaching within schools

Ring the bells that still can ring
Forget your perfect offering
There is a crack in everything
That's how the light gets in

CHAPTER 5

Utilizing Applications

'We do not rise to the level of our expectations.
We fall to the level of our training'

Common Misconceptions

There are a multitude of misconceptions or problems that exist due to the way techniques or patterns are trained that are present within the Taekwon-do world today, these are:

- **There is only a single application to each technique**: *This reasoning is usually apparent due to the encyclopedias. If taken word for word and picture by picture, yes this can be the case, but upon deeper exploration or even if being taught by different instructors, you will notice differences, not only in the execution of the application, but the way they are performed and their purpose.*

- **A block is a block and a punch is a punch**: *Again, if the patterns section of the manuals are followed word for word, with a few exceptions, this is the case. But if you look at the Hosinsol sections, you'll see a multitude of applications that consist of releases and break techniques. Furthermore, following Taekwon-do's roots or listening to other first generation instructors, we clearly see that both a block or a strike can be something different.*

- **A blocks application is the end of the movement**: *On the contrary, even if you did feel a block is just a block, as Taekwon-do blocks are meant as interceptions of attacks, the point of impact will not always be where the block finishes in the pattern but somewhere between the chamber and the finishing motion. In this book, we further expand on this to take into account the whole of the technique, from the chambering to the finish position of the block.*

- **A kick should be held out**: *This is a problem that has occurred with the relevance of competition in Taekwon-do and because grading examiners need to actually see techniques. In patterns, kicks are left out to show the artistic side, in sparring kicks are soft, or flicked, as scoring is more important than technique. In reality, both ways would mean trouble and that the leg would be easily caught. Students should always bear in mind, if the leg travels 60 mph to kick, it should travel back 70 mph and never be held out longer than a split second.*

- **A movement finishes at point of impact**: *A problem with practicing patterns solo is that we are trained to see each movement with a start and finish point. IE. When our punch is out, that is the finish. But in actuality, a technique finishes at the chamber for the next movement. In reality, this would allow our technique not to be grabbed, the same way in which I have mentioned the kicks above. I was always taught to flow between movements and never remain static or solid after a technique, this goes in line with this as well as the 'water' principle mentioned under the scientific applications section of this book.*

- **Black Belts should spend their time perfecting techniques**: *This is true in a way, but also seen out of context. Yes, we should all endeavour to make our techniques better, faster, stronger etc, but how much better is your front punch going to get as you progress up the dan grades? Black belts have the time for exploration, change 'perfecting' to 'inspecting' and we can see the direction a black belt should be heading with regards to the patterns in Taekwon-do.*

- **Every technique has a combative purpose**: *Through my research for this book, I have found that certain movements contained within the patterns are not intended to have actual combative purposes, though they often include a secondary application that could be utilized if* *desired, but their main function was not one of combat, but more for specific training of an individuals body.*

- **To block you move back**: *Ask a student to show you a block from Taekwon-do and they inevitable perform it moving backwards. Within the coloured belt patterns, there is not one block that takes the student in a backwards direction and this is because blocks, when used as blocks, should intercept an attack (as detailed in Chapter 2) to nullify the power of any incoming attack or strike before it reaches its peak of full power. To do this to a live opponent takes a high degree of skill and confidence, never the less, one step and hosinsol are usually introduced at 4th kup (blue belt) levels, where skill and confidence are coming along nicely, not to mention technique, timing and co-ordination, so this element should be continued in such practices.*

The Bottom Line

Though many will quote it as such, patterns, especially for black belts (but not just black belt patterns), are there to be explored. There is no totally right way and consequently there is no totally wrong way, however, should an application seem really implausible or doesn't adapt to the movement practiced, then it probably is and we should look else ware. Patterns can be a journey of self discovery for the enlightened student, or they can simply be a journey bogged down with little irrelevant details and neither enhance the student, nor the art and simply follow political lines and wrangling's of associations as they vie for power or claim to be '*the one*'.

The Applications Themselves

As we progress onto the actual patterns and the applications section of this book, all the things I have noted will be born in mind, but each application wont necessarily fit every one of the above. For example a change might have been instituted based on military rather than scientific approaches etc. However, we do need to also apply the following principles:

1. **Movements and Techniques should follow the same paths and motions as those practiced in solo patterns:** *There is no point practicing a movement/combination thousands of times only to alter it when its needed after our muscle memory has attuned to it and our thought process (or lack of it as should be the case through consistent training) has taught us to do it a certain way. The application must fit the techniques we practice, with only minor alterations acceptable. By minor alteration I refer to things like the reaction hand not going all the way back to the hip, or using the chambered hand to secure the grip rather than pulling it away, by major I refer to things like a low section block suddenly changing the start position to compensate for the application – bottom line is, the jigsaw piece should fit the puzzle and not be forced.*

2. **When we look at the technique, the whole of the technique is inspected**: *Applications appear throughout techniques with the 'point of contact' at different places. Applications can take place utilizing the start position (chamber), the end position (point of impact), or at any point throughout the technique. When students practice a block, they usually*

only look at the start position and the end position, after all, it's the end position that makes a block a block! However, when looking at applications, we must look at the path it takes, not just from the chambered position, but as we set up the chamber and all the way through to the end of the motion. Much of the final motion is actual follow through, needed for when we perform a break for example. Think of a boxers punch, it doesn't stop when it makes impact, but goes through the target, this is the same for many applications.

3. **Standard, Original, Intermediate and advanced applications**: *For the purpose of clarity in this book and when teaching applications to my students, I like to refer to the applications by the above terms. By **standard** (sometimes referred to as basic) I refer to the applications as often taught and as detailed in General Choi's encyclopedias. By **original**, I refer to the applications as they were originally taught, sometimes these do not appear in the manuals due to updates to the system or other unknown reasons. By **intermediate** and **advanced** I simply refer to techniques that are either not basic and can be considered too in-depth to be a basic application. This in no way infers they are superior, just that they are more difficult or a deeper understanding is usually required to perform them*

4. **Intermediate and advanced applications should also follow, in the main, the same paths and motions as those practiced in the patterns, though slight variations may be employed**: *Intermediate and advanced applications are categorized as such as they are a step up from basic applications, often utilizing more parts of the whole technique, have finer details and thus harder to perform. The actual part of the technique that makes contact with the opponent isn't necessarily the same as in the basic or standard application*

5. **The purpose of the opposite (reaction) hand should be considered**: *The reaction arm often has a major purpose or role in the application and shouldn't be ignored.*

6. **The stance and direction of movement need to be considered as well**: *Stances, movement to and from stances and pivoting motions in stances often have a major purpose or role in an application and shouldn't be ignored, though from my study they seem less relevant (but not irrelevant) than they do in Karate katas.*

7. **In actual combat situations things do not have to be perfect**: *Fighting, self defence or combat are scrappy. In actual use in real life situations, it is to much to expect the student to perfectly adhere to the patterns. When practiced as a pattern, they should be seen as perfect examples, or as a two man drills they should be close but not perfect if we are using resistance, but in essence real combat rarely allows perfect uses, intermediate and advanced applications can reflect this, but I refer to using your applications for self defence; allow yourself some freedom*

In summary, some intermediate and advanced applications presented in this book may not have been the original intent, but based on research we can make educated guesses on what else fits the puzzle that will be enhancing our art. They *may* have originally been part of the system, but dropped due to the need of soldiers on the battlefield, dropped due to civilian needs or General Choi *may* not have known them in the first place. We will never really know I'm afraid as unfortunately, General Choi passed away in June 2002, so knowing if the patterns originally had more to the applications than shown in the encyclopedias is also impossible; exactly what colours he used to paint his picture in this part are lost, but it makes our art much more open to study and thus enjoyable as well as ever expanding.

What it does do however, is allow those that want to, to work within the framework of Taekwon-do and create a picture with our own colours. Perhaps this was General Choi's intention all along? Either way, it allows us to add further depth to our martial art, add new levels and perspectives that keep it interesting and practical, whilst still retaining its shape, form and essence.

When To Teach Applications

Before we move onto the actual applications themselves, we should quickly cover the area of when is the best time to teach or learn more advanced applications. Though this is entirely up to the instructor, I personally believe that teaching more advanced applications too early has a negative effect. Referring back to my romanticised definition of why the encyclopedia contains basic applications, it is these applications the student should be visualizing when practicing techniques contained within the patterns. This way, they not only practice the impact points of the multiple applications but learn the follow through as well. Taught too early and a student will simply stop where he/she visualizes the application working, which in turn loses the follow through and thus actually makes the application unworkable in the end!

So once a student has a solid grasp on the patterns, then applications can be introduced. Senior coloured belts or 1st degree black belt levels spring to mind for learning applications contained within lower grade patterns, like Chon-Ji, Dan-Gun, and Do-San for example. Add snippets along the way to show there is more to everything being taught (hang the carrot in front of the donkey so to speak), but in-depth study and practice in these areas should concern the higher level students, not beginners.

Saburn Stuart Anslow explaining applications from the patterns

This also adds to the enjoyment of being a senior grade because as you accumulate more knowledge than you first thought and learn new things, plus the time between dan grades indicates that we *should* be researching and refining things, so this is possibly the best place to do it as we literally have the time!

Personally, its seems easier to show an application, then refer it to what pattern contains it and where, as students seem to pick it up much faster this way, as in essence, they have already practiced it by training the movement just not the application. Plus, they don't have to worry about actual performance issues (such as is their knife-hand block travelling correctly or not being able to perform fundamental movements) as they can already do the technical side to a certain efficiency and skill, so can concentrate on simply applying the application shown.

Consequently, junior grades often enjoy being privy to that extra little snippet of information, it gives worth to their study and allows senior grades to keep them informed of particular movements if asked, though at junior levels it not ideal for them to get bogged down with the applications above and beyond the manual interpretations as there is plenty of time for that later.

When Are Applications Applicable to Self Defence

Contrary to what many are told, I don't believe patterns as a whole were designed as fighting at all, well not what most would consider fighting. To me, patterns are the first instances of self defence, not fighting, not squaring up, those first few seconds when someone grabs your arm (but has darker intentions), thus the heavy emphasis on training them over and over, to make movements instinctive in these instances (hence visualization is essential to correct solo patterns practice). Of course, applications can be used within a fight should the situation occur, but they mainly concern themselves with *first instances* rather than a fight, where, if all goes well, the fight is actually over before it begins fully and if not, this is where sparring, real sparring, all in sparring, comes into play[39]. Patterns are more akin to one step and hosinsol than free sparring, especially the competitive form of free sparring practiced in many dojangs.

Pattern applications are not fighting, neither is sparring, fighting is fighting period. Real self defence should last 5 seconds or less - after that its a fight! The idea behind patterns is to make that 5 seconds count. Consequently, when *'in fight'* so to speak, opportunities can and do present themselves, its up to the student to capitalize on them! Running through patterns over and over with no basis wont help, learning, practicing and testing applications will!

5 seconds

[39] Sparring has many different variations. By *'all in sparring'* I am referring to the type of sparring practiced mainly by the red and black belt levels in my dojang. All in sparring allows the students to grab, sweep, take down and throw as well as strike and they are sometimes allowed to continue on the floor. Contact levels can vary, though control to a certain degree is also emphasised on certain techniques that are obviously dangerous (elbows, eye gouges etc), though these techniques can be used, the defending student needs to be able to acknowledge their effect, rather than feel it first hand.

The application on the last page is taken from Joong-Gun tul and is shown in detail in chapter 14. It involves just 3 techniques and moves forward by two stance lengths. It starts by the defender (the student) being shouted at, then grabbed by the aggressor and finishes with the attacker being choked out! The pictures are slightly off-set in the hope that you can see how the applications flow from one to another.

Here is the actual breakdown, step by step.

An opponent starts to become aggressive. Shouting, swearing and posturing aggressively as the student puts up a fence

The situation quickly develops and the aggressor becomes frustrated and moves forward to attack, grabbing the defenders 'fenced' arm to move it out of the way to initiate a strike

The defender quickly steps forward to nullify the attack, performing Kaunde Palmok Daebi Makgi to lock up the attackers arm and off turn him to render any strike ineffective.

The immediate follow up is the next motion in the pattern (the chamber). Used to push the attackers shoulder down and pull on the attackers arm

The actual pattern technique is brought into play, locking the opponents arm behind his back.

Keeping hold of the attackers arm, the defender slips round and chokes the opponent out. The opponents arm is still held and pulled across his back

The bottom line is that patterns taught with no application knowledge in ITF or any other schools have little use but to help make technique better, but with minimal realism due to lack of resistance - visualization in patterns performance cannot be emphasized enough as it is so important when practicing solo.

Knowing The Application Isn't Enough

The master said, "I will not be concerned at men's not knowing me, I will be concerned at my own lack of ability." - Confucius

We can look at training applications in the same way as training a single technique. To get a grasp of a technique, you need to practice it over and over, the more you do it, the better it gets, the same applies to applications. When an instructor teaches a student a side piercing kick, they break it down to teach the basic elements, then it is practiced, only then is can be applied, but even the most technically correct side kick has no value if it can't be used to hit the target, this is where partners come into play, at varying levels of resistance until you are able to shoot off your side kick at full speed and hit your opponent. Its not applied via sparring straight away... the mechanics need to be learnt in order to think less and deliver faster, almost instinctively. So when practicing applications we must learn the mechanics, practice the applications over and over, then apply them to resisting partners at varying levels of resistance. If you know the application, you no longer have to think about it, so it can be applied quickly without thought when needed, the more you practice the better it becomes!

Applications do need partner work, with varying levels of resistance, then the field needs to be widened in scope, as it is almost impossible to apply an application to a fully resisting partner if they know exactly or even partially what you are going to do. This is where hosinsol comes into play. You may also like to consider '*kata based sparring*' or in our case '*pattern based sparring*' a term coined by English martial artists Iain Abernethy.

I feel patterns were simply drills of one, two or a few movements, that were meant to be practiced solo and with partners. By combining lots of small drills into a pattern, they were easier to remember and allowed practice when solo, allowing someone to train when not at a school or club or when in a suitable location like a park or at home etc.

Back then, when Taekwon-do was formulated, competition was low or non existent, pads weren't invented and ways of training/fighting safely were not modern like today, thus it was considered a safer environment to train what was considered dangerous moves (i.e. arm breaks, finger jabs etc.) that pertained to these first instances. With the advent of sport, sparring evolved to be safer and thus fighting (in training) has evolved to be safer as well, and sadly in many schools the only form of sparring practised now is sport based competition sparring, which although highly enjoyable, disallows most of the pattern applications as they are too dangerous because of the target areas (vital points) or had to be struck to an ineffective area (as far as actual combat is concerned). Modern patterns training has evolved to a point where apart from not knowing proper applications or even any real application, the emphasis is again on winning competitions, so placing your block X amount of inches from the floor at X angle, is more important than what that block actually is for.

Properly taught patterns still retain many benefits if trained properly and both patterns and fighting work hand in hand for combat. Patterns (with visualization) is a valuable resource for self defence, after all, you cannot practise an arm break over and over without going through a multitude of unhappy partners, even in hosinsol you must pull your movement before your partners arm is broken, pattern practice allows the full motion, with follow through. Patterns do not replace partner work, pad work, fitness work, basics, fundamental training, sparring, hosinsol or live opponents, they run concurrent with them, with each overlapping and complimenting the other, forming the whole: what we know as Taekwon-do.

Teaching Patterns Applications

Pattern applications, rather than patterns themselves should be taught stage by stage:

1. **Learn the pattern**: *Students should learn the pattern movements. Where to step, what block is performed, what punch is performed at what point etc*

2. **Learn the pattern**: *You'll notice how I put this twice. There is a difference between learning and really learning a pattern. This is a stage many instructors miss in an effort to get students to their next belt level. The shell of a pattern is practiced, but not the finer details. Little things like using the knee spring properly when performing circular block, dropping into your stance so its timed with the execution of the technique, correct breathing and the fundamentals of basic movements. This process takes a long time if done correctly.*

3. **Teach the application/s**: *Once a student really knows a pattern, then its time to teach the applications properly. As mentioned before its fine to give students insights or snippets of applications, but in-depth study is needed later on. This time is rarely afforded to junior ranks, so is really the domain of the seniors. Teaching applications above and beyond basic block / punch scenarios requires a partner and should be further divided into stages*

   a. Learn and run through the application with no resistance: This allows the student to see how it works in relation to their techniques in their patterns, where to place the hands, how to use the block etc

   b. Practice the applications with low or minimal resistance: This allows the student to start to feel how the applications works, they start to gain faith in it's use and in their own ability to use it. This can be the students simply running through them but also allows groups to be taught using drills based on the applications.

   c. Practice the application with high resistance: this way of practice lends itself to certain applications better than others. For example, release techniques can be easily applied, as can locking techniques if care is taken, however one cannot fully or partially apply a break technique, an eye gouge etc without some form of compliance from a partner. However, by this stage, the students should have developed a good sense of control, thus allowing more dangerous applications to be practiced in relative safety. This is the point where applications can successfully be applied with hosinsol practice, if hosinsol is performed correctly and not like a semi-modified form of one step sparring, though on occasion an application may have to be pulled or slowed down to enable full control – this should be recognized by a partner

The problem with practicing applications with a fully resisting partner is not that they won't work, but apart from what I've stated about not being able to follow through with some of the more dangerous applications, the element of surprise is lost. In all the stages of part 3, the partner knows full well what application is going to be used, except for 'C' where it creates a more unknown element, but the consequence is that students have to be careful and thus cannot always apply applications at full speed, full power or with full intensity, which nullifies some of the techniques. Furthermore, the defending student, even if they do not know what defence is going to be used, they do know a defence is coming and often compensates in readiness, again nullifying some of the effects that an application can produce. This final part can be solved, to some degree by instituting a form of pattern based sparring as detailed below, though this is not without its difficulties as well. We can see there is no 100% ideal way of training many applications full out, with full speed, full power and full intensity, though in training, we should try and get as close as we safely can by utilizing both pattern drills, hosinsol and sparring.

4. **Pattern Based Sparring:** *'Pattern Based Sparring' is the Taekwon-do equivalent of 'Kata Based Sparring', introduced by martial artist and author Iain Abernethy in his many books on Karate techniques and their hidden applications. It bridges the gap between solo pattern practice, self defence and sparring, enabling the student to utilize applications from within their patterns, in a free, resistive, flowing, sparring environment.*

   'Pattern Based Sparring' not only includes the kicks and strikes from Taekwon-do, but also the throws, sweeps, locks and take downs found within the patterns and with the exception of safety considerations, is limitless. As Iain states "The most difference is intent. The aim of sport sparring is to win tournaments, the aim of 'Kata Based Sparring' is to enhance and improve real combative skills."

   A student does not have to jump in at the deep end with regards to 'Pattern Based Sparring', as it can be done in stages until we reach the ultimate level of freedom, where all techniques and applications are allowed. It is whilst performing this type of sparring that a student is able to test which applications best suit them, how to utilize them quickly in order to ensure they are successful and how important certain elements of the overall techniques are, like leverage, use of the reaction hand and stances.

   Of course, it goes without saying that *'Pattern Based Sparring'* should be properly supervised and safety considerations made for dangerous techniques. For example, in our school, three heavy blows to the mats next to our opponents face is equal to being 'punched out' and the fingers lightly pressing on the eyes indicates an eye gouge and partners must respect theses parameters for everyone's safety.

Teaching Applications To Children

First give them roots, then give them wings

When teaching pattern applications to children, common sense should prevail. Original Taekwon-do was formulated for soldiers, not children. Many of the applications are not appropriate to teach children period. Though a couple of the applications can transcend into this area, in the main, most do not, as they are about destroying an opponent, in a vicious way, as quickly and effectively as possible. Children simply do not need to learn this, their bodies are not ready and their minds are even less ready. Even older children (14 years and upwards) should practice with due care and even then, they should only be taught dangerous applications if an instructor deems them responsible enough to learn them.

As a general rule, no children should learn any applications that contain chokes, strangles, breaking techniques (arm, neck or anything else), pressure point applications or any technique that is potentially fatal. Along with striking and blocking, they can learn releases if supervised, so as not to put undue pressure on their partners bones or joints, they can learn break falling and basic throwing. Even then, control should be emphasized at all times and all young students should of course be properly supervised. Throwing in Taekwon-do is often taught as a rear defence first, unlike in Judo where it is taught from the front. Even with the danger points being pointed out clearly and safe practices like reaching round to the shoulders employed, students can often take it upon themselves either by accident or not, to have their arm round the throat/neck of the thrower, so we have to be mindful of such things.

As a rule, I always tell students the dangers of reaching or grabbing the neck when practicing and employ a known rule that if they are found to be choking others (a knock on effect from throwing) outside the dojang they will be expelled permanently from the dojang, this has worked thus far and I see no reason for it not to continue to do so. Of course, very young children do not really even need to learn such things and their time would be much better spent simply practicing the standard techniques associated with Taekwon-do.

As mentioned previously, it isn't hard to employ the applications at later stages and this can be done as the children mature as students, both in age and body. An upshot of the encyclopedias having mainly basic applications is that most of this can safely be taught to children as they are more accepting of things and tend to think less in-depth about them than adults, yes they question, but if we simply say General Choi said this block is to stop two flying kicks (like the application shown of 'W' block) a child will be happy with the explanation, where as an adult would think about it and come to the conclusion that this type of application, in reality, is highly unlikely.

'The dojo is the place where courage is fostered and superior human nature is bred through the ecstasy of sweating in hard work. It is a sacred place where the human spirit is polished'

- Master Nagamine Shoshin

CHAPTER 6

Bringing It Altogether

**'Things which of themselves avail nothing,
when united become powerful'**

As we move onto the tangible sections of this book; sections that show how the applications are utilized within the patterns and thus, how they relate to reality, we are going to find:

1. Applications to movements within the patterns based on their original intent

2. Applications to movements within the patterns that differ from previous Taekwon-do reference manuals

3. Applications to movements within patterns that make more sense in a combat situation and thus real life, than previously detailed in previous Taekwon-do reference manuals

4. Historical changes in applications referenced

5. Technical changes in applications referenced

6. More in-depth applications than you may have previously learnt

7. Techniques that work together to perform the overall desired applicational effect

8. Applications you may already know – providing that they are practical in application

9. Explanations of applications that many seem not to understand

To make a complete picture and add details to the patterns, I have gone through a number of sources in the order listed here:

1. My own experiences and training in Taekwon-do

2. In-depth research into certain areas or certain patterns, to try to determine the exact usage of a movement if none had been previously found that fitted the bill properly. This included fellow instructor and friend Yi, Yun Wook and web based research

3. My own experiences training with other instructors of other arts

4. Martial Arts related books that I have read over the years (and remembered the details)

5. Original Kata from which many movements in the Ch'ang Hon patterns were based upon (remaining mindful of the profile I laid out)

Modus Operandi

Taekwon-do was designed for soldiers and battlefield tested to be devastatingly effective, immediately. If a technique or combination of techniques didn't do major damage, pretty quickly, it was discarded or listed here as an alternative application, unless the primary purpose of the application wasn't as a combat technique (where I may mention its primary purpose and add the next best combat application).

What I Did

All applications had to fit the Modus Operandi (M.O.) above, and take into account the criteria listed in Chapter 4. Though these are not always applicable or found but never the less taken into account when looking at some of the more obscure techniques. Within the following pages you will see I have detailed many differences from what is often taught or seen in many standard Taekwon-do books. I have formalized the patterns applications so each technique shows realistic and useful applications rather than the customary block/strike variety. Any changes are based on either historical or technical changes that occurred within Taekwon-do's history or simply applications that are more realistic than the standard block/strike variety taught, this is based on applications I have been taught, studied or researched in the course of this book.

Finally, when representing the pattern applications, I have shown them in the order of the pattern diagram. I have tried to make each application flow into the next and a knock on effect of this is that some good applications do not fit the flow of the pattern and are thus relegated to the 'additional applications' section of each chapter. They remain useful none the less and deserved to be taught, often it's the better of the standard applications taught that end up here. Consequently, by looking at the patterns in this way, applications often become apparent that take in parts of the preceding or proceeding technique.

What I Didn't Do

- I didn't immediately assume the commonly taught applications had no value – Instead I looked for a different or even higher value applications, unless the application I was taught fitted the profile.

- I didn't try to make every technique into a grappling application, though many simply fitted that way best.

- I didn't discount a block being a block, just the fact that every block isn't meant to be performed always at arms length and to the lower part of the arm or leg (forearm or shin)

- I didn't discount strikes as simply being strikes, though often offer viable alternatives to many of them.

- I didn't presume that everything had a complicated pressure point application, though many techniques lend themselves to pressure point strikes.[40]

---

[40] As a note, I was taught many strikes and blocks to hit pressure points, though they weren't referred to as lung 5, Triple Warmer etc, just simply pressure points – which hurt when struck. However, knowledge accruement has evolved and information on such pressure points are more widely available, so if you care to research, you may find many useful pressure point applications above and beyond this book if that is what you like or enjoy. To me, pressure points are a bonus and a technique needs to have a decent effect without them even being involved, however some that I learnt are included on the following pages. That said, in the main chapters of this book I have referred to anything that relates to a pressure point in the way I was taught i.e. *"hit the pressure point in the forearm"* - but I have listed their TCM (Traditional Chinese Medicine) in appendix iv for reference.

- I didn't try to make a 'square peg fit in a round hole'. The technique had to fit the way the movement is practiced in the pattern to a high degree, as detailed in Chapter 5.

- I didn't find a conclusive answer to every single technique and don't believe there is one.

- I didn't discount the encyclopedia of Taekwon-do explanations of applications, just looked beyond it, around it and in some of the gaps.

What We Find

- There is no one way. Despite in-depth research, there is simply no way to know what was and what wasn't the original applications of the Ch'ang-Hon patterns if you wish to go above and beyond the basic applications of techniques; unfortunately many have ideas but few have concrete proof – though maybe this was the way it was meant to be.

- Of the applications I list, some are original applications, others are researched but fit the MO.

- Extra applications listed in the '**Alternative Applications**' contain some commonly taught applications that either don't fit the MO or do not flow with the patterns diagram, but are useful applications none-the-less.

- Extra applications listed in the '**Alternative Applications**' contain alternatives and also references to similar applications found in other patterns (hence they can be reused or included again when teaching applications to a specific pattern).

- In the main, applications that take a reasonable amount of skill to apply (hence reasonable amount of training time) appear later in the patterns as this makes sense from a training point of view.

- I have tried to make the pattern diagram part of it, although I don't believe this was really the intent as General Choi referred to patterns training, not the patterns themselves as '*Platoon Tactics*'. I originally looked into this area as most books (on finding applications to Karate katas) that I've read state that the direction and angle of the technique is part of the overall application. I have tried to apply this principle in most cases as it helps with the flow of the pattern. Though feel free to replace the applications with any you prefer from the '**Alternative Applications**'. By using the diagram and continually flowing through it, it allows groups of students to practice in the way the pattern is laid out.

- Many applications flow onto the next, or from the previous move, this is indicated in the forth coming chapters, utilizing parts of the proceeding *or* preceding movements as part of the application itself.

- Though similar/same movements can be found time and time again in the patterns, it is the combination of movements (either before or after) that can dictate what its purpose is and thus, where the difference lies from a previous similar technique.

- Patterns applications are designed to be delivered against a multitude of opponents (rather than multiple opponents, which implies they are all attacking at once). A few techniques are meant to be executed at lighting speed before moving onto the next, hence the change of direction in the patterns (this indicates this, but you should not be tied to it). This makes much more sense from a fighting point of view, as no matter how skilled the student, it is improbable to think a martial art student (under a high dan grade level at least) is capable of dispatching multiple opponents with much luck (though multiple techniques that have combat value are included). It is also highly unlikely that a twin block can be executed successfully as the odds of two opponents attacking at exactly the same time are too minute to calculate. This is further confirmed by General Choi in his encyclopedia[41], where he says *"the 1st degree black belt holder has usually learnt enough techniques to defend himself against a single opponent"*

- A block can still be a block, but the basic usage of interception should be applied, along with a skilled student who can react quick enough and the realisation of thought that a block should not intrinsically attack to the end of an arm or leg, but rather strike inside of them (this goes hand in hand with interception)

- A block has other usages, above and beyond blocking

- A strike can still be a strike and in many instances in this book, often is

- A strike is utilized in other ways to help the applications and may not actually strike as it is commonly taught

- Certain movements contained within the patterns are not intended to have actual combative purposes, though they often include a secondary application that *could* be utilized if desired, but their main function was not one of combat, but more for specific training of an individuals body. These are specified, though secondary applications are shown in the 'main' sections to allow practical applications to be obtained from every movement.

---

[41] Volume 1, System of Rank: Significance of 1st Degree

Final Thoughts Before We Move On

Before we move on to the actual applications and usage of the patterns and their techniques, there are a couple of things to think about, that need to be mentioned.

6th Sense Applications

Firstly, pattern diagrams and the combinations of techniques within them fail on a very basic level. And that is that to apply many applications as just blocks and strikes, you would have to have a highly developed 6th sense. As large portions of the patterns require the student to turn and block behind them, meaning as an effective self defence application the student would have to feel an attack coming from the rear, turn, appraise the situation and block appropriately – hence why many applications in this book show more realistic defences from grabs (especially in relation to those expected to be performed by turning 180 degrees) as opposed to 6th *sense* type scenarios. As I mentioned before this may simply be because of the pattern diagrams not being part of the actual combative portion of an application or even an oversight of some sort or alternatively they could have been placed as defences from a rear attack, just not a striking attack, though even this is doubtful as there are so many turns in all the patterns. However, as we are trying to follow the pattern diagrams I have taken this into account.

Aligning Ourselves For Combat

Another point about turning into movements as if they were to block strikes, is if you think of nearly all self defence situations, they start from the front. They only usually start from the side if:

1. **We are sucker punched**: then we'd mentally be to slow to use a block

2. **We are caught in a pincer movement**: As if in a multiple person's scenario and the attackers have manage to circle around us unnoticed. Even then, they are more likely to grab you so the other can attack – but our awareness level wouldn't allow that to happen would it?!!

3. **We are grabbed in order to be attacked**: for example walking past an alley way

4. **We are grabbed from behind**: for example, a woman being dragged away to be attacked further

Though I've probably missed a few out, in most other cases, we line our attackers up at the front and we'd need very fast reactions to perform a full power block at the instant an attack goes from verbal abuse to physical assault, especially a block that performs as we'd like it to. I'm not saying that sort of reaction is impossible, but in most cases the mind simply doesn't work that fast. Sparring and hosinsol contain training attributes better suited to dealing with a frontal striking attack, as in these situations, we know an attack is imminent and are therefore a little more prepared. Patterns are great for developing defences for attacks that are not particularly imminent or catch us off guard a little.

Strikes As All First Attacks

Even if a strike is the first attack initiated, they are often directly followed up by grabbing as the opponent moves in on us, this is often a natural defensive motion of an attacker. On the whole, grabbing to nullify counters is natural human response, so if by our training we can minimize the effects of a first blow, either by parrying, avoiding or simply moving back (all training attributed to sparring), as soon as the grab takes hold, we can apply a response practiced in our patterns to take out the attacker.

However, most common attack scenarios follow a basic course and this can be broken down into key stages. World renowned Self Protection instructor Geoff Thompson[42] refers to this as the four D's:

- Stage 1: Dialogue (Verbal)
- Stage 2: Deception
- Stage 3: Distraction
- Stage 4: Destruction

Both stage 1 and stage 2 allow us to strike pre-emptively, however, this doesn't utilize blocking motions as blocks, though we can utilize them as strikes and it doesn't really go inline with the 'block/counter' train of thought. As a personal note, I teach and emphasis pre-emptive striking to my students, however, this book is not about self protection per se, so we wont go into other points relating to it.

Stage 3 and stage 4 both allow the pattern applications shown in this book to be used. If the distraction in stage 3 takes place as any form of grab – BANG – we apply our application. Even on stage 4, a grab is highly likely to precede the strike, so if quick enough, we can apply it here or as mentioned, survive the first attack and apply it afterwards. Even within fights, opportunity's would arise via grabbing where we can apply applications, though of course, a well trained student could possibly just batter an attacker into submission, but then why train so many blocks! Ideally, we want to apply them in the *first instances* (which, in relation to application execution usually present themselves somewhere between stage 3 and stage 4), to end an attack quickly, rather than having to slug it out. If we get to end part of stage 4, we are usually taken out ourselves or struggling for survival. We do not want to get there.

Strikes Or Grabs

A grab by and large, is only slightly different from a strike, so many applications can be utilized for defences against striking just as easily as they are against grabbing if the student so chooses. In all honesty and with regards to what we just discussed, except for a portion of applications, most seem more appropriate for a grab anyway and many of the applications serve to nullify a

---

[42] Geoff Thompson 'Dead Or Alive', p17

strike that follows a grab. Vis-à-vis this works the opposite way around in relation to punching in the patterns.

Verbal

Grab

Strike

Verbal

Strike

Grab

Chapter 7 Onwards

As we move on to the next chapters, its important to understand the layouts. With the exception of Chapter 7 itself, each of the proceeding chapters are split into 5 sections. These are:

1. **Chapter Title**: This serves as a general introduction page, with the most commonly learnt pattern meaning.

2. **Pattern Layout - *Step By Step***: This is simply a step by step layout of the pattern. I haven't followed the way conventional pattern books lay these out, as I felt it would be used more as a reference on certain series of movements and as such, the movement needs to be clear. The problem with conventional layouts is that half the pattern is often shot from the rear and thus, you only see the models back. In these images, all movements are clear and visible, as the models used for the shots have been rotated if needed, to show a decent shot of the techniques involved. To follow the pattern direction, simply follow the arrows. Though rotated, all shots use the

correct sides, which can be a little disorientating at first when they are turned, but you soon become accustomed to it and can see how useful this way is for reference.

3. **Pattern Introduction**: This is historical details of the pattern in reference to the historical figure (or other name) it was named after. It is also an overview of the pattern itself and the movements contained within it, as well as any interesting or obscure features within the pattern. Any referral to movements applications are based on either how they are usually taught or how they are depicted in the Encyclopedia of Taekwon-do.

4. **Applications**: This is the bulk of each chapter. The pattern is dissected and applications are shown based on the Modus Operandi previously mentioned. In an effort to maintain pattern diagram continuity, the applications of techniques try in the main to follow the flow and steps of the pattern as much as possible, this is simply to aid practice and visual reference. It should be remembered that actual combative situations are never ideal and this section tries to bridge the gap between technically perfect patterns and rough, scruffy use of the applications in a live situation. In other words it tries to cover a bit of both but is not totally either and many of the pictures reflect this deliberately. Though all the applications may not be the originals, they offer practical and realistic interpretation of the movements and techniques. Historical aspects are mentioned in the text, as are some of the more complex or lesser known original applications, which also include those that have changed over time.

5. **Alternative Applications**: This final section of each chapter list applications that either do not flow with the pattern diagram, do not fit the Modus Operandi but are still interesting and useful applications, less well known original interpretation of applications, or applications that are too complex to feature in the main section. Many applications listed here use the movements but ignore the pattern diagram, hence why they have ended up here.

'We are what we repeatedly do.
Excellence then, is not an act but a habit'

- Aristotle (384-322 BC)

CHAPTER 7

Basic Movements

'The whole is simpler than the sum of its parts'

Willard Gibbs

Before we go any further we need to discuss some basics. This is necessary due to Taekwon-do's evolving history. Although much of it stays the same, especially the actual pattern techniques, some things have changed and are taught differently. In this section, we break down the basics contained within the pattern and discuss how relevant or irrelevant each area is.

Movement And Sine Wave

To clarify: in this section I am simply referring to moving from once stance to another between the techniques associated with each pattern.

Though moving forward and backwards in each pattern is often intertwined with the application (allowing addition strength or leverage to the technique), the *way* we move is not so vital for many applications listed here. Dropping into the movement, which is the norm in many cases, aids the power of the application or has an effect on the application itself, though whether we chose sine wave or the new version of sine wave[43] (or even) horizontal wave, is purely in the realms of the instructor or student, although I believe the normal sine wave motion or natural motion of dropping into the movement is more than sufficient.

Apart from basic blocking or striking, extra movement above what is natural body motion (as opposed to actually moving itself) will hinder the speed at which the application can be applied and thus cause problems when executing the applications, which should be instantaneous for the desired maximum effect and efficiency. It is up to the individual to decide which way is preferable to them, although as mentioned in *Appendix vi*, excessive movement beyond the original sine wave has its own problems even with regards to basic blocking and striking.

Pattern Diagrams

Unlike Karate, the pattern diagrams in Taekwon-do seem to represent the ideology behind the pattern more so than playing an intrinsic part in applications. However, not all the diagrams are unique to Taekwon-do as many are in fact identical to the diagrams of the Karate katas that General Choi learnt. For example, the pattern diagram for Dan-Gun tul, Do-San tul, Won-Hyo tul etc are identical to that of Jion kata. Yul-Gok tul's diagram (right) is identical to one of the Heian katas that General Choi leant, plus there are many others that match, up to and beyond dan grade patterns, though I'm sure there are possibly some unique diagrams as well which will be revealed in volume 2 and 3.

That said, in the forthcoming chapters you will see I have often utilized parts of pattern diagrams, purely from a training and flow perspective as discussed previously. If the diagram of the pattern isn't so important to you, feel free to swap and change with the many other applications offered in the alternative applications section of each chapter as many of these simply use a combination of the techniques within the pattern, rather than insisting the pattern diagram be intertwined with them.

Ready Postures

Though I know of instructors that teach some applications to these movements (or actually non-movements as is really the case), I have found no real evidence of any application that involves a ready position as a self defence technique. They are simply the part of the pattern where you begin.

Though there are no practical applications taught, as there is no preceding movement into them in patterns except those used for uniformity or pre-readiness, the relevance of the ready postures I believe is in the ideology of the pattern as well. Unfortunately, these are not documented in any of General Choi's text that I have read, so we can only assume this from the different descriptions banded about. Where relevant, if they meet with the ideology, I have offered reasonable explanations, though in no way are these concrete and are often simply romanticized.

Many of the Ready Postures like the pattern diagrams, bear striking similarities with their kata counter-parts. This is further re-enforced in General Choi's 1965 Taekwon-do manual, where he lists the movements for Kouh-Shang-Kouh kata and writes under movement *#1 'Raise both hands describing a straight line in front of the forehead at the same time look up through the triangle formed with the hands'* and underneath (before movement #2 is described) he further highlights *'*see the ready stance of Po'Un pattern'*. So it seems that ideologies, if in fact they are prevalent, have been added to existing ready stances in line with the *'Korean Identity'* mentioned in the previous chapters. Though once again, like the diagrams, I'm sure there are ready stances unique to Taekwon-do as well.

Stances

The stances in the various Ch'ang Hon / ITF factions seem to remain similar throughout, all stances referred to are basic Ch'ang Hon / ITF stances. If you are reading this book and practice a different style of Taekwon-do (for example WTF), or another art, you need to check you know which stance I am referring to (this can usually be found easily on the internet). As an example, a walking stance in Taekwon-do is one and a half shoulder widths long and one shoulder width wide, where-as in WTF Taekwondo a walking stance is considered much more upright and about a single step in length. In Karate the walking stance is referred to as 'front stance' and the L Stance

referred to as 'back stance'. Stances are often intrinsic to the applications shown and its effect as they aid angles of attack or allow pressure to be applied into the technique. Stances, when used in Self Defence, are only used for a split second to aid forward power, defensive positioning or other reasons related to the application itself, until a conclusion is reached – meaning the opponent has been nullified.

The Fist

Before we carry on with the applications and usage of the reaction hand, we should discuss the fist closing on many techniques as its vitally important to many applications. Whether it closes as the actual technique is employed or is already deemed closed doesn't matter, as minor changes throughout the years means students do this differently.

The general rule is that at any point where a fist is closed in a technique, the purpose can be one of the following:

1. **It is a grip or a grab**: utilized with either the reaction arm or the attacking/blocking arm. For example, we have grabbed onto something (clothing, hair, arm) and have closed the fist to form a grip. In patterns, due to the solo nature, the fist is closed tightly. In actual applications which utilize this, it is showing us we should be gripping tightly, though if its holding something like an arm, it is of course impossible to close it fully.

2. **A tension motion**: The closing of the fist is designed to tense the arm (often utilized with the grip), either in preparation for a release or in preparedness to make impact, for example in a block. This tenses the muscles in the arm and allows it to become stronger on impact momentarily.

3. **Protection**: Protection of the fingers etc.

4. **A Strike**: of course, it can be used as a striking surface.

Reaction Hand/Arm

The reaction hand involves the part of any application where the opposite arm/hand is withdrawn to the hip (or another place). So called as it is meant to be performed as an equal and opposite reaction to the hand/arm performing the actual technique.

Most students think it does very little except withdraw to the hip, many overlook it and apply more force to the actual arm performing the technique, making it an unequal and opposite reaction anyway! However, that aside, although the reaction arm/hand is often employed simply as an *equal and opposite* reaction to blocking and striking techniques, in the following chapters it is a lot more involved in how an application works, more so than simply withdrawing to the hip. Which from a combat point of view is a dangerous habit to get into without realizing the differences between training reaction and application of a block or strike in combat.

As this movement is constantly practiced in patterns, it becomes second nature, though this is wasted if it is not practiced with usage in mind (IE. not forceful, visualized or focused in application). The reaction hand aside from being utilized in pattern applications also has uses on its own, which I shall discuss next.

Applications Of The Reaction Hand Itself

In solo patterns practice, the reaction arm is mostly employed to create an equal and opposite reaction to our strikes and blocks. However, when there is an actual opponent, the equal and opposite reaction takes place within the opponent themselves, so where as in training, the reaction hand has a purpose, in combat, the purpose is voided as to pull the arm back to the hip is dangerous as it leaves us exposed. However, all that training isn't wasted as the reaction arm has applications in its own right, some aid other movements as you'll see in forthcoming chapters, but here we break down the reaction arm motion to its basic form of withdrawing and examine its usefulness in relation to a real opponent.

- ## Motion of the Reaction Hand/Arm as a release

On its own, the sudden motion of withdrawing the arm, whilst twisting can be utilized as a basic release. The arm is withdrawn fast whilst twisting towards the weak point of a grip (between the finger and thumb of the opponents hand) often securing a release, the corkscrew motion making a grip on it even harder to maintain.

This is useful when employed with a strike as it makes the strike more unexpected or allows less attention on the release, depending on what part of the overall technique the opponent responds to.

• Motion of the Reaction Hand/Arm as a grab

The motion of this movement can also be to facilitate a number of other things. It is employed in many applications as part of the overall technique, often either as part of a grip or grab, to accentuate the opposite arm performing another part of the application or to hide or cover another application. This is often seen with close range techniques.

• Motion of the Reaction Hand/Arm to off-balance

The reaction hand can (and often is) used as an off balancing motion. Either as described above or after gripping on the opponents clothing, limbs or other part of the body like the hair. A natural reaction of humans is that balance takes priority, this priority to regain balance will almost always supersede the need to protect oneself, thus, by using this motion to pull an opponent off balance, we force a guard to weaken or disappear altogether and add to the effectiveness of a strike or other motion.

• Motion of the Reaction Hand/Arm to aid an application

The reaction hand is often employed to aid the opposite arm in regards to an application. A common example is that after blocking, parrying or grabbing the opponents arm, the pulling back of the reaction hand helps to firstly lock it straight, so the elbow joint is weak enough to break and secondly to turn the joint to the appropriate angle for the actual break to be performed. In the case of the elbow break, the motion is used to straighten the opponents arm, prior to destroying it with a break. This is important as an elbow is strong when bent and weak when straight. This is just one example of many.

• Motion of the Reaction Arm as an elbow strike

The reaction arm motion can also be utilized as an elbow to the rear, though this should be seen as a secondary application, as there are specific applications for rear elbow strikes contained within the patterns. It has function non-the less.

• Tensing The Back Muscles

Though not an application in itself, one other purpose for drawing the arm to the hip was to tense the back muscles completely. This made the back solid when a strike hit home as well as ensuring the muscles in the back played their role properly in any powerful movement. This is required to make the shoulder joint solid to ensure all our force is utilized in a blow to our opponent. The shoulder works like a shock absorber unless it is made rigid, this adds vital power into the technique, hence why the hand retracts back to the hip at *'point of impact'* exactly.

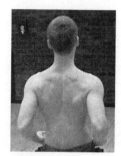

Chambering Positions

Chambering positions by and large play a big part of any application beyond basic blocking. On a basic level they serve to grab and off balance an opponent, increasing the effects of any strikes (be them official strikes or strikes via blocking). On a more advanced level they serve to lock joints in preparation for breaks and torque the body to enable body torque to be used to increase an applications effectiveness.

There is a reason different blocks chamber at different places and its because in many applications when the reaction hand it utilized as a grabbing or pulling motion, it allows the striking arm (the block) to be allowed to follow through to the intended target, if they were reversed the defenders arms would get caught up and make the application ineffective.

On the surface the chamber positions seem to make little difference, for example, Kaunde An Palmok Makgi (*Middle Section Inner Forearm Block*) and Bakat Palmok Yop Makgi (*Outer Forearm Side Block*) as a blocks, seem to do basically the same thing, but once applications are revealed you will see how the chambering positions affect how the block, and thus the applications work.

'You may train for a long, long time, but if you merely move your hands and feet and jump up and down like a puppet, learning Karate is not very different from learning to dance. You will never have reached the heart of the matter; you will have failed to grasp the quintessence of karate-do' - Gichin Funakoshi

And so it is with Taekwon-do

CHAPTER 8

Saju Jirugi

사주 찌르기

Saju Jirugi is the first of two basic exercises designed to introduce beginning students to various basic elements of Taekwon-do.

Saju Jirugi is split into two parts and the same combinations of techniques are performed anti-clockwise and then repeated clockwise so all techniques are practiced on both sides.

Saju Jirugi has 7 movements repeated in both directions

Saju Jirugi – *Step By Step*

As Saju Jirugi repeats movements it was deemed better to show the direction.

Saju Jirugi has 7 movements repeated in both directions, shown here as *start* to *15* and includes the return position between each set of movements. The 1st and 9th movements are performed by stepping forwards from the start position (8), movement 7 returns to Narani Junbi Sogi (8)

Where the student turns 90 degrees, it is perform with a pivot, rather than a step.

Photos are for reference and clarity.

Saju Jirugi – *Introduction*

Saju Jirugi is deemed a basic exercises taught to the beginning student of Taekwon-do. It is not considered a pattern, though is similar in both appearance and execution.

One of the main points of Saju Jirugi is to teach the student how to utilize the hip properly. By utilizing hip power into blocks it enables the student to block (or indeed use any of the applications) using full body mass rather than just the mass of one arm.

This is why, in the first basic exercise, we withdraw a leg half way back and pivot into the block throwing the same leg back in the process. Rather than just turning or pivoting, what we should be doing is utilizing the hip properly to add power to the block. This is a fundamental point that is all to often over looked when trying to teach the students Saju Jirugi in the quest to get them ready for their first grading.

Techniques within Saju Jirugi are interchangeable. It is well known that they are not restricted to just the actual techniques listed and can be swapped and adjusted with nearly any type of block, strike, stance and even kicks. That said, they are most commonly (99.9% of the time) taught with the techniques shown here.

As mentioned, Saju Jirugi is usually one of the students first introductions to utilizing the hip to gain power and though considered just a basic exercise that, as well as teaching basic principles core to the art of Taekwon-do, we can also use it to show the deeper side of Taekwon-do that a student may experience as they progress.

Saju Jirugi encompasses a movement not often found in the patterns and that is where you pull your front leg in half way, pivot 90 degrees and then thrust it backwards as you block. It is the A B C of hip power training.

A. Withdraw leg half way

B. Pivot and set up block (Keeping it at the side)

C. Thrust leg backwards as we twist into the block

Aside from the vital hip power practice directly following the hip twist motion, students are further taught how to drive forward and lock at the correct point, not for maximum power, as this comes with practice, but to ensure the available force (that of the student) is driven in a forward direction into our opponent, hence the locking of the rear leg.

Students should also start learning about correct breathing and when (and when not) to tense their muscles to create maximum effect. Plus we can also use Saju Jirugi to demonstrate other principles associated with Taekwon-do as well as some basic applications and more advanced applications if desired (it is an ideal way of training for more senior students to reflect back on later and to emphasis the importance of keeping up basic training) as Saju Jirugi, unlike patterns, is really only meant to train basics for beginners and the patterns is where the real application training comes into effect as students progress further up.

During the course of performing Saju Jirugi students use the following techniques, stance and movements:

- **Kaunde Baro Ap Joomok Jirugi** *(Middle Section Obverse Fore Fist Punch)*
- **Najunde Bakat Palmok Makgi** *(Low Section Outer Forearm Block)*
- The ready posture: **Narani Junbi Sogi** *(Parallel Ready Stance)*
- All movements are performed in: **Gunnon Sogi** *(Walking Stance)*

With it mix of striking and closed handed blocks we can utilize these basic exercises to demonstrate not only the basic principles but also a few more advanced applications for non-beginners – depending on the instructors preference and as the students standard improves.

The ready posture Narani Junbi Sogi *(Parallel Ready Stance)* used for Saju Jirugi is a basic posture utilized in many martial arts, especially Karate; the only difference being that instead of the arms pointing downwards with the fists towards the floor, they are turned slightly inwards with the knuckles of the fists pointing almost towards each other. The arms are slightly bent and the student relaxed. This motion has been deemed to make the student appear physically bigger.

Applications from Saju Jirugi

Though Saju Jirugi is not a pattern, but a basic exercise and it is designed to introduce new students to the basic elements of the first main stance, of pivoting/turning, of stepping to increase power, of basic offence and countering and as an introduction to the power of hip twist (and how to do hip twist), it is ideal as an introduction to the striking of pressure points and to emphasise blocking by interception, which is a point where many schools fall down; by teaching each block to stop a technique at the end of the motion rather than intercepting an attack.

In the exercise below we can see how Saju Jirugi can be utilized to demonstrate the different points at which a block should intercept an incoming blow, strike pressure points and be used for varying applications such as releases, locks and throws, as well as the normal blocks and strike associated with patterns.

The first movement of stepping forward into:

- **Kaunde Baro Ap Joomok Jirugi**

  (Middle Section Obverse Fore Fist Punch)

It is ideal to demonstrate the use of the reaction hand as a release and to describe how off balancing an opponent increases the effect of a strike. Simply have the student hold out his reaction hand, let the attacker grab it with one hand at first.

The student then steps forward, withdrawing the reaction hand to the hip and striking his opponent (practice first without the actual strike). With practice, this release works from a two handed grab, especially when using the strike motion as well.

Points to note at this stage are how the twisting of the reaction hand ensures we attack (as well as pull back on) the weak area of our opponents grip, between the forefinger and thumb and combined with the fast pull back motion of the arm, it makes it extremely hard to hold on to. Add the strike to this and it makes it twice as hard to maintain as well as increasing the effect of a strike by pulling the opponent off-balance slightly, meaning their guard is down as their body tries to ensure it maintains stability and balance.

The first movement of Saju Jirugi can also be used to point out about pre-emptive striking, though I don't believe that was its original function when it was created being that Taekwon-do is considered a defensive art form, though its a useful lesson to teach in today's modern environment none-the-less.

From here we pivot 90 degrees into:

- **Najunde Bakat Palmok Makgi**

(Low Section Outer Forearm Block) using our left arm.

- **Kaunde Baro Ap Joomok Jirugi**

  (Middle Section Obverse Fore Fist Punch)

This is a good chance to demonstrate a throwing technique. More precisely what is termed a '*body drop*' throw.

Following the last movement, the student is grabbed around the neck by an aggressors right arm. The student then grabs hold of the attackers arm (the chambering position), pivots and throws their right leg back, throwing their block forward at the same time.

Following the curved motion of the block, we thrust the leg back (as in the exercise), making contact with our opponents leg whilst performing the block and the attacker is thrown over our leg in front of us.

The chamber creates the grab, the downward motion of the block creates the twist and pull for the throw, whilst the right leg going backwards creates a point where the opponent looses balance and the opponent is thrown.

We then follow up with the next movement by stepping forward and striking with our punch as our opponent attempts to regain their footing. Here we demonstrate the reaction hand being utilized to increase the impact by grabbing our opponent and pulling him into the oncoming punch.

Again the student pivots 90 degrees into:

- **Najunde Bakat Palmok Makgi**

  (Low Section Outer Forearm Block) using our left arm.

- **Kaunde Baro Ap Joomok Jirugi**

  (Middle Section Obverse Fore Fist Punch)

We can use the second block of Saju Jirugi to demonstrate another easy release technique.

The students right arm is grabbed, from here we chamber the block and pivot, raking the blocking arm straight down the reaction arm, which at the same time is pulled back to his hip – thus a basic release is performed by simply ripping off our attackers grip. Alternatively, the smallest knuckle of the closed fist can be driven into the opponents hand to break the small bones in the back of the hand or at least cause a pain driven response. Like before, the blocking motion is followed by the punch to finish our opponent.

Though this release doesn't require the pivot, when it is used, it actually serves to weaken the grip as it forces the opponent to try to maintain a grip from a funny angle, so serves to demonstrate another useful purpose of the body mechanics associated with the basic movements of Taekwondo.

Once again we pivot 90 degrees into:

- **Najunde Bakat Palmok Makgi**

(Low Section Outer Forearm Block) using our left arm.

- **Kaunde Baro Ap Joomok Jirugi**

  (Middle Section Obverse Fore Fist Punch)

This time we can use the block to show an effective choke that utilizes the chambering motion of the block.

To start this application we use the chamber position. Our right fist grabs and grips our opponents lapel, whilst at the same time we chamber our left fist above. As we go into the chamber, we use our elbow to strike our opponent which disguises our grab and turns their head. The strike should be with the elbow, to the jaw.

From here we simply attempt to complete the blocking motion, keeping our forearm on the jaw line of our opponent and our reaction hand gripped onto their lapel which we attempt to pull back to our hip as we force our block out, which by doing so, results in a rather effective collar choke.

Then we step back to Narani Junbi Sogi *(Parallel Ready Stance)* and perform it all in reverse, working the same applications on the opposite side or including different applications.

Of course there are many other applications to low section block, but as Saju Jirugi is taught to very beginners, its stands to reason, only basic, low level applications would accompany the techniques, however, Intermediate, Advanced or Alternative Applications should be made available by those who have gone up the ranks.

Alternative Applications To Saju Jirugi

Alternative Application to movements 1/2:

- **Ap Joomok Jirugi** *(Forefist Punch)*
- **Najunde Bakat Palmok Makgi**

  (Low Section Outer Forearm Block)

If we are fortunate enough to drop our opponent with our punch
after they have grabbed us, provided we have used the reaction hand to keep hold of our
opponents arm, as we pivot into our next movement, Najunde Bakat Palmok Makgi *(Low
Section Outer Forearm Block)*, we use both the blocking motion and the stance to snap our
opponents elbow, thus rendering them useless to continue.

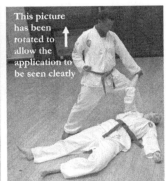

This picture has been rotated to allow the application to be seen clearly

CHAPTER 9

Saju Makgi

사주 막기

Saju Makgi is the second basic exercise designed to introduce beginning students to various basic elements of Taekwon-do.

Saju Makgi is split into two parts and the same combinations of techniques are performed anti-clockwise and then repeated clockwise so all techniques are practiced on both sides.

Saju Makgi has 8 movements repeated in both directions

Saju Makgi – *Step By Step*

As Saju Makgi repeats movements it was deemed better to show the direction.

Saju Makgi has 8 movements repeated in both directions, shown here as *start* to *17* and includes the return position between each set of movements. The 1st and 10th movements are performed by stepping backwards from the start position (9), movement 8 returns to Narani Junbi Sogi (9)

Where the student turns 90 degrees, it is perform with a pivot, rather than a step.

Photos are for reference and clarity.

Saju Makgi – *Introduction*

Saju Makgi (like Saju Jirugi) is also deemed a basic exercise, taught to the beginning student of Taekwon-do. Like its counter-part it is not considered a pattern, though is similar in appearance and execution.

Like Saju Jirugi, one of the main points of Saju Makgi is to teach the student how to utilize the hip properly. By utilizing hip power into blocks it enables the student to block (or indeed use any of the applications) using full body mass rather than just the mass of one arm.

However, unlike Saju Jirugi, Saju Makgi starts off by stepping backwards instead of forwards. It remains a basic exercise and for beginners should be treated as such. It contains (on the surface) no strikes, so serves as an ideal time to mention about how a block can be a strike.

As well as being used to practice hip twist as mentioned in Saju Jirugi, it should be used to explain the important attributes of the blocking tools of forearm and knife-hand.

Like Saju Jirugi, techniques within Saju Makgi are interchangeable and are not restricted to just the actual techniques listed but can be swapped and adjusted with nearly any type of block, strike, stance and even kicks. That said, Saju Makgi is most commonly taught (99.9% of the time) with the applications shown here.

Again, like Saju Jirugi, Saju Makgi also encompasses the movement (pivot) not often found in the patterns; where you pull your front leg in half way, pivot 90 degrees and then thrust it backwards as you block. Again, the A B C of hip power training.

A. **Withdraw leg half way**

B. **Pivot and set up block (Keeping it at the side)**

C. **Thrust leg backwards as we twist into the block**

Aside from more vital hip power practice directly following the hip twist motion, students are taught how to drive forward and lock their mid block at the correct point, ensuring all comes together at the right point for maximum efficiency.

Students should again focus as well on correct breathing and when (and when not) to tense their muscles to create maximum effect. Again, like Saju Jirugi we can also use Saju Makgi to demonstrate other principles associated with Taekwon-do as well as basic applications and more advanced applications if desired (another ideal area of training for more senior students to reflect back later on so as to emphasis the importance of keeping up basic training).

During the course of performing Saju Makgi students use the following techniques, stance and movements:

- **Kaunde An Palmok Makgi** *(Middle Section Inner Forearm Block)*
- **Najunde Sonkal Makgi** *(Low Section Knife-Hand Block)*
- The ready posture: **Narani Junbi Sogi** *(Parallel Ready Stance)*
- All movements are performed in: **Gunnon Sogi** *(Walking Stance)*

With it mix of open handed blocks and closed handed blocks we can utilize these basic exercises to demonstrate not only the basic principles but also a few more advanced applications – depending on the instructors preference and the students standard progress.

The ready posture of Narani Junbi Sogi *(Parallel Ready Stance)* used for both Saju Jirugi and Saju Makgi is a basic posture utilized in many martial arts, especially Karate; the only difference being that instead of the arms pointing downwards with the fists towards the floor, they are turned slightly inwards with the knuckles of the fists pointing almost towards each other. The arms are slightly bent and the student relaxed. This motion has been deemed to make the student appear physically bigger.

Applications from Saju Makgi

In the exercises below we can see how Saju Makgi can be utilized to demonstrate the different ways a block can be used, above and beyond its normal application as just a block.

The first movement from the ready posture is that we step back with our right leg and perform:

- **Najunde Sonkal Makgi**

(Low Section Knife- hand Block) - left hand.

And then step forward into:

- **Kaunde An Palmok Makgi**

(Middle Section Inner Forearm Block)

We can use the first block to demonstrate how to release from a wrist grab into a painful strike.

The attacking student grabs our left arm with their right hand, from the ready posture position. We step back and chamber. The twisting motion of the chamber allows us to pull our gripped hand free by pulling through the weak point in our attackers grip as we twist our wrist. If the grip is solid, it will also move our opponents opposite shoulder so a following punch is made ineffective. We immediately strike low with the knife-hand, into out attackers groin or thigh. If successful, they buckle with the pain of the strike or if not, they move to cover their groin area (a natural reflex in males).

We step forward and strike with our forearm to the side of the neck, to either the brachial nerve or carotid artery. Even if the release wasn't successful, the pulling down motion of the block means we have a clear line of attack to strike and the back/forward motion only serves to confuse and off balance our opponent more.

We then pivot 90 degrees anti clock wise and again perform:

- **Najunde Sonkal Makgi**

  (Low Section Knife- hand Block) with our left hand.

Again we step forward into:

- **Kaunde An Palmok Makgi**

  (Middle Section Inner Forearm Block)

Here we use Najunde Sonkal Makgi in a much more advanced application.

Following our previous defence, an opponent comes in close to attack. From here we perform the chamber by reaching around our opponents head. We use our knife-hand to grip onto (around) our attackers face just prior to completing the block. We then perform the block and crank our opponents head and neck, causing it to break or if not, spin round and drop them to the floor in pain.

From here we move forward, grip their hair and chamber Kaunde An Palmok Makgi quickly to pull the head/neck one way, then we perform the block and crank it the opposite direction, sharply. Even if the first block didn't break the neck, the second block will or at the very least articulate the pain a lot more.

Again pivot 90 degrees anti clock wise and again perform:

- **Najunde Sonkal Makgi**

  (Low Section Knife-hand Block) with our left hand.

Again we step forward into:

- **Kaunde An Palmok Makgi**

  (Middle Section Inner Forearm Block)

This time we are going to use Najunde Sonkal Makgi to release from a grab.

As we are grabbed we chamber in a tight defence. We strike out, first hitting the opponent with the point of our elbow. This can be to the bicep, the chest or the inside front of the shoulder, as all contain pressure points, we continue the block to strike whatever is available (possibly the groin). We step forward into Kaunde An Palmok Makgi, again using the elbow to strike our opponent as we chamber and finish them off by striking the temple with the thumb side of our fist.

Once more we pivot 90 degrees anti clock wise and again perform:

- **Najunde Sonkal Makgi**

  (Low Section Knife-hand Block) with our left hand.

Again we step forward into:

- **Kaunde An Palmok Makgi**

  (Middle Section Inner Forearm Block)

This time our opponent has grabbed us, but has tucked their head in so close we cannot get round to grab their face as we did previously, so we use the chambering motion of Najunde Sonkal Makgi to perform a knife-hand strike to the back of their neck, softening up our attacker.

As we block, we grip or (palm push) the shoulder, spinning our opponent round. This happens so quickly, that on the opposite side they are sill maintaining their grip, so we use Kaunde An Palmok Makgi to step forward and break the elbow joint or lock the arm. The reaction arm should grip the attackers to ensure they cannot release their arm as we strike.

Then we step back to Narani Junbi Sogi *(Parallel Ready Stance)* and perform it all in reverse, working the same applications on the opposite side or including different applications. Of course there are many other applications to low section knife-hand block

and middle section inner forearm block, but as Saju Makgi is taught to very beginners, its stands to reason, only basic, low level applications would accompany the techniques, however, like in Saju Jirugi, Intermediate, Advanced or Alternative Applications should be made available by those who have gone up the ranks.

CHAPTER 10

Chon-Ji tul

the foundation pattern

천지틀

Chon-Ji means literally *'the heaven the earth'*. It is in the orient, interpreted as the creation of the world or the beginning of human history, therefore it is the initial pattern played by the beginner.

This pattern consists of two similar parts, one to represent the heaven and the other to represent the earth.

Chon-Ji has 19 movements

Chon-Ji tul – *Step By Step*

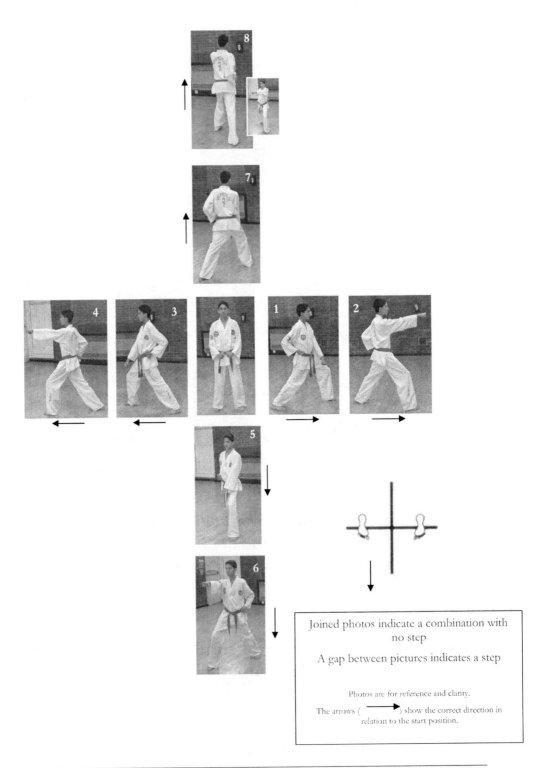

Joined photos indicate a combination with no step

A gap between pictures indicates a step

Photos are for reference and clarity.

The arrows (————▶) show the correct direction in relation to the start position.

Chon-Ji tul – *Introduction*

Chon-Ji is named after a lake on the Paektu Mountain in the Ryanggang Province of what is now North Korea and is actually an extinct volcano crater.

Legend has it that it was where Dan-Gun, Korea's legendary founder, first lived and is the highest peak in Korea and often refered to as the *'Roof of Korea'*.

Chon-Ji actually means *'Heavenly Lake'* and it is said that General Choi, Hong-Hi named the pattern after the lake because the water is so clear and calm that you can literally see the Heaven meeting the Earth, the two parts of Chon-Ji tul represent this.

Sunrise over the Paektu plateau sets the eastern sky ablaze in the colours of molten iron, tinting it in a gold and silvery glow, as the dazzling rays from the sun spread out across the sky

Even though Saju Jirugi and Saju Makgi's main focus is on hip power, Chon-Ji takes us a step further. Again, it is used to teach hip power, but it isn't as broken down as in the Saju's which can be seen as the A B C of hip power training, whereas Chon-Ji teaches how to achieve maximum power into the hips by use of full body rotation and pivot.

In Chon-Ji, we learn how to adapt the hips fully by using the 180 degree turns. This forces our hips to add as much power as possible to movements, as ideally we need 180 degrees of motion to achieve maximum power or follow through, besides it is not always viable to chamber a block behind us with regards to using it against an opponent and Chon-Ji allows us to gain this maximum by forcing the student to turn the 180 degrees of motion and thus use the hips as fully as possible as we pivot into the block.

Chon-Ji also teaches the student how to utilize their body mass correctly by introducing Niunja Sogi *(L-Stance)* to direct force backwards as well as keeping Gunnon Sogi *(Walking Stance)* for projecting force forward. The student should try to co-ordinate his blocks with dropping into the stances and thus gain advantage of his full body weight into movements, this is essential to some of the applications you will learn in this book as it can often mean the difference between breaking an elbow or injuring your own arm.

It is simply bad practice to allow the student to turn or move into a stance and then block. The motion of the block should be co-ordinated with the finalities of the stances as this is the training we seek.

Once the principles are learnt and put into practice each and every time, we can use Chon-Ji to teach basic applications because despite the low block being seen as a basic block that is used all the time, it actually only appears in two patterns (Chon-Ji and Dan Gun) and then disappears until 3rd kup (in Toi-Gye tul and then as part of a combination where the main focal point is the back fist strike and *officially* it is not even a block, just the arm moving downwards). It actually only appears as a solo technique again at 2nd kup, in Hwa-Rang tul. For most students Hwa-Rang tul (or Toi-Gye tul) is many years away and Najunde Bakat Palmok Makgi *(Low Section Outer Forearm Block)* contains many applications which can keep Chon-Ji fresh and in a sense new, in the years to come.

Though we can vary what applications we use, for this chapter I will list some useful ones that also utilize the pattern diagram, some which appear in the black belt patterns but can be taught early on if required (or interchanged depending on the grade of the student). All of this encourages the student and shows there is more to it all than basic blocking and striking and interesting things to advance to as they progress or for more senior students to keep their lower grade patterns in top form and revitalise their thought process by going back to an in-depth look at Chon-Ji tul.

Applications from Chon-Ji tul

We start in Narani Junbi Sogi *(Parallel Ready Stance)*, from here we pivot 90 degrees and perform:

- **Najunde Bakat Palmok Makgi**

  (Low Section Outer Forearm Block)

  with our left arm.

- **Kaunde Ap Joomok Jirugi**

  (Mid Section Fore Fist Punch)

We can use the first application to demonstrate an easy take down from a bear hug.

Have the attacker bear hug the student from behind (over the arms). Use the chambering motion of the block to secure some room to manoeuvre as you pivot, whilst at the same time stepping your left leg behind the attacker. Ideally, the chambered position should be sought as soon as you feel your opponents arms reach around you. From here, simply perform the block and down the attacker goes. The punch can be shown anyway you like, perhaps as a follow up to a second attacker.

From here we turn 180 degrees clockwise and again perform:

- **Najunde Bakat Palmok Makgi**

(Low Section Outer Forearm Block), with our right arm.

- **Kaunde Ap Joomok Jirugi**

  (Mid Section Fore Fist Punch)

We can use this to show an easy wrist lock application.

We have showed this attack from the rear as it aligns with the pattern, though of course the application is easily performed without the turn.

Have the attacker grab the students right shoulder, from there turn and chamber your block with the right elbow over the attackers hand. As you turn, use the block to grip the hand by placing the thumb of your right hand on top of your opponents with your fingers the same direction that the fist would be but use them to peel off the attackers hand.

Continue the blocking motion and this forces the attacker downwards in an effort to alleviate the pain from you twisting their arm. From here we follow up with the punch to the side of the jaw or the floating ribs depending on their position.

Next we turn 90 degrees anti-clockwise and perform:

- **Najunde Bakat Palmok Makgi**

  (Low Section Outer Forearm Block) with our left arm.

- **Kaunde Ap Joomok Jirugi**

  (Mid Section Fore Fist Punch)

For this one we can use it to demonstrate a simple pressure point release.

Have the attacker grab the students dobok at about solar plexus height, at the side.

We pivot and chamber, as we block we strike the gripping arm at a straight 90 degree angle close to the radial pressure point, a couple of inches away from the wrist.

This is an excellent example to give of why follow through is so important. Again, we follow up with the punch to finish the defence.

The radial pressure point is actually further up the arm but by striking just below the wrist, we utilize the pressure point and ensure the grip is hard to maintain due to the lack of

flexibility around the grip. If we struck the point directly we *could* secure a release, but its by-product is that the attacker would usually jolt forward and may actually head butt us, in practice I have also found that despite the pain, the attacker is actually able to maintain their grip pretty often as well.

We then turn 180 degrees clockwise and again perform:

- **Najunde Bakat Palmok Makgi**

(*Low Section Outer Forearm Block*), again with our right arm.

- **Kaunde Ap Joomok Jirugi**

    (*Mid Section Fore Fist Punch*)

For the final low block of Chon-Ji we demonstrate a much more advanced technique by using it to break the attackers elbow.

As the student turns, their wrist (left or right) is grabbed. The student immediately attempts to chamber the block and the reaction hand pulls the attackers arm straight, whilst the blocking arm attempts to reach the chamber position through the attackers arm. Of course this is impossible, but trying 100% should be there in order to create the follow through (this time within the chambering motion) to ensure a successful elbow break.

Following the elbow break, the student finishes off the technique by stepping forward and striking a hammer fist to the opponents groin and follows up with the punch, the reaction hand of the strike helping to exaggerate and increase the pain on the broken elbow joint.

From here we turn 90 degrees anti-clockwise into **Niunja Sogi** *(L-Stance)* whilst performing:

- **Kaunde An Palmok Makgi**

  (Middle Section Inner Forearm Block) with our left arm.

- **Kaunde Ap Joomok Jirugi**

  (Middle Section Fore Fist Punch)

This is an excellent point to demonstrate that a block needn't just be used at the forearm as a block. As an opponent attempts to grab us, we fall back in a defensive stance, forcing them to over-reach and we use the block to strike to the upper arms in order to turn our opponent as they attempt the grab. The punch that follows can be applied to the floating ribs or side of the jaw as these are now exposed.

Next we use a 180 degrees turn clockwise again forming:

- **Kaunde An Palmok Makgi**

  (Middle Section Inner Forearm Block) with our right arm whilst dropping into **Niunja Sogi** *(L-Stance)*.

- **Kaunde Ap Joomok Jirugi**

  (Middle Section Fore Fist Punch)

This time we can demonstrate how we use the stance and block in combination if we didn't manage to turn our attacker as previously demonstrated. We turn and are grabbed into a front choke. We utilize the dropping into L Stance to demonstrate how it locks straight the opponents arm for the intended break and how the block is applied to break the elbow and strike again to finish our opponent. The pull back motion when we drop into Niunja Sogi locks our opponents arm straight, which is essential for breaking the joint. Again, we finish them with the front punch, perhaps to the throat!

Next we use a 90 degree turn anti-clockwise.

- **Kaunde An Palmok Makgi**

  (*Middle Section Inner Forearm Block*) with our left arm.

- **Kaunde Ap Joomok Jirugi**

  (*Middle Section Fore Fist Punch*)

This time we can demonstrate the use of Kaunde An Palmok Makgi (*Middle Section Inner Forearm Block*) to throw an opponent off balance and at the same time nullify a strike.

The opponent grabs the students wrist in order to initiate a strike.

The moment the grab is felt, the student pivots and starts the chamber as he drops away from the opponent, this pulls the attackers shoulder sharply forward. The student then immediately locks out the block and drops into the stance. This quick motion foils what the attacker intended; which was to grab the student and punch him. The sharp pivoting motion as the chamber and block are employed nullifies the strike by sharply jolting the attackers shoulders, forcing the shoulder of the striking arm in the opposite direction meaning the punch either stops altogether or if thrown lacks power and reach to do any damage. Using this application also throws the attackers grabbing arm across their own body, leaving it in a prize position for an arm lock or elbow break, or simply a front snap kick into the abdomen or solar plexus, though Chon-Ji simply shows a forward punch, which would hit the attackers jaw bone at the side. In the pattern, the reaction hand for the block is usually withdrawn to the hip but in this case we use it to clamp onto the attackers hand to ensure it doesn't remove itself with the sudden jerk.

We could also further demonstrate how a strike can be applied to other parts of the body, like the back of the shoulder to aid in damaging the arm, we could even strike the joint directly if we wanted to.

We utilize the final 180 degree turn clockwise into:

- **Kaunde An Palmok Makgi**

  (Middle Section Inner Forearm Block) with our right arm.

- **Kaunde Ap Joomok Jirugi** (*Middle Section Fore Fist Punch*)

The final block can be used to demonstrate the old adage of '*when is a block not a block*', the answer being of course '*when it's a strike*'.

Here the student uses the chambering motion of the block as cover to an incoming punch (in this case its a right hook). After we have covered or parried and ensured we are not struck by the blow, we use the reaction hand to grab hold of the attackers arm and use the blocking arm to strike either under the arm pit, the exposed floating ribs or even to the side of the neck depending on where our blocking arm is positioned after we parried.

Of course, the follow up punch can be used as a further strike if needed.

We finish the pattern by performing:

- **Kaunde Ap Joomok Jirugi**
  (*Mid Section Fore Fist Punch*)
  moving forwards twice

- **Kaunde Ap Joomok Jirugi**
  (*Mid Section Fore Fist Punch*)
  moving backwards twice

The final four punches of Chon-Ji (two forward and two backwards) can be used to demonstrate driving forward into our attacker and not relying on just one blow, especially for junior grades, following a successful blocking application, with the last two demonstrating striking whilst retreating. They are of course a basic exercise to allow the beginning student to practice punching on both sides and in both directions.

Alternative Applications To Chon-Ji tul

Alternative Application to movement 3 or 7:

- **Najunde Bakat Palmok Makgi** *(Low Section Outer Forearm Block)*

This application not only uses Najunde Bakat Palmok Makgi but also the 180 degree turn found in the pattern. The student is grabbed on the shoulder from behind. The student starts to turn and uses the chambering motion of the block to strike the attacker with his elbow. As he continues to pivot the block opens out and is thrust against the attackers neck, whilst the reaction hand grips the attacker and the downward motion of the block applied to take the attacker down.

Reversed View

Alternative Application to movement 1,3,5 or 7:

- **Najunde Bakat Palmok Makgi** *(Low Section Outer Forearm Block)*

One of the more commonly taught applications to Najunde Bakat Palmok Makgi is that of an arm lock.

Personally I feel there are better techniques to facilitate this type of application as its awkward to apply due to the positioning required. Nether the less, it may prove useful so it is included here.

As the students arm is grabbed, he steps forward and chambers the block over the attackers grabbing arm. The block is then applied with speed to the attackers triceps or rear shoulder, producing an arm or shoulder lock.

Alternatively, if the student has pulled the arm straight enough, he could apply a breaking technique to the elbow.

CHAPTER 11

Dan-Gun tul

the throat striking pattern

단군틀

Dan-Gun is named after the holy Dan Gun.

The legendary founder of Korea in the year 2333 B.C.

Dan-Gun has 21 movements.

Dan-Gun tul – *Step By Step*

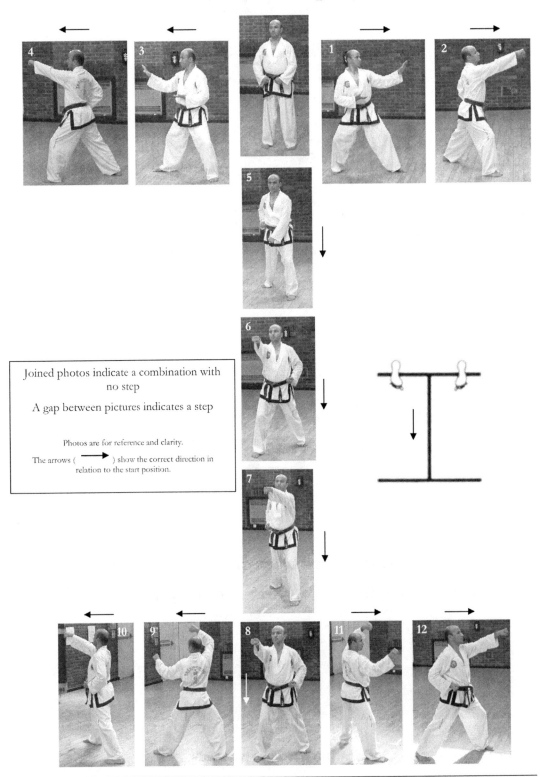

Joined photos indicate a combination with no step

A gap between pictures indicates a step

Photos are for reference and clarity.

The arrows (——→) show the correct direction in relation to the start position.

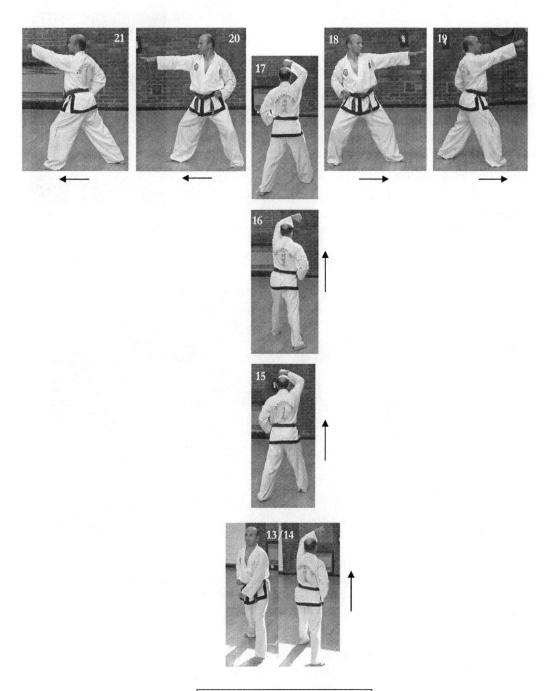

These movements are a combination with no
step between them – both should be
performed facing the arrow direction

Dan-Gun tul - *Introduction*

Dan-Gun is named after the legendary founder of Korea.

The legend goes that there was a time when heaven and earth were one and animals could speak like humans. The god Hwanin sent his son Hwang-Ung to the East to build a new country. Hwang-Ung settled on the Paektu Mountain (see Chon-Ji), the highest peak on the peninsula in what is now North Korea. This was in 2,333 B.C. during the 25th reign of the Yao Emperor in China.

The picture[44] below is a depiction of the Dan-Gun legend and shows Hwang-Ung (son of the God Hwanin) under the Sandalwood tree (mentioned in Kim Pu-Sik's version of the legend) with the tiger and the bear that wanted to become human.

One day a tiger and a bear appeared in front of Hwang-Ung and asked if they could be transformed into human form. After much thought Hwang-Ung informed the animals that their wish could be granted, but it would be difficult and would take much patience. The animals agreed that they would do whatever it took to become human and make their wish a reality.

Hwang-Ung gave the tiger and the bear twenty cloves of garlic and some mugworts and they were told to eat them whilst they stayed in a cave and prayed earnestly for 100 days.

---

[44] Photographs in this chapters introduction are by courtesy of David A. Mason, *www.san-shin.org*. Reproduced with permission and thanks.

After twenty days the tiger became hungry and could no longer continue, so he left the cave the next day in search of food and so stayed a tiger. When the 100 days were almost at an end, the bear began to lose its fur and its rear feet began to change, until at the end of the 100th day the bear had fully transformed into a beautiful woman. She became known as Ung-Yo which means *'the girl incarnated from a bear'*. Hwang-Ung, so taken by her beauty, married Ung-Yo and she gave birth to a son, who they named Dan-Gun. This child gave rise to the first Korean Dynasty, called Chosun, literally meaning *'Land of the Morning Calm'*, now known as Korea.

Another version of the legend (possibly the very first), by the 12th century scholar General Kim Pu-Sik, who wrote the *'Sam-Guk-Sagi' or 'Annals of the Three Kingdoms'*; the earliest surviving source of history on the three kingdoms of Korea, tells a similar story except that Hwang-Ung told the tiger and bear to retire from the sunlight for 21 days with the food, in order to become men.

The tiger, because of his fierceness, could not endure the entire 21 days and came out whilst the bear, with greater patience and faith, stayed for the duration and was transformed into a perfect woman.

It is said Dan-Gun introduced the rite of marriage, the subject-king relationship, the arts of cooking and house building, cutting of trees and agriculture, and how to bind up their hair with cloth to the men of the 'Nine Wild tribes' after they found Dan-Gun sitting under a tree. He also introduced religious worship and is said to have built the first altar in 2265 B.C. on the highest peak (Muni-San) of Kang-Wha Island. This is known as Dan-Gun's Altar. Dan-Gun is reputed to have lived with his wife, Pi So-Ap, and his sons, who are said to have built the fortress of Sam-Nang at Chung-Dung Island.

In 1122 the uncle of the Shang King of China, Ki-Ja, escaped the overthrow of the Shang Dynasty and migrated to Korea with 5,000 followers. After reigning for 1,211 years, Dan-Gun fled from Ki-Ja's army to the town of Mun-Wha, resumed his spirit form and disappeared from the earth. The Ki-Ja ruled Korea from 1122 B.C. to 193 B.C. teaching the people Chinese culture in the form of letters, reading, writing, medicine, and art. The shrine in Mun-Wha today contains his 410-foot (in circumference) *'grave'*.

The Tomb of Dan-Gun (left) and the reputed original stone monument telling the history of the 'Tomb of King Dan-Gun' (unverified by archaeologists outside of North Korea), found at the site with the buried ruins of the original tomb. Two large skeletons are now enshrined inside the reconstruction; they are said to be King Dan-Gun and his wife.

통일기원국조단군상

Statue of Dan-Gun

Dan-Gun is known as the grandson of the Lord of Heaven, founder of Korea's first Kingdom and is said to have *'retired as a Mountain-spirit'*, probably at Kuwol-San (Nine-Moons Mountain) in Pyeongyang, Northern Korea. Dan-Gun remains a spiritual figure that has helped maintain a strong Korean culture and it is this strong belief in identity that has helped Korea protect itself from invasion throughout its history. October 3rd is celebrated as a national holiday, commemorating the founding father, Dan Gun.

The 21 movements in this pattern refer to part of the legend of Dan-Gun (depending on which version you go with), where the mythical tiger either couldn't persevere and only hibernated for 20 of the 100 days he needed to or couldn't endure the 21 days he was meant to, for transformation into human form.

Dan-Gun, being one of the lower grade patterns initially seems to involve very basic movements. Basic punches are employed at high section throughout; the pattern involves a couple of low section and mid section blocks but many more high section blocks like rising blocks and twin forearm blocks (though this is mid and high). Blocks that have two hands involved (i.e. knife-hand guarding block or twin forearm block) are only shown employing the front hand in the application in most other books.

Basic applications for the high section punches include a high section punch to a taller opponents jaw (which doesn't really make sense considering all pattern techniques are supposed to be performed in relation to your own body size), to a jumping opponents ribs or a jumping opponents solar plexus, some of the pictures in the encyclopedia do not show an application to the punching techniques at all. The low section blocks are employed against front kicks for both, the twin forearm blocks against a side kick (the upper hand isn't utilized at all) and the rising blocks against downward strikes from knife-hand and a pole attacks. The final knife-hand strikes are employed in one picture against a bicep of an arm by the body from side on (as it would be in a boxers stance).

In the applications section to Dan-Gun tul, we see that it offers many striking techniques, though often employed in the same way most students are taught. It concentrates on attacks, throws and striking to vital points around the head, neck and throat including the larynx, the carotid artery, the temple and the jaw line and the use of the head and thus the neck to perform vicious takedowns.

Dan-Gun starts in Narani Junbi Sogi (*Parallel Ready Stance*) and I can find no written historical relevance between the pattern meaning and the ready posture. Dan-Gun is a mythical figure but if we look at the depicted drawings of him we can see his arms are turned inwards like in the ready posture, around the same height as used in the ready posture and it could be contrived that its just the robe that meets in the middle and his fists are closed in the ready posture position, but this is no more than an offered *guess* and not in any way conclusive.

Applications from Dan-Gun tul

From Narani Junbi Sogi (*Parallel Ready Stance*) we use the following techniques:

- **Kaunde Sonkal Daebi Makgi**

(*Mid Section Knife-hand Guarding Block*)

- **Nopunde Baro Ap Joomok Jirugi**

  (*High Section Fore Fist Punch*)

We start from a wrist grab to our left hand, with either hand of the opponent. As we turn into the block we chamber our knife-hand guard block, then step forward.

No matter which hand has grabbed us, the chambering motion:

1. sets our block up for its intended purpose
2. would make the opponent pull harder, thus making the completion motion of the block easier, as we don't have to force it forward as hard.

From a left hand grab (to our left side), we simply pivot and chamber, ensuring our actual knife-hand is to the outside and step forward into the block, locking or releasing the grab. If grabbed with the right hand, we drive the block forward towards the attackers mid section and obtain a release through the weakest area of the fore finger and thumb. Though later on (in higher grade patterns) I will show how the chambering motion on its own is used as an actual release, I don't believe we have enough body motion to perform this block effectively each time, as we only half turn, meaning we don't have a full, from front to back, chambering motion.

Following this, the student steps forward with the high section punch. As all applications in Taekwon-do patterns are supposed to be performed on imaginary opponents of equal size to the defender, striking to the eyes with a Fore Fist doesn't make much sense considering the amount of other options available to hit (throat, jaw, solar plexus etc) and a punch to the eye would possibly be rendered ineffective due to the angle of the arm (your unlikely to hit with the knuckles as opposed to your fingers). Instead, the angled direction of the punch indicates a strike to the throat, the whole technique contains follow through to engage the technique at maximum power, thus destroying our opponent.

This application can of course be repeated on the opposite side, but as we actually turn with a step, rather than simply pivoting in to the block like before, there may actually be a different application contained within the whole motion.

Next we see:

- **Kaunde Sonkal Daebi Makgi**

(*Mid Section Knife-hand Guarding Block*)

- **Nopunde Baro Ap Joomok Jirugi**
  (*High Section Fore Fist Punch*)

- **Najunde Bakat Palmok Makgi** (*Low Section Outer Forearm Block*)

- **Nopunde Baro Ap Joomok Jirugi** (*High Section Fore Fist Punch*)

If we a grabbed from behind, our hands are already close to the chambering position so we simply turn and strike. Targets points would most likely be on the opponents body rather than the arms as we cover a fair bit of ground by stepping, so we turn and strike the opponent, striking to any available target (carotid artery, triceps, floating ribs etc), we *can* finish with the high punch to the throat like before or we can utilize the proceeding low section block (*Najunde Bakat Palmok Makgi*) to get rid of our attacker. The block allows a different approach and as we do not come across this block again in another pattern until Hwa-Rang tul, I think it pertinent to mention this application now.

If our first strike (using the knife-hand guarding block) was successful, we can employ the low block application here straight away (the high section punch being used to simply manoeuvre into position or to grab the hair - see **Alternative Applications**), if not we can strike as pictured, then utilize the application, either way the proceeding application is utilized in the following way: As we turn into the next block and we chamber to the side, we are chambering at the same position as the head of the opponent we just struck. The high section punch is withdrawn to the chamber position but we grab onto the opponents face or jaw (hence the fist is a clasping motion – telling us to close the fist into a grab), the reaction arm can also be used to strike the throat as an extra. The block is then followed through with. The fist is kept clenched and the opponent is flung rather unceremoniously to the floor in front of us, possibly cranking the neck en-route.

The relaxed defence of our opponent following a strike gives this a better probability of working more easily. We can use the next motion (stepping forward in walking stance) as a low section kick to the ribs, groin or head of the downed opponent (depending on how they fall) just to ensure they don't get back up or when they try to get back up. Ap Joomok Jirugi (*Fore Fist Punch*) can be seen as the back up strike, if our take down technique didn't work properly.

The next movements are:

- **Nopunde Baro Ap Joomok Jirugi**

  (*High Section Fore Fist Punch*) X 2

Apart from the obvious; that they are a multitude of strikes, there is no interpretation of these movements which prove them better, though here a small alternative is offered. Therefore, in light of no different applications, we are forced to conclude that these are best utilized as strikes, although we should bare in mind they are most likely to be to the throat to instantly crush our opponents wind pipe with the force of the blow rather than a punch to the head. The step is demonstrated here as a kick to the floating ribs, just as a little *extra*.

This is followed by:

- **Sang Palmok Makgi** (*Twin Forearm Block*)
- **Nopunde Baro Ap Joomok Jirugi**
  (*High Section Fore Fist Punch*)

In this instance, we utilize twin forearm block as an alternative to a release. From our previous position our left arm is grabbed. From here we pivot the 270 degrees into Sang Palmok Makgi. Our right hand pulls in to chamber then raises above our head, allowing us to pass under it as we strike to the neck or face with the front hand or forearm.

This motion allows the following actions:

1. It opens up the front of the attacker to our counter attack by pulling the opponent forward slightly and keeping her side on as we strike

2. It keeps one arm of the attacker occupied as well as the attacker themselves momentarily as they are pulled off balance

3. The turn is a surprise movement that goes some way to disorientating the opponent

Reversed view

We follow up again with the high section punch to the throat as previously described and we begin to turn to face another opponent.

Again we use:

- **Sang Palmok Makgi** (*Twin Forearm Block*)
- **Nopunde Baro Ap Joomok Jirugi**
  (*High Section Fore Fist Punch*)

From here we perform the block again in the opposite direction.

Like most repeating blocks it can be used to simply practice on the opposite side, but we are going to use it to perform an Aikido type throw in an advanced application

After finishing off the previous opponent our arms are grabbed, we turn (as if to go quietly). As we start to chamber our arms, the motion of bringing the arms together and twisting at the wrists should help to cause the opponent to grip tighter. We immediately raise the block, and in doing so the strength of our opponents arms is placed in a weaker position, we immediately step forward and perform our punch (sharply). The sudden change of direction of our arms (up, then down whilst moving outwards as well), coupled with the stepping forward motion brings the attacker over our right leg as we pull forward into the punch and the attacker is thrown forward.

This should of course, be considered an advanced application as it relies very much on surprise and speed, as the attacker needs to remain gripped onto you. It is similar to a throw found in Aikido and it is placed here to demonstrate one of the most obscure applications that can be found within the Ch'ang Hon patterns and to give an alternative to this technique.

We then move onto:

- **Bakat Palmok Makgi** *(Low Section Outer Forearm Block)*
- **Bakat Palmok Chookyo Makgi** *(Outer Forearm Rising Block)*

The student is grabbed by an attacker at the front or side, by either a choke or lapel grab, single or double handed. The low section block is used to strike to the elbow joints, this releases any pressure if choked and allows the follow up. This block should hit directly horizontally (as it travels mid way through the blocking motion) to the opponents grabbing arm/s as if struck at an angle, it may not cause the response required to make an opponent release, hence why it may not actually create a full release from the choke on its own (as the

position is high and thus harder to hit horizontally). Either way, if we secure a release, that's great, if not, the following motion will clench it. Straight from the low section outer forearm block we immediately perform Chookyo Makgi (Rising Block), up to the opponents throat. We utilize knee spring for added power, this also allows to drop down and then lock out straight under the opponents jaw line.

Next we use:

- **Bakat Palmok Chookyo Makgi**
  (Outer Forearm Rising Block)

- **Bakat Palmok Chookyo Makgi**
  (Outer Forearm Rising Block)

- **Bakat Palmok Chookyo Makgi**
  (Outer Forearm Rising Block)

The first rising block is used to cover a strike or grab to our head (not face, but the top of our head, like a hair grab or downward strike), we block, twist our arm slightly more to secure a grip to stop the arm being withdrawn, then move into the next block and strike upwards to the attackers elbow, the final rising block again be utilized as a strike to the throat or jaw.

Unfortunately the actual chambering position of this block has been changed for Taekwon-do so that it chambers above the reaction hand for speed which means to be absolutely precise, we cannot use the reaction hand as a grip. However, this change was instituted somewhere along the line rather than at the beginning, so the original way still fits with our modus operandi, and single applications of this block can be found in the **Alternative Applications** section. For now, the three blocks can be used as training to work this combination on both sides or one of the blocks can easily be utilized with single applications of this block found in the **Alternative Applications** section or within other patterns that utilize it, like Do-San tul.

We pivot and perform:

- **Sonkal Yop Taeragi** (*Knife-hand Side Strike*)
- **Nopunde Baro Ap Joomok Jirugi**
  (*High Section Fore Fist Punch*)

As we will see in more senior patterns, the knife-hand chamber and strike can be used to throw the opponent, but in this case, we have just broken the opponents arm and struck his throat so these techniques can be used against a new opponent or to finish off our previous one.

We finished the previous movement with the right foot forward and perhaps even crushing our opponents wind pipe against a wall (see **Alternative Applications**). We turn and strike to the throat of our attacker with our left knife-hand, finishing him off with the high section punch.

We complete the pattern by using:

- **Sonkal Yop Taeragi** (*Knife-hand Side Strike*)
- **Nopunde Baro Ap Joomok Jirugi**
  (*High Section Fore Fist Punch*)

Having turned to finish our opponent, we are now attacked from the rear (this is a good defence for people with long hair). We pivot 180 degrees, striking the throat of our attacker and ensuring we finish them with the high punch to the throat.

Alternative Applications to Dan-Gun tul

Alternative Application to movements 1/2 and 3/4:

- **Kaunde Sonkal Daebi Makgi**

  (Knife-hand Guarding Block)

- **Nopunde Ap Joomok Jirugi**

  (High Section Fore Fist Punch)

A turning kick to the ribs is caught on the rear arm, taking the impact on the shoulders and the rear knife-hand guard simply hooking or grabbing under the leg, with the front hand maintaining a safe gap and cover for any strikes that may come after being grabbed. From this position the student simply walks forward into the punch. This punching motion is again high section, meaning the punch is not only going forward to push the opponent over, but also upward, almost like a flipping motion, so the defender doesn't simply fall back but is helped to land on their neck or head.

Alternative Application to movements 1/2 and 3/4:

- **Kaunde Sonkal Daebi Makgi**

  (Mid Section Knife-hand Guarding Block)

- **Nopunde Baro Ap Joomok Jirugi**

  (High Section Fore Fist Punch)

Many years ago I wrote an article on pattern interpretation where I touched upon using Kaunde Sonkal Daebi Makgi as a *'fence*[45]*'* type technique – this was for those who had problems incorporating more modern self protection training methods into their dojangs. I simply said if using a *'fence'* is a problem, simply utilize Kaunde Sonkal Daebi Makgi instead – though in a slightly relaxed manner so it is not so obvious. As you can see from the pictures below, they are not too dissimilar.

The purpose of a *'fence'* is to maintain a distance between an aggressor and the student. The front arm is used to keep the attacker at arms length, with the student moving forward or backwards to maintain the distance between an aggressor and himself. The lead arm is also used as a distance calculator, after all, if you can touch it, you can strike it.

Here we see the student using a finished Kaunde Sonkal Daebi Makgi as a *'fence'* and realizing the aggressor is about to attack, he launches a pre-emptive strike using Baro Ap Joomok Jirugi. In a real situation, the fence would most likely be performed closer, touching the opponent.

Alternative Application to movements 1/2 and 3/4:

- **Kaunde Sonkal Daebi Makgi**

  (Knife-hand Guarding Block)

- **Nopunde Ap Joomok Jirugi**

  (High Section Fore Fist Punch)

Nopunde Ap Joomok Jirugi, when utilized with Gunnon Sogi *(Walking Stance)* and even be used to effect a basic takedown, in the form of a tripping technique.

Following a successful block, the student steps forward ensuring his leg goes round the outside of his opponents leg. The punch is used to grip the shoulder as he thrusts it forward, forcing the opponent to trip backwards over his leg.

---

[45] The 'fence' was a phrase first coined by British martial artist and Self Protection expert Geoff Thompson. It is possibly the most important technique developed in martial arts in the last 10 to 20 years and should be a part of all students martial arts repertoires.

Incidentally, this could be used to demonstrate the three consecutive punches in Dan-Gun tul!

Alternative Application to movements 9 and 11:

- **Sang Palmok Makgi** *(Twin Forearm Block)*

Sang Palmok Makgi is possibly a better application to a front choke than the more commonly used Hechyo Makgi *(Wedging Block)* found in Do-San, but as this doesn't utilize the turn (as in the pattern diagram) it is found in this section.

As we are grabbed around the throat from the front, We immediately drop into L-Stance Sang Palmok Makgi with each of the forearms striking against our opponents forearms. One strikes the inside (moving outwards) and the other under (and upwards) of our opponents forearms, just above the wrists.

The L-Stance also has the role of helping increase the effectiveness of the application as, whilst our block is forcing our opponents arms away - upwards and outwards, our body moves in the opposite direction, helping to pull out of the choke. The turn (that is used when we step into L-Stance also helps to decrease the pressure off the choke as well as twisting us out of it slightly.

Alternative Application to movements 9 and 11:

- **Sang Palmok Makgi** *(Twin Forearm Block)*
- **Ap Joomok Jirugi** *(Fore Fist Punch)*

An attacker has grabbed our students lapel. The student immediately counters by grabbing onto the attackers lapel (inside of the attackers arm) whilst at the same time using the upper part of the block, at a slightly inverted angle, to grab onto the attackers arm. Keeping a tight grip on the attackers arm, the student then chambers for the next movement, bringing his right arm (in this case) to his hip which in turn rotates the attackers arm into a locked position. The reaction arm (left), extends, stopping the opponent from locking his bent arm as well as causing him to be pushed slightly and re-address his position, providing cover for the lock. The reaction arm is also used as a fulcrum to help with the lock.

Alternative Application to movements 14/15 or 16/17:

- **Bakat Palmok Chookyo Makgi**
  (Outer Forearm Rising Block)
- **Bakat Palmok Chookyo Makgi**
  (Outer Forearm Rising Block)

Two Bakat Palmok Chookyo Makgi's used together enable the student to turn a block into a painful lock, that usually results in taking a opponent down to the floor. From an overhead strike (this could just as simply be a released grab or a loose arm) the student performs or rather positions the first Chookyo Makgi by placing it under the attackers arm. The second Chookyo Makgi is then placed over the top of the elbow joint and the student attempts to switch each blocks position. In turn the higher of the two Chookyo Makgi's creates a fold in the attackers arm (at the joint) by striking down onto it and the lower Chookyo Makgi pushes upwards, helping the fold before pushing the attackers forearm back on itself. This locks the arm in a position and pain is created from pressure points in both the attackers forearm (radial nerve) and bicep. Coupled with this, the student should step forward as in the pattern, which takes the attackers arm beyond his head alignment and thus forces him backwards and down to the ground if required.

Alternative Application to movements 14, 15, 16 or 17:

- **Bakat Palmok Chookyo Makgi**

  (Outer Forearm Rising Block)

If the student has their opponent against a wall, Chookyo Makgi is an ideal finisher as a choke technique. Simply force our opponent onto the wall and lock out Chookyo Makgi in a solid forward stance as shown in the pattern (i.e. Walking Stance). The reaction hand can be used to grab onto the opponent if desired.

CHAPTER 12

Do-San tul

the releasing pattern

도산틀

Do-San is the pseudonym (pen name) of the patriot Ahn Chang Ho (1878 - 1938)[46] who devoted his entire life to furthering the education of Korea and its independent movement.

Do-San has 24 movements

Do-San tul - *Step By Step*

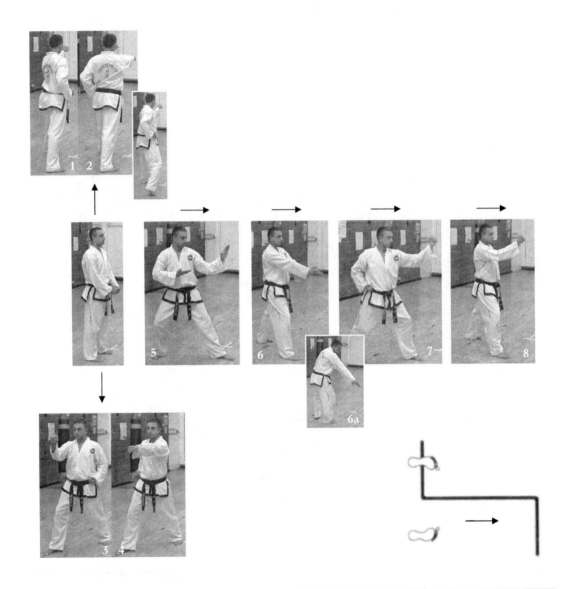

Joined photos indicate a combination with no step

A gap between pictures indicates a step

Photos are for reference and clarity.

The arrows (———→) show the correct direction in relation to the start position.

Do-San tul - *Introduction*

Do-San is indeed a celebrated figure in Korean history as he played a major part in Korea's independence, but was imprisoned by the Japanese and remained there until his death in 1938.

The 24 movements of this pattern are said to represent Ahn Chang-Ho's entire life devoted to the education of Korea and its Independent movement. However, as Ahn Chang-Ho's lifeline dates are given as 1876-1938[46], this means he was 62 (or 60 – *see footnote*) when he died, which can be a little confusing. Some feel the 24 movements are in reference to General Choi stating that the 24 patterns of Taekwon-do represent *'One day in the universe or an entire lifetime'*, which many now include in the short descriptions of Do-San tul, stating *'the 24 movements of this pattern represent his entire life which he devoted to furthering the education of Korea and its independence movement'*, however, when Do-San was formulated there were only 20 patterns of Taekwon-do and the added *'24 hours represent..'* (in reference to Do-San) was not included in any descriptions until around 1983 - so this cannot be the original reason. I feel (initially at least) the 24 movements were in reference to the age at which Ahn Chang-Ho became nationally recognized as a leader of his countrymen, something which occurred not in Korea, but actually in the United States of America.

At the age of 18, Ahn Chang-Ho became a member of *Tongnip Hyophoe* (Independence Association); the year was 1894. In 1902, he emigrated to San Francisco in the United States with his newlywed wife, Lee Hae-Ryon and was one of the first Koreans to emigrate to the United States of America. It is said that as he arrived on a steamship approaching via Hawaii, he decided to call himself 'Do-San' (Island Mountain), resolving to *'stand tall above the sea of turmoil existing in Korea at that time'*

By the age of 24 (the number of movements in the pattern), Ahn Chang-Ho was known as a leader of his countrymen within the United States as he organized the *Kungminhoe* (Korean National Association) which inspired his fellow countrymen (in the United States) to hope for national independence. In 1906, he returned home to form an independence group known as the *Shinmin-Hoe* (New Peoples Association) after learning of the Japanese Protectorate Treaty. A treaty which enforced the right of the Japanese to legally occupy his country. *Shinmin-Hoe* promoted Korean independence via the cultivation of nationalism in education, culture and business.

By 1910, the *Shinmin-Hoe* had grown in size considerably and soon became the focus of the Japanese occupiers attempts to close down such organizations as they threatened the occupation. In December of the same year a fake plot was fabricated of an assassination attempt on Terauchi,

---

[46] The Encyclopaedia of Taekwon-do and countless other references are wrong, as Ahn Chang-Ho was actually born in the year 1878 (9th November) and not 1876. http://www.ahnchangho.or.kr

Masatake, the Japanese Governor-General of the time, who was due to attend a dedication ceremony of a bridge on the Amnok river. The Japanese used this fabricated plot as an excuse to arrest every one of the *Shinmin-Hoe* leaders as well as six hundred innocent Christians. One hundred and five Koreans were tried after horrific torture in which many of those arrested died. This incident and the fact that the charges and plot were obviously fabricated concerned the worldwide community so greatly that they applied international pressure on the Japanese which eventually allowed most of the defendants to go free.

Terauchi Masatake [47]

After the assignation of Hiro-Bumi Ito (by Joong-Gun) Japan tightened its grip on Korea's leaders and Ahn Chang-Ho, was forced into exile in Manchuria before finally ending up again in America.

Whilst in America, he was elected chairman of the Korean National People's Association which negotiated with the US government. During this time he formed the '*Hungsadan*', a secret organization of patriots. This and other organizations put pressure on the US President (Woodrow Wilson) to speak on behalf of Korean autonomy at the Paris peace talks in 1918.

The '**Hungsadan**'. *Circa 1917*

Paris Peace Talks - 1918

In 1919, Ahn Chang-Ho travelled to Shanghai to form part of a Provisional Korean Government and help draw up a Democratic Constitution for Korea but after two years, he resigned his post after becoming disillusioned with the provisional Korean leaders and their in-fighting.

On 1st March, 1919, the Provisional Korean Government declared independence from Japan, calling for a massive resistance from the Korean people. Though thousands were killed, arrested and tortured during unarmed demonstrations in which the Japanese police fired into the crowds, Ahn Chang-Ho was not deterred and continued his work in the US, even creating a village in Manchuria for wandering Korean refugees.

Political unrest continued in Korea throughout Ahn Chang-Ho's life, which saw him arrested and released by the Japanese on a

[47] Picture: Carl Prinz von Hohenzollern, *Meine Erlebnisse während des Russisch-Japanischen Krieges, 1904-1905*, Ernst Siegfried Mittler und Sohn, 1912

number of occasions until he past away in Seoul on 10th March 1938, a national hero.

Whilst in America the first time, Ahn Chang-Ho's wife, Lee Hae-Ryon gave birth to their son Philip (29th March, 1905). Born in California, Philip became an actor and is well remembered for his famous role in the 1970's series *'Kung-Fu'* (starring David Carradine). Philip Ahn played Master Kan, the wise monk who was in charge of the Shaolin Temple and *'Grasshoppers'* mentor. Philip Ahn's acting career lasted over forty years until he passed away on 28th February, 1978.

Ahn Chang-Ho
Memorial, Riverside,
California, USA [48]

Do-San sees the student introduced to inside blocks, the straight finger-tip thrust, 360 degree spinning motions and their purposes. It also introduces the students to split second counter striking and starts to teach the student how to use techniques that flow into each other via the use of body mechanics rather than shifting stances.

This pattern is split into combinations, mainly of two or four (2 x 2) movements and allows defences to be practiced to both sides. This pattern seems to concern itself chiefly with releases from wrist and arm grabs, followed by fast counter strikes. Do-San tul starts from the ready posture Narani Junbi Sogi *(Parallel Ready Stance)*. Though there is no record of this ready posture having any significance, some believe it signifies a man in hand cuffs. However, subsequent patterns with the same ready posture (Yul-Gok, Choong-Moo etc) have no mention of the figure they describe being imprisoned so the reason is tenuous at best. Nevertheless, it remains a nice way to describe the posture.

---

[48] Picture courtesy of the International Relations Council of Riverside, CA

Applications from Do-San tul

Do-San tul starts from the ready posture Narani Junbi Sogi *(Parallel Ready Stance)*

We begin Do-San using the following techniques:

- **Nopunde Bakat Palmok Yop Makgi**

  (High Section Outer Forearm Side Block)

- **Kaunde Bandae Ap Joomok Jirugi**

  (Middle Section Reverse Fore Fist Punch)

We will utilize the first set of combinations as a release and counter attack from a wrist grab. Though these releases can be used if grabbed by either hand, we will use the first set to show the effect from a cross grab and the second for a *same side* grab (i.e. left hand to left hand or vice versa).

From the ready posture the attacker grabs the students left wrist with their left hand. The student immediately pulls the wrist to the chambered position (inside of the reaction arm) and then drops into the walking stance whilst performing the block. When applying the technique, the students arm is bought up beyond the attackers arm (the chamber) to enable the lock/release motion and then sharply put into place. I refer to a lock as if the attacker doesn't release, the arm becomes locked (the attackers arm can also be clasped if needed). The chamber position not only raises the arm to the correct point to apply the release/lock, but also has the effect of nullifying an incoming strike by sharply twisting the opponents shoulders and thus, throwing the opponents right shoulder backwards, taking power away from the opponents other arm in case an attack was imminent.

Chambering may also have the effect of actually making the attacker pull harder (which helps the application flow even more smoothly) but even if not, the fact that its high section when applied means we are in the correct position to apply it anyway. The reason we chamber inside of the reaction hand is because we do not use it as a grab or pulling motion and to chamber the block in another way restricts both the height and the angle plus it is also free for the next movement to be performed quickly. The actual blocking motion either releases the grip from the students arm or locks the opponents arm across their own body, nullifying a second attack and in most cases locking their elbow joint. The following reverse punch can be used as a vital point strike to the opponent's floating ribs, under the arm pit, the jaw or even to attack the elbow joint if it is locked straight.

Alternatively, the block can be used to *sweep* a grab off the shoulder before counter attacking with the reverse punch. We can utilize the chambering motion of the block as a release, but as the block chambers to the side rather than right back like a knife-hand in Dan-Gun it seems unlikely, as there is insufficient follow through to get a good release this way (as part of the chamber), though it is not unachievable.

For the second set of combinations, again we use:

- **Nopunde Bakat Palmok Yop Makgi**
  (High Section Outer Forearm Side Block)

- **Kaunde Bandae Ap Joomok Jirugi**
  (Middle Section Reverse Fore Fist Punch)

The second combination in this set sees us utilize the block as a release from a grab from behind. It could of course be used to simply brush off a rear grab, but we should try to hurt our opponent in the process to fit in with the modus operandi (M.O.) we set.

As our shoulder is grabbed, we turn on the centre line. The fact that we do not step indicates this is for a limb, rather than as an actual attack to the body, as the distances involved in each would be different, a step leaving us closer to our opponent than a centre line turn. However, if the opponent is close enough, we should attack the head directly as discussed later on in this chapter.

As we turn, we chamber our block, then as we drop forward we strike to the pressure point on the triceps or biceps, depending on which arm grabbed onto you, immediately following up with a reverse punch, which would be either the floating ribs or the solar plexus depending on which arm you struck with the block. We could also attack the elbow joint as the neck would serve as an anchor point, whilst the block would strike in the opposite direction, though it would be wise to strike above or below the elbow, as if the elbow is bent, the student is likely to damage their arm more than the attackers. This applications works the same for a double grab from behind.

The next set of movements we see:

- **Kaunde Sonkal Daebi Makgi**

(Middle Section Knife-hand Guarding Block)

- **Sun Sonkut Tulgi**

(Straight Fingertip Thrust)

- **Dung Joomok Nopunde Yop Taeragi** *(Back Fist High Side Strike)*

- **Dung Joomok Nopunde Yop Taeragi** *(Back Fist High Side Strike)*

The pivoting motion we use from the previous movement sees us turning 90 degrees straight into the next movement (rather than foot to foot or stepping).

The fact that we are using a knife-hand rather than forearm block leads me to believe we are moving away from our original opponent, rather than grabbing and breaking their neck (which we could do with this block – *see Won-Hyo*) but the direction and angle of the knife-hand would possibly require more body motion to generate power for a throw using only the head. Plus, the fact that the block chamber doesn't start from a forward position first means we are not using the chamber as part of the block, but the end motion to strike into our opponent (of course, you can simply block if you want).

This knife-hand can be used as a release from a grab or to nullify a strike like a hooking punch. So, for this next application we see the knife-hand guarding block used to strike the pressure point on the bicep of the incoming opponent.

This has 6 effects:

1. It allows us to nullify the attackers main attacking tool (the arm – possibly his strongest)

2. In the process it causes a pain sensation, momentarily covering us for the next movement of what we are going to do in the next split second

3. As the brain focuses on the pain it causes a break from a secondary attack so disorientates what could have been multiple attacks (i.e. two punches)

4. As we strike close to the opponent, most of the momentum is taken out of the attack, making it easier to stop i.e. it doesn't drive through our block due to the generation of force on the outside arc of the attack

5. If a secondary attack does come, we are close enough for it to have minimum effect

6. It also opens the opponent for the next movement (the straight fingertip thrust)

The following motion, Sun Sonkut Tulgi *(Straight Fingertip Thrust)* is used to slip under the opponents arm, under the armpit, with the palm of the left hand used to brush the arm aside if needed. The release motion (the way we turn the hand and move our feet closer together) gives us some idea of what comes next and can also be used to *drill* our way through, though this is unlikely to be needed. The hand turns 180 degrees, the feet come close together in classic throwing position and we pivot 180 degrees + 180 degrees (360 degrees in total) in the course of the next movement. The left arm is closed/clench to a back fist meaning we grip onto our opponent (the arm), as well as using the chambering motion of the right arm to grip at the front, rising up around our opponents arm/shoulder, as we perform a shoulder throw before proceeding onwards, the back fist being kept up to avoid being clobbered by anything as we continue.

As a note, this is not the primary application taught for this movement, which I believe is one of the better applications often taught throughout the coloured belt patterns. The primary application is detailed in the **Alternative Applications** section for this pattern. I simply thought it interesting to list an alternative.

The second back fist could be a reminder that the application can be performed on either side, however, I believe it's possibly a secondary attack for another opponent coming in. i.e. we have thrown one, and we strike to the second. The back fist should be *whipped* out as we strike to the temple. The reaction hand can be used to increase the overall effect by grabbing the opponent if we used the first as a cover (thus trying to nullify any incoming blows) and using the reaction principles to pull whilst we strike, causing the attacker to lose momentum and balance as we strike to the temple. However, if used this way it is in opposition to how a back fist is usually chambered.

After the two back fist strikes we are back to the same combination at the start of the pattern:

- **Nopunde Bakat Palmok Yop Makgi**

  (High Section Outer Forearm Side Block)

- **Kaunde Bandae Ap Joomok Jirugi**

  (Middle Section Reverse Fore Fist Punch)

This time we see the side block utilized as an inside block to a double grab from the side. This could be a double shoulder grab or even a side choke. For this example we will use a side choke.

As the attacker moves in to choke us, we spin 270 degrees and strike the triceps pressure point with the block. The spinning motion is away from the attacker, releasing pressure from the front hand of the choke, which is the most dangerous as it is on our larynx. The spinning motion also loosens the choke.

As we spin we build up momentum for the block, which strikes the attackers arm to the pressure point on the triceps, above or below the elbow (forearm), this is immediately followed up with a reverse punch to the floating ribs vital point. Like before, this is actually a dual purpose strike. It strikes the triceps pressure point as well as indirectly attacking the elbow joint as the neck would serve as an anchor point, whilst the block would strike in the opposite direction creating tremendous pressure on the elbow.

We turn 180 degrees and again we use:

- **Nopunde Bakat Palmok Yop Makgi**

  (High Section Outer Forearm Side Block)

- **Bandae Ap Joomok Jirugi**

  (Middle Section Reverse Fore Fist Punch)

The second combination is the same as the first, allowing for the student to similarly practice on both sides, though from slightly different positions of side choke/grab and choke/grab from the rear, alternatively it can be used the same as the second combination at the beginning. However, here we show it utilized as a parrying motion to a punch. When a standard punch (cross or hooking punch) travels towards you, the bicep is turned inwards and striking it with the outer forearm causes considerable pain, but to the seasoned student it will numb the whole area, whist still maintaining enough closeness to guard the face if needed. The punch is the counter attack.

The centre line turn is apparent on these combinations. The fact that it has been changed a number of times since Taekwon-do was formulated leads me to the conclusion that the way it is actually performed is not a major part of the applications and just indicates how to turn without moving in either direction whilst still increasing power (hence whys its been changed a number of times, as better ways have been derived for this to increase power). This way we can turn into an opponent who is close, but not be so close as to nullify our own strikes.

Following the previous combinations, we then withdraw our rear leg and pivot into the next movement. We then step foot to foot and move diagonally using:

- **Bakat Palmok Hechyo Makgi** (*Outer Forearm Wedging Block*)

- **Ap Cha Busigi**

  (*Front Snap Kick*)

- **Doo Jirugi**

  (*Double Punches*)

A common misconception to Hechyo Makgi *(Wedging Block)* is that this block is designed to release from a double grab. However, if you try it against a resisting partner who has a secure grip, you will see that it actually hits at the elbow joints and only bends the elbows, rather than securing a release.

It is actually intended to stop a grab before it takes hold, thus creating a wedge and allow the follow up kick to take place. The wedge is kept there so the kick is not blocked, the closed fists possibly indicating we should grab our opponents arms so they can't block (not shown in pictures). The front snap kick is to the solar plexus, which has the effect of either directly dropping the opponent on the spot or doubling them over (if done correctly), ready for the next combination of techniques, the double punches. Some feel the pattern application is too close, but it takes into effect the follow through of the kick, allowing the student to attack the opponents inside and explode the energy into out opponents body, which is why they drop rather than simply fly off backwards.

The double punches represent a neck break, the reaction hand reaches past the opponents (to the front of the opponents head) and grips on at the front, the double punch motion is cranked forward, then back again sharply, thus breaking the opponents neck. The closed fists represent a grip, though there is some leeway on this as it can be done using the inside of the fists rather than actually grabbing on if desired.

This should be viewed as an advanced application, the basic application being two simple punches after the kick. The same motion is employed on the opposite side and allows practice to either side and with either leg.

Next we use:

- **Bakat Palmok Chookyo Makgi**
  (Outer Forearm Rising Block)

- **Bakat Palmok Chookyo Makgi**
  (Outer Forearm Rising Block)

The two rising blocks *(Bakat Palmok Chookyo Makgi)* employed afterwards can be used as in Dan-Gun. The first blocking or covering a strike or grab to our head (not face, but the top of our head, like a hair grab), we block, twist our arm slightly more to secure a grip to stop the arm being withdrawn, then move into the next block and strike upwards to the attackers elbow. As mentioned in Dan-Gun, its unfortunate that the actual chambering position of this block has been changed for Taekwon-do but the original way of performing the block fits with our modus operandi and single applications of this block can be found in the **Alternative Applications** section.

We follow on with:

- **Sonkal Yop Taeragi** *(Knife-hand Side Strike)*

The pattern finishes off with a knife-hand strike in sitting stance in both directions. The rising block is followed by turning into the first knife-hand strike. This can be utilized to attack an incoming opponent, much like the second back fist strike, but an advanced application of this motion is a tripping type throw to break the opponents neck.

As we have just attacked the elbow joint, we are very close to our injured opponent with our right leg forward. The raised right hand (from the rising block that broke the elbow) drops down as a guard or spacer between us and the opponent, whilst the knife-hand chambers by reaching round to the attackers jaw or face (or we can grab clothing). The students pivots (as if performing the next strike) and the pivoting motion employs the throw or trip, pulling and twisting the opponents head. As the knife-hand moves further than 180 degrees, it separates the top vertebrae from the rest – most people can turn their head almost 180 degree, but further, performed fast will break it. The front leg remains where it is so the opponent is thrown over it (the tripping part).

We finish the pattern using:

- **Sonkal Yop Taeragi** *(Knife-hand Side Strike)*

Between the two knife-hand strikes we step foot to foot, unlike in Dan-Gun, this possibly meant that the legs are employed in the applications in a more active role than simply stepping forward to add power. For this application we will use a wrist grab again.

The release works similar in application to some others, but finishes with a different intent. What makes this application different is that though we release by chambering the strike (by pulling the gripped hand into chambering position whilst twisting it), at the same time we step sideways towards our opponent. As the hand is released, we drop down behind the opponent, immediately throwing out knife-hand across their throat or chest as we step one leg behind, both striking and tripping them in one motion.

Alternative Applications To Do-San tul

Alternative Application to movement 4:

- **Kaunde Sonkal Daebi Makgi**

  (Middle Section Knife-hand Guarding Block)

Again, the knife-hand is employed to strike a pressure point in order to thwart a grab attempt.

We use the front knife-hand of the knife-hand block as a strike to the bicep pressure point. Of course it is employed close to the opponent rather than to the forearm.

The guard arm (the right in these pictures) is there in case we need a cover of some sort. Its ideally placed at mid section to move up or down quickly and is also there for a follow up strike.

Alternative Application to movement 6 and 7:

- **Sun Sonkut Tulgi**

  (Straight Fingertip Thrust)

- **Dung Joomok Nopunde Yop Taeragi**

  (Back Fist High Side Strike)

In the pattern, after the knife-hand strike we perform a releasing motion, followed by a 180 degree turn to end up with a back fist strike.

As our arm is grabbed, we firstly thrust forward and twist the hand in order to loosen the attackers grip.

Following this we change direction and pull the fingertip thrust away from our attacker as we pivot and strike with the back fist. The push then pulling of the hand will either release our hand completely or it may not, either way it occupies our opponent for a split second or two.

We then confuse the opponent by spinning and striking with the back fist, whist pulling our fingertip thrust back. If attacker actually managed to maintain his grip, the pulling back motion of the fingertip thrust opens our opponent by turning him side on and off balance, allowing for our back fist to strike as we continue round and release our hand.

Alternative Application to movement 6 and 7:

- **Sun Sonkut Tulgi**

  (Straight Fingertip Thrust)

- **Dung Joomok Nopunde Yop Taeragi**

  (Back Fist High Side Strike)

Here we show standard taught application for **Sun Sonkut Tulgi** *(Straight Fingertip Thrust)* as a release technique. It works really well in this respect, the only issue with it is the following strike which necessitates you turning your back on your opponent which many don't like, however, if performed quickly, we can facilitate a strike halfway through the spin, so our exposed time is considerably less. The opposite arm is there to protect against a knee strike as you push through with the release.

As our arm is grabbed, we shift all our body weight forward, whilst at the same time dropping lower (by bending our knees, not our back) and twisting our fingertip thrust 180 degrees. All this added together, when performed sharply as it is supposed to be, makes it almost impossible for our attacker to keep a grip on our arm. Immediately following the release we go into the spin motion and as we spin, we chamber (for the back fist) and strike with our elbow. If the opponent draws away, we have a longer reach technique and can then utilize the back fist if required.

A common practice today is to simply pivot on the balls of the feet and turn the fingertip thrust 90 degrees. But this is not enough to secure a release, as the twisting motion isn't enough, but more importantly it does not drive the body weight forward enough to push the arm through to the full release.

Alternative Application to movement 6 and 7:

- **Sun Sonkut Tulgi**
  (Straight Fingertip Thrust)
- **Dung Joomok Nopunde Yop Taeragi**
  (Back Fist High Side Strike)

Another application of the twisting motion associated with **Sun Sonkut Tulgi** *(Straight Fingertip Thrust)* in this combination is to create space in a closed in situation, like being grabbed. As the student is grabbed, rather than striking the solar plexus, the fingertips are placed on to them and the twisting (and body) motions are used, creating space for a follow up, in this case the standard back fist strike. The sudden pain induced by this application is shocking to the opponent and helps loosen the grip as well as creating the space.

Alternative Application to movements 13 and 17:

- **Bakat Palmok Hechyo Makgi** *(Outer Forearm Wedging Block)*

This is another close range application.

When in close, grab your opponent by the collar in a cross hand grab (the chambering motion of Hechyo Makgi). Then as you drop into your stance, pull the hands apart as if you were performing the 'block'. The block should be pulled as hard as possible to try and form it. The opponent experiences a choke via their own collars.

You could of course follow up this technique with a front snap kick, just like in the pattern.

Alternative Application to movements 21 or 22

- **Bakat Palmok Chookyo Makgi**

  (Outer Forearm Rising Block)

This is a great technique for simply pushing the opponent back. When attacked or overwhelmed, we dig deep into our stance, place our arm across the opponents chest, under their arms or anything else that is available and push up into the block, using not just out arms, but the large muscles of the legs as well. As this block comes up at an angle, it has the effect of not only pushing backwards, but upwards at the same time, meaning our opponent finds it impossible to drop his weight down if the block is performed quickly.

Alternative Application to movements 23 or 24

- **Sonkal Yop Taeragi** *(Knife-hand Side Strike)*

In this application it is the actual chamber motion that we use. We chamber this strike by bringing a knife-hand inside of our reaction hand.

For this example, it is the reaction arm that has been grabbed. Utilizing our knife-hand, we simply strike to the inside of the attackers arm, to the pressure point, which has enough shock factor to secure a release. We immediately pull our reaction arm away once the grip is loosened as we then follow on the strike to ensure we finish our attacker.

CHAPTER 13

Won-Hyo tul

the close quarters pattern

원 효 틀

**Won-Yo was a noted monk who introduced Buddhism to the
Silla dynasty in the year 686 AD.**

Won-Yo has 28 movements.

Won-Hyo tul - *Step By Step*

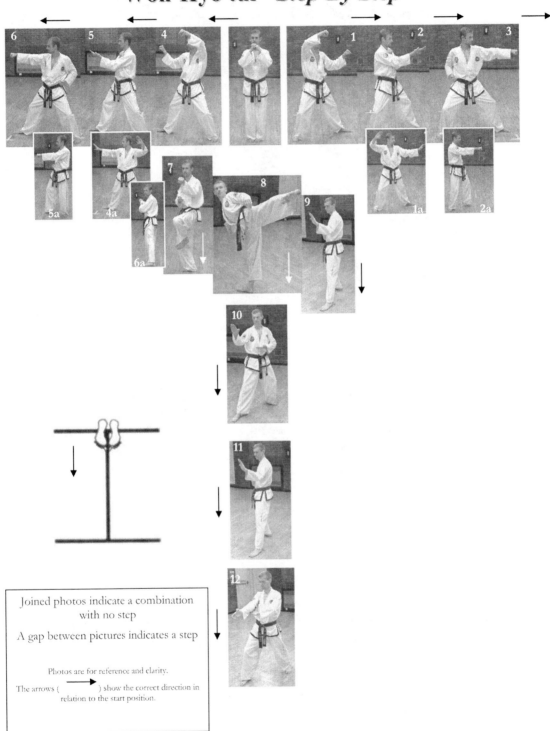

Joined photos indicate a combination
with no step

A gap between pictures indicates a step

Photos are for reference and clarity.

The arrows (⟶) show the correct direction in
relation to the start position.

Won-Hyo tul - *Introduction*

Won-Hyo tul starts from the ready posture Moa Junbi Sogi 'A' (*Closed Ready Stance 'A'*). Won-Hyo was the noted monk who introduced Buddhism to the Silla Dynasty in 686 AD, this ready posture represents this as it is similar to a Buddhist salute (a way of showing respect to another and often seen in Chinese styles when they bow, though there is no bow here) or even the hands in prayer. Another common train of thought with regards to ready postures where one hand is place over the other is that they are symbolic to the very nature of Taekwon-do. The fist represents the strong attack that can be utilized if required, whilst the open hand over the fist represents restraint.

Won-Hyo

Won-Hyo was born in Kyongsang Province in 617 AD by the name of Sol Sedang. Won-Hyo is a penname, derived from his nickname '*sedak*' which means '*dawn*' (Won-Hyo means the same). Civil war between the three kingdoms (Silla, Koguryo and Paekche) was rife in Korea at this time and legend has it that Won-Hyo, as a young man, took part in these civil wars and it was him seeing many of his friends slaughtered that drove him to become a monk and turn his back on violence at the age of 20.

There are many stories of what happened when Won-Hyo became a monk, from remodelling his home to look like a temple, to shaving his head and disappearing into the mountains, and no-one is actually certain whom he studied Buddhism under!

Despite in-depth research, it remained a mystery for a while as to the reason for this pattern having 28 movements, though I now believe it may relate to the last two digits[49] of the year 528 AD when King Pop-Hung was pressured by his court to execute a 22 year old monk by the name of Ichadon in order to convince the court that Buddhism was a worthy religion. Stories from the scene of Ichadon's death said of his blood being '*white as milk*' and led to Ichadon becoming a martyr and King Pop-Hung granting mandates on the freedom of Buddhist belief, whereby Buddhism became accepted more readily by the people.

The picture on the following page depicts the well known story of Won-Hyo's '*sudden awakening*' when in 650 AD, Won-Hyo, aged 33, and his friend Uisang travelled towards China to study under the famous Buddhist scholar Huan-Tchuang. As they neared the Chinese border they were mistaken for spies and just managed to escaped with their lives. During the long journey to China, Won-Hyo had rested in a cave. During the night he was thirsty and in the darkness he fumbled around only to find a vessel with water in to quench is thirst. When he awoke in the morning he realized the vessel was a rotten skull which had collected rain water

---

[49] General Choi has used two digits of a three digit number with regards to the number of movements in other patterns on numerous other interpretations. For example; Kwang-Gae tul, Yoo-Sin tul, Yong-Gae tul and Moon-Moo tul all use this type of reference

and was swarming with maggots and he fell down and vomited. Afterwards he realized that without the minds pre-conceptions it was a well placed, cool and delicious thirst quenching drink, but in the light of day it was the rotting skull. His 'awakening' was the inner enlightenment that *'everything is created by the mind alone'*!

Upon this, Won-Hyo[50] decided that there was no need for him to find a master, as he now understood *'life and death'* and considered there was no more to learn. Whilst Uisang continued to China, Won-Hyo headed back towards Korea. On his return Won-Hyo undertook large amounts of scholarly work and became well known to both the public and royal family, often being asked to conduct service and give sermons within the royal courts.

In 660 AD, he was asked to go and live in the royal court by King Muyo and while there he had a relationship with Princess Kwa, which lead to marriage and the birth of their son Sol-Ch'ong. Following this, Won-Hyo toured Korea and hating the fact that all the different religions constantly argued with each other over their differing beliefs, he devised his own ideology to reconcile the differences between the religions.

In 661 AD, Won-Hyo had a revelation that changed his Buddhist philosophy. From this he developed the Chongto-Gyo or *'Pure Land'* sect. This new philosophy didn't require long study of Chinese literature for the sect members, just diligent prayer and it made his branch of Buddhism philosophy easily accessible to the lower classes, thus making it popular among the entire population.

Won-Hyo left the priesthood in 662 AD and spent the rest of his life travelling the country teaching the philosophy of his sect to the people. During his life, Won-Hyo authored around 240 works on Buddhism and twenty still exist today, in 25 volumes. His son Sol-Chong, grew up to become one of the ten Confucian sages of the Silla era

Punhwang-sa temple

---

[50] Picture courtesy of Wonkeun Nam, Korean Buddhist Monk. Reproduced with permission and thanks.

In 686AD Won-Hyo passed away, aged 70 and his body was laid in state by his son, Sol-Ch'ong, at Punhwang-sa temple. In his lifetime, Won-Hyo had seen the unification of Korea's three kingdoms (Koguryo, Silla and Paekche) and brought about a magnificent culture change in Korean society through his Buddhist philosophy which had far reaching effects not only in Korea but Japan and China as well.

Won-Hyo consists of sets or combinations of movements (one set is repeated four times), one legged stances, three continuous blocks in a row, as well as repeated moves. The applications in the encyclopedia simply dictate a block is to block a hand (usually a punch) or kick, double blocks like twin forearm block are used against multiple opponents and the strikes are simply that… strikes!

On closer inspection you will see that Won-Hyo is a close range pattern. The techniques contained within it are mostly concerned with close quarter techniques and the combinations in the patterns work together to form the overall final effect.

The first combination of movements are repeated four times throughout the pattern. This indicates that they should be practiced on both sides and the possibility of more than one major set of applications. Furthermore, the grip which was still taught until recently is often left out altogether (it's now simply taught as a fist pulled to the shoulder) and it's a vital component of the original applications.

The bending ready stances as depicted in the encyclopedia actually miss out a vital photo during the chamber of how the movement builds up. In practice, it is a jamming motion, followed by a counter kick off the same leg. The three knife-hands as you move forward can indicate working both sides, or three different applications.

The basic application of the fingertip thrust is a simple parry and strike, which is a good application, however, here it is utilized as a throw which is more in-line with the close-counter techniques of the rest of the pattern. The following sequence of the circular block, front snap kick and reverse punch combination are utilized as a lock and counter strike, rather than blocking two opponents simultaneous.

The final forearm guarding blocks can serve a dual purpose. Here we see them employed as actual combative take-down techniques, as a physiological technique and other applications.

Applications from Won-Hyo tul

Won-Hyo tul starts from the ready posture Moa Junbi Sogi 'A' (*Closed Ready Stance 'A'*)

The pattern immediately starts with a combination of three movements:

- **Sang Palmok Makgi**

  (*Twin Forearm Block*)

- **Sonkal Nopunde Anuro Taeragi**

  (*Knife-hand High Inward Strike*)

- **Gojang Sogi, Kaunde Joomok Jirugi** (*Fixed Stance Middle Fore Fist Punch*)

This combination is intended for a close range attack. The opponent grabs you with both arms (or even one), strike just below the wrist to secure a release (you can hit pressure points, but the speed of the technique and closeness to the wrist will often secure the release anyway). Then the front arm reaches out and grabs the opponent (this part of the technique is often missed out totally these days), as it is clenched and pulled in sharply, you simultaneously strike to the carotid artery.

The pulling motion has three effects:

1. It displaces the opponents equilibrium, this drops his guard as his body automatically tries to regain balance

2. It pulls the opponent close for the strike

3. It allows for the next technique to be used in a more forceful manner as we literally punch the opponent away.

Example of the missing grab

As this punch is really a pushing strike, the follow through of the technique and the change of stance to a more forward position (*L Stance to Fixed Stance*) means we get a longer pushing motion, rather than an impacting motion.

The momentum force is transferred to the punch as it accelerates to a sudden stop (as you complete the stance) transferring the energy of the punch into the opponents body, thus creating even more force.

This combination is repeated on the opposite side to allow the student to practice no matter which way they are facing when attacked or to add different combinations as shown later in the pattern, when these combinations repeat themselves.

The next set of movements consist of:

- **Gorboryu Junbi Sogi 'A'**
  (Bending Ready Stance 'A')
- **Yop Cha Jirugi** *(Side Piercing kick)*
- **Kaunde Sonkal Daebi Makgi**
  (Mid Section Knife-hand Guarding Block)

The previous combination is immediately followed with Gorboryu Junbi Sogi 'A' (Bending Ready Stance 'A'). Many students miss out a small but vital element of this stance, and this is the way the leg forms, then travels to the ready position. This technique is a *jamming* technique, designed to stop an incoming opponent travelling closer towards you, whilst the chambering of the leg is the preparation for the counter attack, which of course follows this motion in the form of a side piercing kick, finally landing with a knife-hand guarding block.

The knife-hand is the finishing technique, designed to utilise the dropping of the body weight, to increase the power of the strike to the opponents neck (side/back), thus finishing off the opponent. The rear hand is in a guard position for defence and in case a second attack is required.

We can finish the application here, but as an alternative, after the first knife-hand block, we can utilize the chambering of the next block to grab the opponents head (which will be around the level of our hands due to the kick and knife-hand strike) and, as we step past, we crank it violently (into the next knife-hand block) and break the neck.

The next we use:

- **Kaunde Sonkal Daebi Makgi**

    (Mid Section Knife-hand Guarding Block)

- **Kaunde Sonkal Daebi Makgi**

    (Mid Section Knife-hand Guarding Block)

- **Sun Sonkut Tulgi** *(Straight Fingertip Thrust)*

The fact that another two knife-hand guarding blocks follow the first often confuses students. However, if we look at a more advanced application of this block we can see why they follow.

We can utilize the neck crank or use the second and third knife-hand guarding blocks in the following way. First of all, in the heat of battle, a fellow soldier of the one you just downed isn't going to stand around after you have just finished off his mate, he is going to attack. The next two knife-hand blocks are simultaneous parry and strike counters, that can be used against swinging fists or even a circular attack with weapons such as clubs, the two handed approach makes blocking a weapon not only easier, but safer too.

These photos are taken from an above angle to show the strike/parry – follow through – and final finishing strike

As the opponent swings in a right hook punch, the chambering motion of the block allows you to strike pressure points in both the lower and upper arm simultaneously, often rendering the arm immobile, whilst the completed motion strikes the opponent. The arm is struck at the pressure points and the opponent is finished with a strike to the carotid artery vital point.

The third knife-hand guarding block can be utilized in the same manner, or as a neck break to finish off this opponent, as previously described.

The final motion in this set, sees us employing Sun Sonkut Tulgi *(Straight Fingertip Thrust)*, then turning into the first combination we performed. Again, a military tactic is employed here, as well as a more advanced applications than simply striking the opponents solar plexus with our finger tips.

Our previous strike may have killed or stunned our opponent, either way, this next applications goes in line with the rest of the pattern applications we have performed so far.

The technique is actually a hip throw. The forward hand goes past the opponent to wrap round his waist at the back (this is why there is no release motion like in Do-San). The front hand (palm) is used to move any protruding limbs out the way and if needed, grab onto the opponent to assist the throw.

The turning motion is part of the throw but also allows us to throw our second or third attacker into the first one/two should any be recovering enough to continue attacking, thus creating an avenue of escape or evasion or allowing us to gear up for another attack or perhaps even time to get a weapon. The fact that is turns more than 180 degrees indicates a hip throw, rather than a shoulder throw, as a hip throw is more circular in motion.

This brings us back to the combination we used at the very beginning of Won-Hyo consisting of:

- **Sang Palmok Makgi**

  (Twin Forearm Block)

- **Sonkal Nopunde Anuro Taeragi**

  (Knife-hand High Inward Strike)

- **Gojang Sogi, Kaunde Joomok Jirugi**

  (Fixed Stance Middle Forefist Punch)

This time we can utilize it in an intermediate type application. A shoulder is grabbed, we perform Sang Palmok Makgi with the front arm inside of the opponents arm, we can, if close enough, use the front arm as a side fist (Yop Joomok) to the opponents jaw and the following chambering motion to either hide our intent or simply push the face further away (this is not a major point), as we rise up again. As we drop back into our L-Stance, our opposite arm (the reaction hand) secures the attackers hand ensuring it has no way of moving and stays where it's grabbed. This causes the opponents arm to be locked straight, thus making it weak for the break, the knife-hand strikes immediately as we drop (think split second timing), we strike directly to

the elbow joint creating a break.

The final punch as in the first example, has a more forward stance than the previous L-Stance. We draw back slightly then drop into Gojang Sogi (fixed stance), which means we are closer to the opponent than when we applied the application and it is designed again, to get rid of him quickly by sharply punching (pushing) him away.

As a reminder, the momentum is transferred to the punch as it accelerates to a sudden stop (as you complete the stance) transferring the energy of the punch into the opponents body, thus creating even more force. An opponent with a broken joint doesn't fight, but he is still in the way, think of this as a punching push to get rid of the opponent and create some space. This is usually a strike to the floating ribs vital point to cause further damage.

The same motion is employed on the opposite sides to allow us to practice a reasonably complicated combination without having to switch sides if used for real. This block on its own (also found in Dan-Gun) or with the following motions as shown in the applications to the first set, can also be used to stop a hook/swinging type punch instead of striking after a grab, with the block chambering to stop the incoming blow and the rear (high section) arm grabbing onto the attackers striking arm we strike simultaneously with the side fist.

Next, we concern ourselves with close range counter techniques to kicks. Taekwon-do, when created was advanced in kicking but opponents were not. They would utilize basic kicks like a rough front kick or a stomp at best. The next position used is stepping foot to foot, indicating we are moving from one opponent to a new one.

We now utilize the following combination:

- **Dollimyo Makgi** *(Circular Block)*
- **Ap Cha Busigi** *(Front Snap Kick)*
- **Ap Joomok Jirugi** *(Fore Fist Punch)*

As we move forwards we perform Dollimyo Makgi *(Circular Block)*. The fact that we move from a foot to foot position, then out into our stance means we are actually moving diagonally body wise, away from its initial direct path, this is further enhanced by chambering the block as we twist our body (plus the reaction hand is there just in case and to help guide the opponents leg into the trap). The forward motion means we move inside the kicks range, thus catching it before it reaches it full power and the diagonal motion compliments the first part of the circular block by adding momentum, making it more equal to a stronger attacking tool (the leg), as we make contact. As the block scoops low, it indicates as mentioned; to grab hold of a basic kick or stomp and hook it. The first part of the block allows us to connect with the opponents kicking leg, (moving it slightly more in line with our twisting body), but the arm is hooked or scooped around the leg as we perform the second part of the motion, this is performed in a *snap* like manner, using the knee spring to straighten up quickly and the leg is locked in place or is twisted throwing the opponent off balance by the crank at the end, disrupting our opponents equilibrium.

You will notice also that the shoulders are very much off turned when performing this block. This is the final way of ensuring our bodies are clear of the opponents kick and allows us to fully lock the leg, the side step, the first point of contact and the shoulders all work to ensure we remain close enough to employ the technique, whilst suitably turned to avoid it or take a slight blow to a muscled part of the torso/shoulder as opposed to a vital area like the solar plexus. As the leg is longer than the arm, if we were straight in front we could catch the full force of the kick whilst employing the technique. This is also a lesson on how powerful the reaction principle is and how torque can be applied into blocks.

This is followed up with a front snap kick to the opponents testicles (as the opponents leg is caught and raised to allow us to attack here).

The final part of this combination is a reverse punch. This can be to the opponents vital point, such as the floating ribs but it seems reasonable that a kick to the testicles would virtually force the opponent to squeeze his legs together or double up in pain and turn to drop to the floor. Though solar plexus or throat could equally be used, depending on which leg they attacked with in the first place. This punch allows us to help them on their way or finishes them and stops then getting up again too quickly, if at all.

The punch should be employed a split second before landing, thus utilizing full body weight (that is why there is no knee spring here, as you are still moving forward).

Following on we use:

- **Gorboryu Junbi Sogi 'A'**
  (Bending Ready Stance 'A')
- **Yop Cha Jirugi** *(Side Piercing kick)*
- **Palmok Daebi Makgi** *(Forearm Guarding Block)*

This is the first pattern where we come across two blocks at the end, one after the other, to finish. This is repeated in other patterns later on and is a good combination of movements to utilize against two or even three opponents that are closing in from all sides.

First we again use Gorboryu Junbi Sogi 'A' *(Bending Ready Stance 'A')*. We can perform the jamming and counter kick motion on the opposite side that we previously practiced, to ensure both legs are trained to jam and then counter kick. The only differences are that it's the opposite leg and it comes from the rear, rather than the front like before, which may indicate it's a more aggressive kick such as a shin strike, designed to damage, rather than simply jam, so we utilize it to strike one attacker and counter kick him.

We complete this combination by utilizing Palmok Daebi Makgi *(Forearm Guarding Block)* as a rudimentary throw. Following the side piercing kick, the student is taught to step down and pivot round into Palmok Daebi Makgi, but there is no set measurement to this distance[51]. The reason that there is no set measurement maybe in order to make the next application workable!

We'll say for this instant that the previous combination utilizing Gorboryu Junbi Sogi 'A' and Yop Cha Jirugi has not fulfilled the modus operandi this time. So following the side piercing kick we step down, judging the distance so the students lead leg is close to the opponent. As he steps down, he grabs the opponent with both hands and pivots into Palmok

---

[51] The foot positions found in the Ch'ang Hon patterns are usually very precise as to where the foot is meant to be placed

Daebi Makgi (*Forearm Guarding Block*) which has the effect of pulling the opponent over the lead leg and backwards onto the floor – the rudimentary throw!

Following on we use:

- **Palmok Daebi Makgi** (*Forearm Guarding Block*)

The second Palmok Daebi Makgi (*Forearm Guarding Block*) we find in Won-Hyo tul can also be used in a rudimentary throwing fashion or in this case, more of a trip. As the opponent moves towards us, the student steps forward ensuring the lead leg moves behind the attackers, and performs Palmok Daebi Makgi. Stepping forward using our front hand to grip or strike our opponent (with the forearm across their chest), as we strike in with the block it allows us to effect the trip and take our opponent over with the back of their head hitting the ground.

This block is repeated either side, allowing the student to practice the grips and throws using both legs, both arms and on both sides of the body.

Alternative Applications To Won-Hyo tul

Alternative Application to movements 7 or 25:

- **Gorboryu Junbi Sogi 'A'** *(Bending Ready Stance 'A')*

The chambering technique of Gorboryu Junbi Sogi 'A' is ideally utilized to sweep

the foot of a close in opponent. Simply put your foot behind their lead leg and chamber. The forearm guarding block can be used to strike the opponent to help him on this way, or if grabbed, used to exaggerate the movement by adjusting the timing slightly so that you pull back at the same time as sweeping.

Alternative Application to movements 7 or 25:

- **Gorboryu Junbi Sogi 'A'** *(Bending Ready Stance 'A')*

As an interesting aside to my research, I came across an application of Gorboryu Junbi Sogi 'A' as a defending and counter attacking technique employed on a steep hill or stairs.

The student is higher than the attacker and cannot lean forward for fear of being over balanced due to the extended reach needed to land a hand technique or being grabbed and pulled down. So Gorboryu Junbi Sogi 'A' is used to kick and withdraw the kicking leg as needed to defend the position.

Alternative Application to movements 19 or 22:

- **Dollimyo Makgi** *(Circular Block)*

From a grab to the students shoulder the student raises his arm high and circles it over and around our attackers arm. As it circles, it loops back up and successfully locks out the attackers arm and shoulder. As the final motion of the block is employed, it has the effect of not only locking the attackers arm, but forcing them to turn to alleviate the pain, thus opening them up for an easy counter attack.

Alternative Application to movements 19/20/21 or 22/23/24:

- **Dollimyo Makgi** *(Circular Block)*
- **Ap Cha Busigi** *(Front Snap Kick)*
- **Ap Joomok Jirugi** *(Fore Fist Punch)*

Dollimyo Makgi can also be used to simply scoop up and throw away attackers kick. The lower portion of the block makes contact with the attackers leg, scoops underneath it and throws it aside as it continues round, turning the attacker in the process.

This is then followed up with Ap Cha Busigi *(Front Snap Kick)* to the coccyx or floating ribs if the attacker hasn't fully turned and the attacker is finally finished with Ap Joomok Jirugi (Fore Fist Punch) to the base of the skull or the jaw bone.

Alternative Application to movements 27 or 28:

- **Palmok Daebi Makgi**

  (Forearm Guarding Block)

As detailed in more senior patterns, Palmok Daebi Makgi can be used to create an armbar or shoulder lock. From a defensive position our lead arm is grabbed. The student steps forward and chambers the block underneath the attackers arm. This pulls the attacker off balance slightly which covers the students intentions. As the rear arm of the block twists, it grips onto the attackers arm. The student then completes the block by dropping into it and striking the back of the attackers triceps with the lead arm. Or the student can apply the lead arm into the rear shoulder, as shown in the Joong-Gun tul applications.

The fist of the lead arm can further be used to enhance the technique by grabbing onto the opponents clothing to keep the lock secured.

This can be altered slightly for an elbow break by using more follow through or simply striking with the lead forearm directly to the elbow joint, as the rear arm and chambering may have straightened the attackers arm sufficiently to enable this.

Alternative Application to movements 27 or 28:

- **Palmok Daebi Makgi**

  (*Forearm Guarding Block*)

Of course, we can simply use Palmok Daebi Makgi (*Forearm Guarding Block*) to scare any enemies that may be considering attacking. i.e. we turn and face them, ready for action in a fighting pose, the same pose used to start free sparring (or fighting), use one of the more advanced applications to this block (found in Joong-Gun) or simply use the front fist of the block to strike our opponent, though this leaves us rather exposed!

Alternative Application to movements 25, 26, 27 and 28:

- **Gorboryu Junbi Sogi 'A'**

  (*Bending Ready Stance 'A'*)

- **Yop Cha Jirugi**

  (*Side Piercing Kick*)

- **Palmok Daebi Makgi**

  (*Forearm Guarding Block*)

- **Palmok Daebi Makgi**

  (*Forearm Guarding Block*)

As an exercise on how the chambering motions of a block can prove useful as strikes themselves, we are going to show how the last kick of Won-Hyo and the two final blocks can all be utilized against three attackers in quick succession. One in front and two from the side.

As an attacker runs in from the front, we strike out with our side kick, but as we step down not one, but two attackers are closing in, one on either side and if we commit to defending against one, we leave our back (and thus ourselves) exposed to the other.

You will note that there is no set distance here for stepping down after the side kick (though it is not foot to foot and it is roughly 1 shoulder width) meaning we can judge our distance in relation to the other attackers and immediately on landing, we turn to face one opponent whilst chambering our block.

We use the chambering motion of the first block; throwing the right hand backwards and striking the opponent to our rear (originally on our left), as a stunning blow; stunning him for a second as we strike the other

attacker on completion of the block. We then immediately turn and finish off the first attackers with a similar strike (that flows from one to another).

Notice how the chamber for this block, as we turn, is almost the same as when its struck and the closest hand is always guarding our centre, whether we are chambering or striking with it, so in case we misjudge things we have some protection guarding our own body.

This application may seem improbable to some degree, but it goes inline with Won-Hyo being a close quarter pattern and works well

with the two similar blocks successively and also serves to teach how quickness and timing are invaluable.

CHAPTER 14

Yul-Gok tul

the grabbing pattern

율곡틀

Yul-Guk is the pseudonym of a great philosopher and scholar Yi I, nicknamed the Confucius of Korea (1536-1584).

The 38 movements represent his birth place on 38 degrees latitude and the diagram represents scholar.

Yul-Gok has 38 movements.

Yul-Gok tul - *Step By Step*

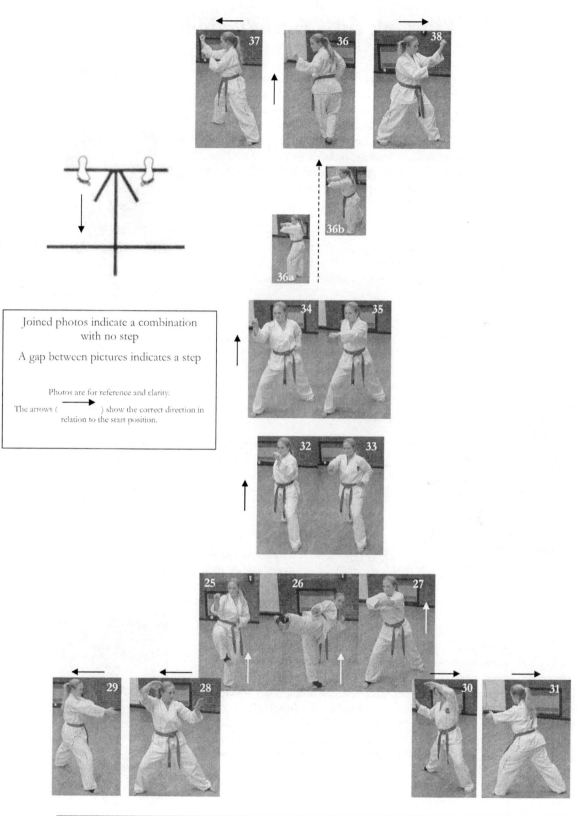

Joined photos indicate a combination with no step

A gap between pictures indicates a step

Photos are for reference and clarity.

The arrows ( ) show the correct direction in relation to the start position.

Yul-Gok tul – *Introduction*

Yul-Gok is named after Korea's great philosopher and scholar Yi I, born in Kangwon Province on 26th December, 1536. Yul-Gok, a child prodigy, learnt Chinese scripts at just 3 years old and by the age of 7 was writing poetry in Chinese. Yul-Gok passed the Civil Service literary examination at the age of just 13 and at 29, after passing a higher Civil Service exam with full marks, he began work for the government, holding many important positions such as Korea's Minister of Personnel and War, Rector of the National Academy and Minister of Defence.

His thesis, *'Ch'ondoch'aek'* showed his profound knowledge of history and the Confucian philosophy of politics, whilst reflecting his deep knowledge of Taoism and is regarded as a literary masterpiece.

Following his mothers death when Yul-Gok was 36, he retreated to the Diamond Mountains for three years and upon his return to society authored *'The Essentials of Confucianism'* (1576) which showed how to lead a good Confucian based life. He become revered as the 'Greatest Teacher in the East'.

Yul-Gok means *'Valley of Chestnuts'* and was the penname chosen by Yi I in his later years as he continued writing many revered text and documents. Yul-Gok lived by how he preached and took sincerity very seriously. He felt *'A sincere man was a man that knew the realism of heaven'*. He once wrote that a house could not sustain harmony unless every family member was sincere and he felt that, when confronted with misfortune, a man must carry out a deep self-reflection to find and correct his own mistakes.

The Diamond Mountains, Korea
(notice the tower in the middle)

Yul-Gok's beliefs in sincerity, loyalty, and the improvement of the individual displayed in his own actions. As an example, Yul-Gok's stepmother enjoyed drinking wine, which Yul-Gok never approved of. Even though, every morning, year after year, he brought her several cups of wine and never reproached her for her habit. She finally decided to stop drinking on her own, without ever having been told of Yul-Gok's displeasure. In gratitude for all those years of non-judgmental dedication, Yul-Gok's stepmother mourned his death for 3 years, clad in white mourning attire.

A year before his death in 1583, Yul-Gok proposed that the government train and equip a 100,000-man Army Reserve Corps. Like many of his suggestions it was undermined by minor Government officials who were caught up in East/West political conflicts within the government. It was unfortunate that this suggestion concerning national security was never allowed to be implemented, as 9 years later Korea was invaded and occupied by the Japanese as the Korean military forces failed to resist the army of Hideyoshi.

Toyotomi Hideyoshi

Even after his death in 1584, Yul-Gok's writings continued to have an effect on Korea and its government because of his dedication to Confucianism and theory of government. Following his death '*Yul-Gok Chônjip*' (The Complete Works of Yul-Gok) was compiled.

Yul-Gok is indeed an interesting pattern as it contains some interesting 45 degree motions early on in it, as well as techniques we have previously covered, possibly meaning different applications for them. We have the quizzical X-Stance with the back fist and the last few movements form a bit of a puzzle, as we have a strike (the back fist) which follows a strike and then we have a block which follows a block, neither following the usual block and counter patterns usually associated with patterns. Another strange occurrence with the Doo Palmok Makgi (*Double Forearm Block*) is the position of the secondary arm, being along side the first. This is one of the techniques that has been changed from how it appears in Karate, where the secondary arm points fist towards the blocking arm. However, that still doesn't explain the application of either the X Stance, the back fist strike or the double forearm block!

Yul-Gok is also an odd pattern. It's the only pattern that has a *'measure up'* as its first movement. Even more confusing is the fact that to many, the measure up isn't centred but inline with the students left shoulder or even when centred in relation to our own body (as I was taught) the target area offered in the encyclopedia is the solar plexus, which doesn't really make much sense. So where did this technique and the confusion with it come from? The confusion about where the measure should align is possibly quite easily solved. In both the versions of the encyclopedia's I have (1993 and 1965) both refer to the measure up as to 'D' (which from the ready position is directly to the students front), the photo in the encyclopedia's has the demonstrator show it to the side, so it seems it's a possible simple photo error, 'D' is in relation to the start position, so the *'measure up'* arm is either at our centre or actually slightly to the right of it (pointing towards 'D'). The *'why'* will be revealed as we run through the pattern applications. However, though many instructors teach the raising of the arm (or extending of the fist as a slow punch) as a preparation technique in order to measure up for the following punch, this reasoning is actually pretty doubtful. Firstly, all the coloured belt patterns up to 3rd degree start with a block (or in Hwa-Rang tul's case, a defensive motion) and even the higher grade patterns, when studied in-depth, start with blocks or defensive techniques (even if they seemingly start with strikes – though there are only a couple of cases like this) as this conforms to the fact that Taekwon-do is a defensive art and also follows the Shotokan principle of *'No first strike in Karate'*. So why would Yul-Gok be any different from the other 23 patterns! Secondly, the raising of this arm is counted as one of the 38 movements of this pattern, which means its much more likely to have an actual application or purpose above and beyond a preparation technique for movement number two. This technique is explored in depth in this chapter and a proper or more plausible explanation reached.

From my own experience of the applications I know for this pattern, or movements contained within it, I looked to see if there were similar applications and low and behold we find them, time after time. In fact we find variations on a single theme so often that I have nicknamed this pattern *'the grabbing pattern'* as nearly all applications refer to not only grabbing your opponent, but also keeping hold whilst we follow up to finish them off.

Applications from Yul-Gok tul

Yul-Gok starts in Narani Junbi Sogi *(Parallel Ready Stance)* and begins by raising our left arm in readiness for the punch as we step into Annun Sogi *(Sitting Stance)*

This is followed by

- **Doo Jirugi** *(Double Punch)* in **Annun Sogi** *(Sitting Stance)*

The student is grabbed by both shoulders, we side step and drop low (and to our left) into Annum Sogi *(Sitting Stance)*, whilst raising our left arm.[52] By doing so we create a release as our body is pulling away and downwards and our arm simply prises the grab off by going upwards, and the side ways movement further increases the difficulty of maintaining a grip. The measuring arm can also be utilized as a grab to our opponent, pulling him into our first punch, then releasing and following up with our second strike. Either way, both strikes seem better suited to the floating ribs vital point (in the fourth picture we have also shown the arm pit vital point, which is also valid as it would depend on the height of your attacker), as that is the position we find ourselves in by dropping into Annun Sogi *(Sitting Stance)*.

You will also notice how we attack just the right side of the body, which falls in-line with the next combination and it is a usual body reaction to pain to withdraw (think of placing your hand on something hot – you feel pain and instinctively pull it away). As this combination is performed again on the opposite side (and then the next set of combinations are repeated also) it is teaching us that we can perform this application and the follow up applications by stepping either way. The actual step between the combinations, taking us from the left hand side over to the right is to slow to be used as a real time applications, but may be used to emphasize the importance of focus, as a focused technique to a small target area is required to ensure

---

[52] The measuring punch is not taught to punch out, but rather to rise up straight (though I was originally taught it as a slow punch)

applications such as these are successful. Though I believe these combinations are indicating use on either side an additional application for this set of techniques (the punches) and the next set (Inner Forearm Block and Front Snap Kick) can be found in the **Alternative Applications** section.

Next we use:

- **Kaunde An Palmok Makgi** (*Middle Section Inner Forearm Block*)
- **Ap Cha Busigi** (*Front Snap Kick*)
- **Doo Jirugi** (*Double Punch*)

Our opponent had grabbed us with both hands and we defended as described above by attacking to his right side floating ribs. This may make an opponent withdraw his right side away from the pain, and whilst stunned his left hand is still upon our right lapel or shoulder (we removed the right as we dropped). From here we pivot 45 degrees and perform Kaunde An Palmok Makgi (*Middle Section Inner Forearm Block*).

As we chamber for the next block, we utilize the reaction hand in the chamber to hold his arm in place which in turn increases the effect and success of using the blocking motion this way. We withdraw our right leg slightly as we chamber and prepare to pivot. Sharply we pivot at a 45 degree angle, locking our block into place. This locks in at our opponents elbow or upper arm and displaces him sharply to our right (his left) where he may be turning subconsciously away from the pain having just had his ribs broken, thus helping the motion. We immediately follow with Ap Cha Busigi (*Front Snap Kick*), the target usually being the solar plexus, however, the block would have probably thrown our aggressor slightly side on, so I prefer to see it as a strike to the inside of the thigh (to the pressure point) or the turned knee. This drops our opponent to a height where we can use Doo Jirugi (*Double Punch*) in the same guise as before (in Do-San), as a neck break or simply punch them a couple more times to finish them off, though the neck break application fits the M.O. more readily.

To break the neck of our opponent we reach round with our reaction arm and using either our palms (as shown in the pictures) or a grab, perform the double punch motion, twisting the neck violently one way, then the other – the last returning all the way to finish the break.

Again we use:

- **Kaunde An Palmok Makgi** (*Middle Section Inner Forearm Block*)
- **Ap Cha Busigi** (*Front Snap Kick*)
- **Doo Jirugi** (*Double Punch*)

The application is then repeated on the opposite side, which allows us to practice the same set of combinations no matter which side we are grabbed .The angles are used to lock an opponents arm and throw them outwards momentarily. Here we see the same application on the opposite size, using double punches instead to finish our opponent off.

Following this we use:

- **Sonbadak Golcha Makgi**

  (Palm Hooking Block)

- **Sonbadak Golcha Makgi**

  (Palm Hooking Block)

- **Kaunde Baro Ap Joomok Jirugi**

  (*Obverse Fore Fist Punch*)

This is a variation of the above, but to an attacker straight in front this time. Though I do like the normal usage of this block, as coming down straight onto the attackers incoming arm, in a realistic combat situation the timing would be very difficult (though not impossible), so its gets relegated to the **Alternative Applications** section for this chapter. The circular motion of this block also indicates we are avoiding something and have to go around it, because in reality we could easily just drop our hand from a greater height from our opponents to grab onto them, there isn't really a need for the circular motion to do this.

This application moves down the body from the shoulders to being grabbed on the upper arm. When our opponent grabs our arm, we circle our palm around our

opponents whilst shifting forward slightly (as in the pattern), as our palm hits our opponent, the combination of moving in slightly, the circular motion of the block and finally our palm wrapping over our opponents creates a lock. Using torque (throwing our shoulder out) the arm is turned as well (as is the attacker) opening up accessible points to strike. The second palm hooking block can be used to strike the throat, artery, as a claw squeeze, to strike the attackers collar bone or to strike the ear causing a painful burst ear drum due to the *'cupping'* position of our hand, with the punch finishing them off.

Following this we use:

- **Wen Sonbadak Golcha Makgi** *(Left Palm Hooking Block)*
- **Orun Sonbadak Golcha Makgi** *(Right Palm Hooking Block)*
- **Kaunde Baro Ap Joomok Jirugi** *(Obverse Fore Fist Punch)*
- **Kaunde Baro Ap Joomok Jirugi** *(Obverse Fore Fist Punch)*

Reversed view

As per usual, this combination is repeated on the opposite side, however, this time we show it using another combination that's closer to what is the standard taught application for this movement.

The combination of palm hooking blocks are used to parry a set of double punches, in this case a jab and a cross. The first punch is parried and held, so a second punch is thrown in frustration to release the first, this is also parried and held just like in the pattern. As per the pattern combination, we turn the first block (the left hand) into a punch and using our attackers bottom arm we punch over the top with it and place pressure on their elbow joint, hopefully breaking their elbow. We then step forward and perform Kaunde Baro Ap Joomok Jirugi (*Obverse Fore Fist Punch*), to ensure we have finished them off.

The next set of combinations use:

- **Gorboryu Junbi Sogi 'A'**
  (*Bending Ready Stance 'A'*)
- **Wen Yop Cha Jirugi**
  (*Left Side Piercing kick*)
- **Ap Palkup Taeragi** (*Front Elbow Strike*)

This combination, though similar to the one in Won-Hyo has some important differences. The bending ready stance, starts off the same, but it comes from the rear leg, making it more likely to be a strike than a simple checking movement.

As we strike with out foot, we draw up into the stance, the arms are flung forward to grab our opponent, ensure they don't get away.

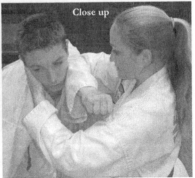

Close up

We side kick, this can be mid section (like in the pattern) or the groin and we follow with the traditional grab to the back of the head and the elbow to the face.

However, if we side kick to the side of their body slightly (which is in fact easier to target at this distance), they turn, allowing us to use the palm and elbow strike to the side of the jaw. If you think about it, after a good side kick the opponent would be either doubled up or falling down and the head position would be a lot lower, thus there would be no back of head to grab and drive onto with our elbow. By grabbing one side and elbowing the other, the jaw is easily broke and we crush the 'U' shape ends of the jaw together, think of squeezing a wishbone.

From our last position we immediately turn and utilize:

- **Gorboryu Junbi Sogi 'A**
  (Bending Ready Stance 'A')
- **Orun Yop Cha Jirugi**
  (Right Side Piercing kick)
- **Ap Palkup Taeragi**
  (Front Elbow Strike)

Reversed view, showing the grab

However, this is slightly different from the previous combination as we tend to bring the rear leg straight up from our walking stance in the previous movement.

Imagine being grabbed from behind after taking our friends opponent out by breaking his jaw. We pivot and use the rising of the leg as a knee strike.

We are pretty close to our opponent at this point which makes a mid section side kick hard (though not impossible) to do, so we'll utilize the kick as a strike to either the groin or to the pressure point on the inside thigh. Again we use the guarding block portion of this movement to grab and keep hold of our attacker and finish in exactly the same way as before with the elbow strike to the side of the jaw.

We then we turn and perform:

- **Sang Sonkal Makgi** (*Twin Knife-hand Block*)
- **Sun Sonkut Tulgi** (*Straight Finger Tip Thrust*)

On the opposite side our attacker throws a left hook at us, we turn in to face the attacker, using our chamber as a guard to catch the strike. As soon as contact is made, we roll into our block. The rising knife-hand turns and grabs onto the arm, whilst the front knife-hand strikes the carotid artery or under the armpit. Notice how dropping into our stance enables us to jolt our attacker and open up the striking points. Of course the front knife-hand could also be used to stop a secondary attack as well, before following up with the Sun Sonkut Tulgi (*Straight Finger Tip Thrust*), in this case I have shown it to the throat, though of course you can follow the manual and direct it to the solar plexus if you want. The left hand clears any objects like arms out the way for the strike.

Reversed view

After this we turn and perform:

- **Sang Sonkal Makgi**
  (*Twin Knife-hand Block*)
- **Sun Sonkut Tulgi**
  (*Straight Finger Tip Thrust*)
- **Nopunde Bakat Palmok Yop Makgi**
  (*High Section Outer Forearm Side Block*)
- **Kaunde Bandae Ap Joomok Jirugi** (*Middle Section Reverse Fore Fist Punch*)

The action is repeated, so it could simply be used for repeat practice from the opposite side or we could utilize a different application for practice.

For this application, we turn to face an in coming attacker and are grabbed. We use one knife-hand to strike to the wrist and the other to strike the pressure point on the bicep (though it could easily strike the carotid artery like before). From here we drive our finger tip thrust into the solar plexus (or throat) and bring our side block *(Bakat Palmok Yop Makgi)* into the chambering position.

Using the side block we could simply hammer fist strike to the face, or more inline with this patterns diagram (and the way this pattern seems to utilize keeping hold of the attacker), grab the attackers clothing, throw him off balance by pivoting round whilst he is stunned (as per the pattern) and then striking him again with the reverse punch (notice its reverse as we are still holding on) to finish him off. Why spin him round? Well, the previous set of techniques are unlikely to be a telling blow (unless we strike the wind pipe), and simply stun him, whilst stunned it enables us to perform the block and the natural reaction of maintaining balance kicks in, thus we regain control and strike. Alternatively, we can throw him to the floor with this motion and strike downwards to finish him off.

These 2 pictures have been re-angled to show the application

This is followed by:

- **Nopunde Bakat Palmok Yop Makgi**

  (High Section Outer Forearm Side Block)

- **Kaunde Bandae Ap Joomok Jirugi**

  (Middle Section Reverse Fore Fist Punch)

Again this motion repeats indicating it can be used either way and that practice on both sides is essential. However, this allows a slightly different application to be shown because in this part of the pattern there is no pivot to throw our opponent round and as we are moving forward we can utilize this to a front facing adversary.

Instead of using Nopunde Bakat Palmok Yop Makgi *(High Section Outer Forearm Side Block)* to grab clothing, we actually use the clenching of

the fist to grab the face (the fist a reminder that we should clench as hard as we can).

The chambering of this block is akin to covering (a natural response is simply to cover with both arms), which we can use to deflect the incoming blow and the block follows on. This block utilizes the elbow to strike into the sternum or chest, whilst we simply claw the face. With face covered (and being clawed), as we rip the block away, the opponents hands will often raise and we strike at a vulnerable vital point, either the solar plexus or the floating ribs as the attacker may have turned sideways slightly either to ease the pressure from the attack on his face or as we rip our reaction arm back. Alternatively, we could just hammer fist his jaw and follow with a reverse punch as well.

Next we use:

- **Kyocha So Dung Joomok Nopunde Yop Taeragi**

  (X Stance Back Fist High Side Strike)

- **Nopunde Doo Palmok Makgi**

  (High Section Double Forearm Block)

- **Nopunde Doo Palmok Makgi**

  (High Section Double Forearm Block)

These last few movements as mentioned in the introduction form a bit of a puzzle. A strike (the back fist) follows a strike and then we have two blocks, one after the other. Another strange occurrence with this block is the position of the secondary arm, being along side the first in Doo Palmok Makgi *(Double Forearm Block)*. This is one of the techniques that has been changed from how it appears in Karate, where the secondary arm points fist towards the blocking arm.

However, that still doesn't explain the application of either the X Stance, the back fist strike or the double forearm block – for that we have to look at the rest of the pattern, which details many

grabs, therefore it stands to reason these techniques follow suit. Granted we can use the back fist strike to cover distance and strike to an incoming attacker, but if we follow the '*grab*' theory and lead on from the previous technique of a reverse punch, perhaps not being as effective as we hoped and leaving us in a vulnerable position, with our arm caught or being grabbed from a distance (as shown in the photographs).

From the previous position our arm is grabbed and our whole body weight is thrown towards the attacker, we use the chambering position of the back fist to pull us towards the attacker and/or turn him side on as well as securing a release from the grip and covering our real intentions.

As we drive forward our shoulder and thigh/hip crash into our opponent, knocking his equilibrium off and backwards. We form our X Stance by placing our left leg in front of the attackers leg and as our rear leg comes up behind we drop into the stance.

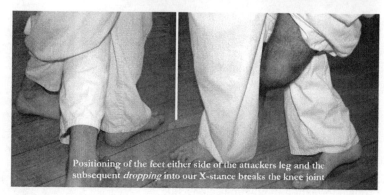

Positioning of the feet either side of the attackers leg and the subsequent *dropping* into our X-stance breaks the knee joint

This forms the grab to ensure our attackers doesn't disappear whilst at the same time severely damaging or breaking the knee joint. By dropping as well as keeping the rear foot on the ball, it also allows us to maintain proper balance. The sudden set up motion and drive forwards causes our opponent to offer the side of the knee, rather than the front. As we drop into the stance the arm of the back fist strike finishes off our attacker, throwing them backwards (we can also strike if the distance is right), whilst the X Stance keeps them close for the follow up if needed.

The chambering of the reaction hand also has another interesting feature. If close enough (or the whole motion is being utilized from a close grab rather than from a distance) we can use the right hand as a strike also, to cover our intentions for our legs, as its doubtful we can gain a lot of power in the punch, so a distraction applications seems more plausible.

Be careful practicing this application with the whole body weight thrown into the motion, it makes a very powerful move, more than capable of destroying someone's knee. Practice with care, as you can see from this photo, even a little more pressure results in a lot of pain and this was performed at no-where near full intensity.

From X-stance position, we *can* grab on with both hands and pivot into Doo Palmok Makgi *(Double Forearm Block)* and the attacker is flung away over our left leg, although the previous movement is more than enough to drop our attacker to the floor with a broken knee.

Doo Palmok Makgi *(Double Forearm Block)* is another excellent example of a two pronged application, by that I mean one that is doing an attack, whilst covering our secondary intention.

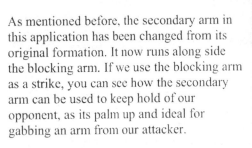

As mentioned before, the secondary arm in this application has been changed from its original formation. It now runs along side the blocking arm. If we use the blocking arm as a strike, you can see how the secondary arm can be used to keep hold of our opponent, as its palm up and ideal for gabbing an arm from our attacker.

In this case, we use the front arm of the block to strike whilst at the same time our other arm secures a grip. We move the top hand into a grip following the strike as we start to turn for the next movement. With both hands clenched into tight grips, one on the clothing, the other on the attackers arm, we pivot into the next movement and as our feet close together whilst stepping into the next stance, we launch our opponent into the throw. The two solid anchor points (strong grips with the hands) and the stepping motion make this a surprisingly easy throw to perform.

Again, the second block shows us that this technique can be used on both sides and is ideal for practicing shoulder throws.

Alternative Applications To Yul-Gok tul

Alternative Application to movements 4/5/6 (or 1/2/3) and 7/8/9/10:

- **Doo Jirugi** (*Double Punch*) in **Annun Sogi** (*Sitting Stance*)
- **Kaunde An Palmok Makgi** (*Middle Section Inner Forearm Block*)
- **Ap Cha Busigi** (*Front Snap Kick*)
- **Doo Jirugi** (*Double Punch*)

I have seen these techniques taught a number of times as a release from a bear hug and though it may prove useful to junior grades, I have my doubts as to how authentic an application it is. I will tell you why I believe this after taking you through the application itself, but I will also add to this often taught defence to make it a little more viable.

Though this application can be practiced on either side, using the first and fourth sets of combinations or, as in this case, the second and third set of combinations so it flows within the patterns diagram.

The student is grabbed in a rear bear hug and immediately drops low by stepping into Annun Sogi (*Sitting Stance*) and raising his arm (in this instant his right, as per the pattern) to aid the pushing upwards of the opponents arms whilst his body travels in the opposite direction to help with the release, at the same time striking with the left elbow.

These pictures run from right to left

Immediately he strikes his opponent again with a right elbow (the reaction arm movement to the left punch), and then again with a left elbow (the reaction hand movement to the right punch) which all helps to dislodge the attacker and create a gap to allow the next phase of the application to take place.

After softening up his opponent with the elbow strikes, the student shifts his body to an angle to facilitate a throw and by moving diagonally he is able to use the grip of Kaunde An Palmok Makgi (*Middle Section Inner Forearm Block*) to grab his opponent and his rear leg to effect a body drop throw by pulling his opponent over it as he slides into his next stance.

These pictures run from right to left

This has the effect of pulling the opponent over and round so their head is directly inline for the next technique of Ap Cha Busigi (*Front Snap Kick*) which should be to the head, or ideally the throat to finish the attacker. As if that wasn't enough, the student can also utilize Doo Jirugi (*Double Punch*) to break the attackers neck, as shown in the main applications section.

Now you may be wondering why I don't consider this an original or even practical application? Well, I am referring to the first part (the release from a bear hug) which, although it may work in practice or even in reality, there are much clearer applications shown for bear hug releases in later patterns, as in they are blatantly obvious, making it unlikely that this is a *hidden* application at all even if it seems like it could be. What's more is that in solo patterns training of these combinations there is no actual focus for the elbow strikes as the P.O.I (Point Of Impact) is focused on the fists, not the elbows, meaning the students thought process is less likely to connect with this application when needed unless the emphasis on his solo patterns training changes, and if we simply take use of the reaction hand as a rear elbow strike, every technique lends itself to a similar application as they nearly all use the reaction hand, though in this case, the dropping into annun sogi makes it slightly more likely. My final reason is simply because its repeated on both sides, which even though this is normal for many applications, that is because a student needs to be able to work defences off of either side for frontal or side attacks, but in the case of a bear hug, there is no 'either side' just the rear, they either grab in the bear hug or they don't, so repeating the combination makes little sense, except to enable the final throw, which is the bit I've included to make it more applicable and is not taught with the 'bear hug' application as standard, in fact I've never seen the throw taught when showing this as a bear hug defence. That said, should you wish to teach this as an application, you now have the means to ensure its fits the M.O. with the follow up techniques included.

Alternative Application to movements 15/16/17 or 18/19/20:

- **Sonbadak Golcha Makgi**

  (Palm Hooking Block)

- **Sonbadak Golcha Makgi**

  (Palm Hooking Block)

- **Kaunde Baro Ap Joomok Jirugi**

  (Obverse Fore Fist Punch)

Here we show the Sonbadak Golcha Makgi combination utilized as a checking technique to parry an incoming blow before striking with the punch. This is another reason for having two blocks, as after grabbing onto our opponent, they may throw a counter attack with their other non-grabbed arm and the side block allows us to parry it and follow with our strike.

Reverse view

Alternative Application to movements 15, 16, 18 or 19:

- **Sonbadak Golcha Makgi** *(Palm Hooking Block)*

Palm hooking block is a great technique to send an opponent crashing to the ground. As a strike is thrown we utilize the block in the circular hooking motion, cupping over our attackers arm as we avoid the blow. However, instead of stopping like in the pattern we continue on our downward path, keeping hold of our opponents arm and using their own momentum against them (the water principle), to send them face first into the ground.

Alternative Application to movements 15,/16/17 or 18/19/20:

- **Sonbadak Golcha Makgi**
  (Palm Hooking Block)

- **Sonbadak Golcha Makgi**
  (Palm Hooking Block)

- **Kaunde Baro Ap Joomok Jirugi**
  (Obverse Fore Fist Punch)

Here we use the first Sonbadak Golcha Makgi *(Palm Hooking Block)* as shown in the main text application, to wrap around the attackers arm following a grab to our own. However, instead of striking to the collar bone, we use the second Sonbadak Golcha Makgi *(Palm Hooking Block)* against the side of our opponents head, forcing his head sharply to the side. As we do, we immediately follow up with the strike.

Alternative Application to movements 15, 16, 18 or 19:

- **Sonbadak Golcha Makgi** *(Palm Hooking Block)*

Palm Hooking Block is ideal to reverse a wrist grab into a wrist lock on the opponent. As the students arm is grabbed, form Sonbadak Golcha Makgi by wrapping the palm around the opponents own wrist. It should be suitably re-enforced with the opposite hand (think chambering motion of the second block) by clamping down onto of the opponents, as sweat can make it slip off and the pushing out of the shoulders helps to augment the lock.

This application is useful as it works with both *'same side'* and *'cross grabs'* of the wrist, though with same side grabs, a quick follow up is essential, as the opponent is still facing you and thus able to use his opposite hand!

Alternative Application to movements 15, 16, 18 or 19:

- **Sonbadak Golcha Makgi** (*Palm Hooking Block)*

Alternatively, instead of hooking and clasping onto the arm as shown previously, we can use Sonbadak Golcha Makgi *(Palm Hooking Block)* as we slip a punch or onslaught of punches from the attacker. Whilst avoiding the blows, the student simultaneously uses Sonbadak Golcha Makgi *(Palm Hooking Block)* to the back of their head, the palm coming up behind them, clasping on (the shape of the block is ideal) and bringing the block downwards to again, sending them face first into the concrete.

Alternative Application to movements 15, 16, 18 or 19:

- **Sonbadak Golcha Makgi** *(Palm Hooking Block)*

Sonbadak Golcha Makgi may well be one of the first anti-rifle technique we come across in the patterns. Though some know that one of the techniques in Joong-Gun was originally a rifle grab, Yul-Gok also fits the mould well. Though I can't conclusively say, I offer this reasons for its inclusion as a possible anti-rifle technique:

1. From my research, Sonbadak Golcha Makgi is unique to Taekwon-do. IE. Before Taekwon-do, this block performed in this way didn't appear

2. The more well known 'rifle' application appears in the very next pattern up – this application is simple by comparison

3. A gun trajectory shoots straight, this block not only grabs the gun, but also alters that trajectory away from the students (or soldiers) body

4. This application falls inline with modern military gun disarms of today[53], so is comparable to it

---

[53] I learnt some gun disarms, albeit with pistols rather than rifles. They were taught by a military unarmed combat instructor (Alan Cain) and one defence he taught was very similar to this application but had a bit more detailed follow-up , possibly as it involved a pistol rather than a rifle

Alternative Application to movements 24 or 27:

- **Ap Palkup Taeragi** *(Front Elbow Strike)*

Ap Palkup Taeragi can be used as an elbow breaking technique. Using the cupping hand to grab our opponents arm, the student simply strikes to the elbow joint, whilst pulling the attackers arm towards them. A slight adjustment in the cupping arms position enables this application to work successfully.

Alternative Application to movements 24 or 27:

- **Ap Palkup Taeragi** *(Front Elbow Strike)*

Ap Palkup Taeragi, as used in Yul-Gok tul (with the additional grab) can also be used to facilitate an arm lock. As the student is grabbed at the front, she pivots slightly and performs Ap Palkup Taeragi, using the supporting hand to keep hold of the attackers arm, and her own forearm and elbow to lock onto the attackers joint. Further or more forceful rotation will cause the attacker extreme pain or break his arm altogether. Here, after the initial lock, she applies pressure downwards and drops back into L-Stance to help maintain a straight arm, driving the attacker to the floor whilst she retains control.

Alternative Application to movements 24 or 27:

- **Ap Palkup Taeragi** *(Front Elbow Strike)*

Ap Palkup Taeragi can also be used to facilitate a release and strike technique.
As the students arm is grabbed, she drives the elbow forward and breaks the attackers grip,
utilizing the grabbing hand to aid the technique and pull the opponents arm downwards. She can
continue driving the elbow forward into the attacker. The bent arm is ideal to flick out and finish
with a back fist strike.

Alternative Application to movements 24 or 27:

- **Ap Palkup Taeragi** *(Front Elbow Strike)*

Ap Palkup Taeragi can also be used to
create space between the student and
opponent from close range.

The point of the elbow is used to strike against the
opponents chest, whilst the other hand can be used to grab
the clothing to enhance the strike. A quick follow up
technique should be used.

Alternative Application to movements 28 and 29:

- **Sang Sonkal Makgi** (*Twin Knife-hand Block*)
- **Sun Sonkut Tulgi** (*Straight Finger Tip Thrust*)

We are grabbed and choked from the side, we turn and drop
into our L-Stance whilst performing Sang Sonkal Makgi (*Twin Knife-hand Block*). The knife-hands strike to the pressure points in the inner forearms (or the bicep) together as we simultaneously drop back into our L-Stance, thus pulling our throat away from the choke as well. From here we can grab our attackers arm or clothing and drive Sun Sonkut Tulgi (*Straight Finger Tip Thrust*) into his throat, or we can move in and perform a shoulder throw as in Do-San. Notice how the opponent reacts when the fingertip thrust is driven forward, by leaning backwards to alleviate the pain, meaning our fingertip thrust ends up at almost the same height as performed in the pattern!

Alternative Application to movements 32 or 34:

- **Nopunde Bakat Palmok Yop Makgi**

   (*High Section Outer Forearm Side Block*)

Bakat Palmok Yop Makgi, being a high section block, is of course ideal as a side fist strike to the face of our attacker, especially due to that fact that it chambers inside and close to the body.

It can also be used to successfully reverse a cross-wrist grab, by using a smaller chamber for speed and moving the fist of our grabbed wrist, under our attackers (the chamber), then up and across into the actual block position. This can easily be followed up with the reverse punch as shown in the pattern, though another technique would be preferable as we ideally need to keep our other hand helping maintain the lock, as its easy for the attacker to let go in order to slip out. Therefore it is advisable to place your opposite hand on top of the attackers and keep it there. This is not designed to be a holding block, but rather a quick technique to aid follow up.

Alternative Application to movement 36:

- **Kyocha So Dung Joomok Nopunde Yop Taeragi**

  (X Stance Back Fist High Side Strike)

Kyocha So Dung Joomok Nopunde Yop Taeragi can be used to teach the basic leg positions of a scissor take down.

The student moves forward on the attacker with one leg in front (the lead leg) and one behind the attackers legs. From here the student only has to jump up and twist anti-clockwise and a scissor take down happens.

The back fist would likely be grabbed by the attacker as the student tangles up their legs, so can be used as an anchor point. Alternatively it can be used to strike across the attackers chest or throat to aid the take down or simply as a follow up technique following successful completion of the take down. Its strange that this is found in Yul-Gok as a more flowing (i.e. correct) version of the scissor takedown is found in the next pattern up, Joong-Gun, so this could be viewed as basic training for a more advanced technique.

Alternative Application to movement 37 or 38:

- **Nopunde Doo Palmok Makgi**

  (High Section Double Forearm Block)

The double motion of this block can be utilized as a double motion technique. If the student is attacked quite close, by a straight technique like a punch, push or grab, as one arm checks, strikes or blocks the attackers main arm, the lower portion of the block simultaneously delivers a counter strike as its at an ideal height to match the solar plexus of our attacker. Of course, we would be moving forward anyway, like in the pattern, so should be close enough to perform this application, with only very slight modifications.

Alternative Application to movement 37 or 38:

- **Nopunde Doo Palmok Makgi**

  (High Section Double Forearm Block)

A more modern variation on the application of Doo Palmok Makgi is to utilize it against a flurry of punches, due to its strength by the way of a supporting arm. Plus, as the there is no reaction arm it means we can throw the whole of our body weight into the application. As the student is rushed by a series of punches he chambers (but not to far back), slips to the side and unloads the full power of the block into the side of our attackers upper arms, effectively redirecting the force of our attacker and turning him away so his back it towards the student, ready for a counter.

Alternative Application to movements 1, 2 and 3:

- **Measuring Arm**

- **Doo Jirugi** *(Double Punch)*

Whilst doing research for this book I came upon mentions in some Karate styles of what they term *'night fighting techniques'*. These are techniques that are useful when having to engage an enemy in subdued light and I feel, whether the General realized it or not, this is where this technique may have originally come from.

In the dark we still need to target to a vital point to take our enemy out properly and if we reach out in front, the area is vast as you have both left and right sides of the chest, the stomach and the shoulders and working out exactly what part is which (quickly, in the dark) takes a little bit of time. We need to work out what part of the body we are touching to know where in relation to it is the vital point to strike. However, by feeling our opponents outline via the side of the body, this process is made so much simpler and quicker, the fist represents finding and keeping hold as we perform our first strike, the second as a follow up to ensure we have done our job correctly.

One other interesting point about the 'night fighting techniques' is that they tend to encourage the student to drop low, out of the range of an immediate strike from the aggressor or below his vision line for a split second (in the dark we take longer to adjust to things, so think of dropping into Annum Sogi (Sitting Stance) as a simple form of protecting ourselves until we can engage. We not only drop but also move side ways, thus our immediate targets (jaw, throat, solar plexus and groin) all move from where they were to a relatively safer position.

So, we are attacked in a darkened atmosphere, we side step and drop low into Annum Sogi (Sitting Stance), whilst reaching out to find our opponent and once we do, we strike and strike again to ensure we have hit the targets. An alternative use of the reaction arm, as detailed at the start of this chapters applications, is to remove a grab from our shoulder, which tends to fall inline with the next set of movements. The measuring punch is not taught to punch out, but rather to rise up, so as we drop into the stance we also rise up the arm to remove it, which works just as well in the dark, as it does in the light.

*'Discovery consists of seeing what everybody has seen
and thinking what nobody has thought'*

- Albert von Szent-Gyorgyi

CHAPTER 15

Joong-Gun tul

the elbow breaking pattern

중근틀

Joong-Gun is named after the patriot Ahn Joong-Gun who assassinated Hiro-Bumi Ito, the first Japanese governor-general of Korea, known as the man who played the leading part in the Korea-Japan merger.

The 32 movements in this pattern represent Mr Ahn's age when he was executed at Lui-Shung prison in 1910

Joong-Gun has 32 Movements

Joong-Gun tul - *Step By Step*

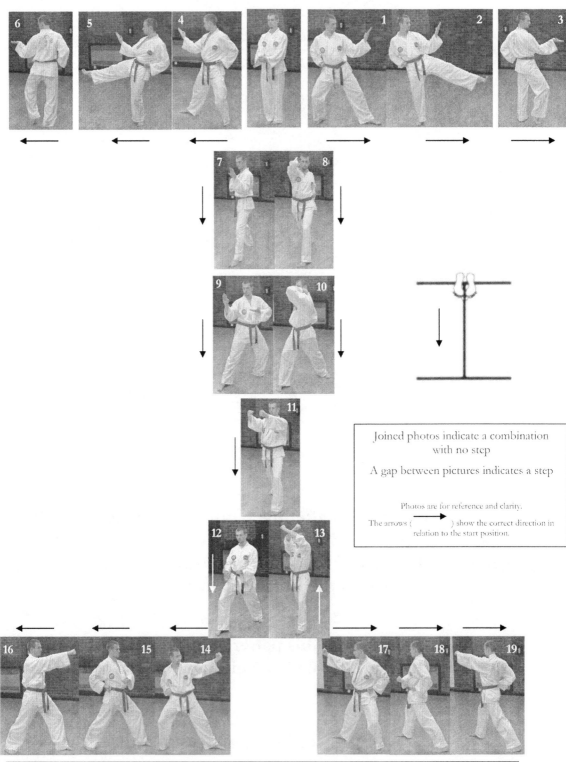

Joined photos indicate a combination with no step

A gap between pictures indicates a step

Photos are for reference and clarity.

The arrows (➔) show the correct direction in relation to the start position.

Joong-Gun tul - *Introduction*

Ahn Joong-Gun was born in the town of Hae-Ju in the province of Hwang-Hae in 1879. He became a teacher, founding the Sam-Heung (three Success) School. Running a school in that era meant many hardships due to the Japanese occupation of Korea.

In 1903, following a French and Russian alliance, troops from both armies moved into the northern parts of Korea, which was taken as a threat by the Japanese due to their intent to claim Korea as part of their empire. Despite protests (in 1904) by the Japanese that the French and Russian forces should vacate Korea, the Russians ignored them and were eventually attacked by the Japanese navy and though Korea tried to remain neutral, it was invaded by Japan in 1905 none-the-less, forcing the surrender of the Russians and firmly establishing Japan into Korea.

Hiro-Bumi Ito, one of Japan's leading statesmen was in charge of taking over the Korean Government as part of the long term occupation plan for Korea. He pressured the weak Korean Government of the time into signing a treaty giving the Japanese legal rights to occupy Korea, this was called the *'Protectorate Treaty'*. He was named the first Governor-General of Korea in 1905 and given total control of all the Japanese forces stationed in Korea, as well as all foreign relations and trade in Korea and was answerable only to the Japanese Emperor himself.

Hiro-Bumi Ito

Upon his arrival in Korea in March, 1906, Hiro-Bumi Ito ordered all foreign delegations in Korea to leave, leaving Korea totally at Japan's mercy, whilst he enforced the *'Protectorate Treaty'* giving Japanese the rights to buy the land from Korean citizens, though in many cases land was simply taken.

The Korean people were incensed by this. The *'Protectorate Treaty'* caused much anger and anti-Japanese violence swept the country. Guerrilla groups were formed to attack the Japanese forces, but they were eventually defeated or hunted down by the much larger Japanese army. However, the violent unrest continued and spread further as many Government Official's, loyal to Korea, committed suicide whilst the Korean Government Officials who had signed the Protectorate Treaty were assassinated

In light of the Japanese oppression of his country, Ahn Joong-Gun went into self imposed exile in Southern Manchuria. Whilst there, he formed a small guerrilla army of around three hundred men, one of which was his brother, which conducted raids across the Manchurian border into northern Korea keeping consistent pressure on the Japanese forces in that region.

As the violent objections spread, Japan became increasing worried by the patriotic Korean organizations and their very vocal Anti-Japanese stance, especially those in the United States. Fearing intervention from outsiders in their control of Korea, the Japanese sent an American, D.W Stevens, to the United States to distribute pro-Japanese propaganda, but he was assassinated by two Korean patriots, outraged at the situation.

In June, 1907, the Korean emperor, Ko-Jong, secretly sent an emissary to the Hague Peace Conference to expose the Japanese aggressive policy in Korea to the world. When Hiro-Bumi Ito learned of this he forced the abdication of Emperor Ko-Jong from the throne and officially took total control of the Korean Government. This incensed the Koreans further and rioting broke out much of which involved Korean army units. Hiro-Bumi Ito's response was to disband both the Korean Army and Police Force, with the exception of Palace guards as well as the handing over of all prisons and courts to the Japanese. Korean troops retaliated, attacking the Japanese troops, but they were quickly defeated.

Though the Korean troops were defeated, the resistance continued for many years, with guerrilla attacks and patriots attempting assassinations on several prominent Japanese leaders and members of the Japanese-Korean Government. Many groups operated out of South East Manchuria, which was close to the town of Kando in Northern Korea. Kando became a breeding ground for the guerrilla forces, so much so that a significant Japanese military and police presence began to occupy the area. The problem was, that around 20% of the 100,000 population of Kando were Chinese and when the police and army cracked down on the population of Kando, Chinese were caught up in the violence which caused a considerable conflict between the Japanese and the Chinese!

In June 1909, in response to the increased Japanese presence in Kando, Ahn Joong-Gun led his forces on a raid which resulted in many Japanese deaths. Even though the guerrilla forces planned and executed their raids from within China, the Japanese and Chinese signed a treaty on 4th September 1909 that granted the Japanese access via the Southern Manchurian Railway, which enabled them to exploit the rich mineral resources in Manchuria. In return, the Chinese received the territorial rights to Kando and this was 'the straw that broke the camels back' for Korean patriots such as Joong-Gun, who headed for his base in Siberia to plan the assassination of the man responsible, Hiro-Bumi Ito!

Russia was already nervous of the increase Japanese activity in Northern Korean and the Japanese setting it sights on Manchuria. It was arranged for Hiro-Bumi Ito to meet General Kokotseff, a Russian representative at Harbin in Manchuria on 26th October, 1909, in order to calm the Russians fears of

Japan's intentions towards annexing Manchuria and the invasion of China.

Joong-Gun was waiting for Ito to arrive at Harbin train station. Despite knowing full well he could never escape and would be tortured severely by the Japanese if captured, he shot and killed Ito as he stepped off the train. He was indeed captured and imprisoned at Port Arthur and tortured for five months but despite this, it is said his spirit never broke. Finally the Japanese executed Ahn Joong-Gun at Lui-Shung prison at 10 am on 26th March 1910, he was just 32 years old.

The sacrifice Ahn Joong-Gun made, his attitude and that of his compatriots symbolized the loyalty and dedication of the Korean people to their country's independence and freedom from the Japanese. Joong-Gun was a patriot who loved his country, so much so that in the end, he gave his life for it. His love was captured forever in the calligraphy he wrote on his cell wall, whilst awaiting his execution, which simply said 'The Best Rivers and Mountains', implying he felt his country to be the most beautiful place on earth, worth dying for.

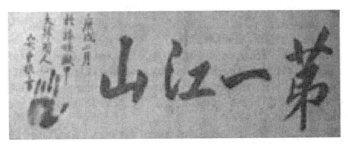

'The Best Rivers and Mountains'

Ahn Joong-Gun went from being a teacher, to a guerrilla leader and freedom fighter but is forever remembered as a famous Korean patriot, who died for the love of his country.

Joong-Gun is the first of the senior coloured belt patterns. It is introduced at 4th kup (blue belt) and as such the combinations and applications increase slightly in skill level to reflect the grade of the student. It is well known that the pattern has 32 movements because that was the age that Ahn Joong-Gun reached before his execution at Lui-Shung prison in 1910, but what you may not realize is that the pattern contains many combinations of three movements at a time which may be attributed to Ahn Joong-Gun's early years as a teacher where he founded the Sam-Heung School. Sam-Heung translates as *'three success'*!

It starts on the ready posture Moa Junbi Sogi 'B' (Closed Ready Stance 'B') and although like in other patterns I cannot find a direct relation between the ready posture and the pattern interpretation, I might speculate a little. The right fist is clenched and is often seen as a symbol of aggression, the left hand is open which is often seen as a symbol for humility, so the left over right could mean humility in the face of aggression, which was part and parcel of Ahn Joong-Gun's life. The hands together may also represent Ahn Joong-Gun's imprisonment (as in hand cuffs, bound etc) before his execution for the sacrifice he made for his country by assassinating Hiro-Bumi Ito. They may also represent his spirit through his torture, which lasted for 5 months in which it was said his spirit never broke throughout.

Joong-Gun contains a palm upward block performed early in the pattern which confuses many students as to its application. It is often shown as a deflection, directing a strike upwards, though this is unlikely as not only does it leave the student in a vulnerable position for a second attack, but we are likely to deflect the punch into our own face as the block is performed inline with our body (thus deflecting the punch up towards our head) in a side on stance.

Further into the patterns many are taught that a twin vertical fist strike to the jaw line is followed up with a twin upset fist to the kidneys, but one is a frontal attack and its immediately proceeded by an attack to the rear, which doesn't really make sense as there is no movement to turn the attacker around in between the two strikes!

We are introduced to another useful release technique as well as counter strikes and follow ups. More release techniques are hidden within the pattern. We also come across what is known to many as Yonsok Sogi (*consecutive stance*).

The double forearm block surfaces again and we utilize side punches in L Stance as well as many combinations of techniques that flow together. Students are often taught that the double palm blocks found in this pattern are to block a simultaneous punch and kick, but the odds of either one person or even two people punching and kicking at exactly the same time are extremely slim indeed, so more practical applications are given.

We are further introduced to a quizzical turn into what is known as angle punch, which extends past our own centre line, almost to the opposite shoulder and the infamous U-Shaped block, which many incorrectly think is to block a pole, but its original application is explained here in its correct detail.

One final thought: It has always been slightly puzzling that the pattern Joong-Gun finishes with two 'blocks' but no following strikes, though I know this is not limited to this pattern. However, if we look at the life of Ahn Joong-Gun, as a guerrilla army leader/freedom fighter and translate his life into the moves of the pattern we can see that block, then (counter) attack - such as the knife-hand guarding block, directly followed by the upward elbow strike - can be seen as symbolic and is a relevant theme throughout the pattern. The Japanese occupying forces attacked Koreans and was often attacked or countered in return by Korean guerrilla armies such as those led by Joong-Gun and the final three moves do not continue this trend! Following this symbolism, I feel that perhaps these last three movements represent the last few months of Ahn-Joong Guns life, where he was captured after the assignation of Hiro-Bumi Ito. The angle punch is not centred, but held just before the shoulder, in fact it is over the heart – the heart of a patriot. The last two movements are both *'blocks'* showing that despite his incarceration he was still attacked (via torture) and still defended (via his spirit) but could not lead a counter attack as he was incarcerated and unable to physically do so!

Applications from Joong-Gun tul

Joong-Gun starts with the ready posture **Moa Junbi Sogi 'B'** (*Closed Ready Stance B*)

From here we use:

- **Sonkal Dung Kaunde Makgi** (*Reverse Knife-hand Middle Block*)
- **Najunde Ap Cha Busigi** (*Low Section Front Snap Kick*)
- **Sonbadak Ollyo Makgi** (*Palm Upward Block*)

From a left sided wrist grab, we utilize Sonkal Dung Kaunde Makgi (*Reverse Knife-hand Middle Block*) to reverse the wrist grab, this turns the arm in preparation for the break we are going to perform and exposes the elbow joint. To cover our movement we use Najunde Ap Cha Busigi (*Low Section Front Snap Kick*) as a distraction. This front kick is low section and off the front leg, meaning its focus is speed rather than power and the movement takes the thought process from upper body, to lower body no matter what target we strike with it. Straight after the kick, we move in with Sonbadak Ollyo Makgi (*Palm Upward Block*) to break the elbow, we only move forward slightly into Dwitbal Sogi (*Rear Foot Stance*), as this keeps us at the right distance for the break. The reaction hand is used to straighten or keep hold off the elbow ready for the break and also helps with the actual motion by pulling the elbow downwards as we straighten it.

This combination doesn't have to be used to destroy. In the **Alternative Applications** section, I show how to can be used as a restraint to take an attacker prisoner for example.

Next we use:

- **Sonkal Dung Kaunde Makgi** *(Reverse Knife-hand Middle Block)*
- **Najunde Ap Cha Busigi** *(Low Section Front Snap Kick)*
- **Sonbadak Ollyo Makgi** *(Palm Upward Block)*
- **Kaunde Sonkal Daebi Makgi** *(Middle Section Knife-hand Guarding Block)*
- **Wi Palkup Taeragi** *(Upward Elbow Strike)*

For the second set of the combination, we are grabbed on the shoulder and we turn and strike the attackers bicep with Sonkal Dung Kaunde Makgi *(Reverse Knife-hand Middle Block)*, again we follow it straight away with Najunde Ap Cha Busigi *(Low Section Front Snap Kick)* to the shin, groin, knee or nerve in the thigh, as a distraction motion.

We then strike to the solar plexus using Sonbadak Ollyo Makgi *(Palm Upward Block)* to double our attacker over. It remains an open handed strike so we can slip it straight round our attackers face to finish them off with the next movement.

Utilizing Kaunde Sonkal Daebi Makgi *(Middle Section Knife-hand Guarding*

Reversed to show application

Block) as per previous patterns, we finish our opponent by breaking the neck using Kaunde Sonkal Daebi Makgi *(Middle Section Knife-hand Guarding Block).* We reach round, take hold of the face on the jaw and rip our knife-hand block into position.

If we didn't succeed in finishing them this way, perhaps we missed our grip or slipped, we have a further back up in place by following up with Wi Palkup Taeragi *(Upward Elbow Strike).* Alternatively, this combination can be used as shown in the next application shown to practice on both sides.

Again we use:

- **Kaunde Sonkal Daebi Makgi** *(Middle Section Knife-hand Guarding Block)*
- **Wi Palkup Taeragi** *(Upward Elbow Strike)*

This time we use Kaunde Sonkal Daebi Makgi *(Middle Section Knife-hand Guarding Block)* to cover and catch an incoming strike. We move into the strike with our guard up (the knife-hand chamber), and block/catch the striking hand. As we pull our reaction hand back to our hip, we grip and twist our attackers arm and use Wi Palkup Taeragi *(Upward Elbow Strike)* directly to the elbow joint, breaking it.

With this break, as the elbow is such a powerful tool, we don't actually need to turn the joint all the way round, as long as its side on, the elbow will damage it severely. We can also use Kaunde Sonkal Daebi Makgi to block/strike to the pressure points in the arm as we chamber, then strike the carotid artery before striking with the elbow. Another alternative is to use the elbow strike of the first combination in this set to strike the body at the solar plexus and use the knife-hand block to break the neck as previously shown.

Next we use:

- **Sang Sewo Jirugi**
  (Twin Vertical Punch)

- **Sang Dwijibo Jirugi**
  (Twin Upset Punch)

- **Kyocha Joomok Chookyo Makgi**
  (X-Fist Rising Block)

- **Dung Joomok Taeragi** *(Back Fist Strike)*

On their own, these twin attacks are useful, but they don't logically go together as per the pattern diagram. In the usually taught applications, Sang Sewo Jirugi *(Twin Vertical Punch)* is a strike to the jaw, then we attack the kidneys using Sang Dwijibo Jirugi *(Twin Upset Punch)*, so we are suppose to somehow turn our attacker round in between the moves, which is unlikely.

We can use Sewo Jirugi *(Twin Vertical Punch)* if both our arms are grabbed. We pull in to our chest, which in turn makes our opponent pull back, as they do so we throw our fists forward between the attackers grip. Using this motion, the grips are hard to maintain as we force our forearms through the weak point of the grip, the gap between the thumb and fingers, driving home our strike in the process.

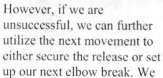

However, if we are unsuccessful, we can further utilize the next movement to either secure the release or set up our next elbow break. We utilize Sang Dwijibo Jirugi *(Twin Upset Punch)* to release by quickly rotating our arms over our attackers, around and down, then we drive them forwards into our attacker, making their grip extremely difficult to maintain, due to the angle of the attackers hand and again, the student exploiting the weak area of the grip.

From here we grip onto the arms an perform Kyocha Joomok Chookyo Makgi *(X-Fist Rising Block)* to bring their arms up and over our shoulder, this rotates their arm to the require position. Keeping hold of our attackers arm, we chamber as if to perform the next movement in the pattern, this brings the locked arm down over our shoulder to break the attackers elbow.

Alternatively we could simply attempt to throw from the X-fist position, which would have the same effect of snapping the elbow joint or use the next move (the back fist) to throw our attacker round over our rear leg.

Then we continue with:

- **Dung Joomok Taeragi**
  (Back Fist Strike)

- **Release Technique** *(Daite)*

- **Nopunde Ap Joomok Jirugi**
  (High Section Fore Fist Punch)

As the standard application taught for this combination is effective in its own right we show it here. Its an effective release technique if used quickly and with a snap. The first technique is the actual back fist, which is a good method of attack. However, should the arm be caught, Joong-Gun shows us how to release the arm quickly and effectively and follow up immediately with a counter attack.

After trying to strike your attacker with the back fist, your arm has been caught. As soon as this is realized we initiate the release by turning your knuckles downward so that we can expose the enemies weakness in the "thumb side" of the hand, which is between the thumb and the index finger. As we twist the fist we rapidly rip our arm in a downward motion towards our opposite hip, as if sheathing a sword. This complete motion turns our arm to its thinnest width, meaning we can create a smaller gap to release through the weak point, it also means we put stress on the attackers thumb as we rip our arm free and follow up with our high section punch to the attackers jaw or throat. Just prior to the release motion being initiated, it is useful to withdraw the lead foot slightly and drop back into Gunnon Sogi *(Walking Stance)* so we can use hip twist to help with the snap of the release.

The actual release technique has been changed over time, originally it drew the back fist down and across the body, as if performing a *sheathing* sword motion as described here. Now many schools teach to drop the whole arm straight downwards and though this works sometimes, it doesn't utilize the weak point in the attackers grip as part of the motion, so in my opinion is less effective!

On the opposite side we repeat the combination of:

- **Dung Joomok Taeragi** *(Back Fist Strike)*
- **Release Technique** *(Daite)*
- **Nopunde Ap Joomok Jirugi**
  (High Section Fore Fist Punch)

As our attacker throws a punch, a hook in this case, we turn and parry with our reaction hand – this forms the chamber position for Dung Joomok Taeragi *(Back Fist Strike)*. The reaction hand grabs onto the attacker arm and we drop into L Stance and perform Dung Joomok Taeragi *(Back Fist Strike)* against the attackers straightened elbow joint, using the forearm, rather than the fist. Its important to remember the follow through, so we should simply try to strike the attackers temple with our back fist as its shown in the pattern.

We could of course use the back fist to strike the pressure points under the arm pit or the floating ribs as shown on the right.

We then slip the back fist from under the broken arm and pull them towards us using the release motion which all intensifies the pain and then we finish them by striking to (and through) the throat with Nopunde Ap Joomok Jirugi *(High Section Fore Fist Punch).*

Next we perform:

- **Doo Palmok Makgi**

  (Double Forearm Block)

- **Kaunde Ap Joomok Jirugi**

  (Middle Fore Fist Punch)

  in **Niunja Sogi** *(L Stance)*

- **Yop Cha Jirugi** *(Side Piercing Kick)*

We can use Doo Palmok Makgi *(Double Forearm Block)* as a covering motion against a quick attack. Its useful as it uses both hands and thus offers extra protection and added force into the block should it be required. With luck we may strike a bicep and damage our attackers arm, though protecting ourselves is the main issue here.

If the arm is grabbed, we rip it back towards us using the twisting motion to release it (shown in the next set of combinations), then we punch back sharply using Kaunde Ap Joomok Jirugi *(Middle Fore Fist Punch),* dropping into L Stance to avoid a blow with the opposite arm as we move out of the original line of fire and stay further back from our opponents reach.

Following the strike we move into our opponent by chambering Yop Cha Jirugi *(Side Piercing Kick),* bringing our kick not into our opponent (though this is a possibility if the distance is there, which it will probably not be) but behind our opponent as we grab onto them and perform a major outer reaping throw sending them crashing backwards to the ground, smashing their skull or injuring their neck. We can of course follow up if need be.

We can use the opposite arm (reaction hand) to cause a confusing strike to our opponent or even cover their face as shown, if we open our fist into a palm. The punch should strike the floating ribs, arm pit, solar plexus or even the groin.

Again we perform:

- **Doo Palmok Makgi** *(Double Forearm Block)*
- **Kaunde Ap Joomok Jirugi**

  (Middle Fore Fist Punch) in **Niunja Sogi** *(L Stance)*
- **Yop Cha Jirugi** *(Side Piercing Kick)*
- **Kaunde Palmok Daebi Makgi** *(Forearm Guarding Block)*
- **Sonbadak Noollo Makgi** *(Palm Pressing Block)*

As mentioned previously, Doo Palmok Makgi *(Double Forearm Block)* is used as a cover, so after taking out our previous attacker, we are immediately attacked again. As we were in a vulnerable position whilst performing our side kick/throw, it may be hard to gauge what attack is coming.

Again we use Doo Palmok Makgi *(Double Forearm Block)* as a general purpose, *cover all* block, as we crash down into our next attacker. The block can either simply cover or used to strike as previously shown in Yul-Gok's applications.

We can use the combination as before, but with a slight variation. After crash landing so close to our opponent, our wrist is grabbed, so we pull back and either reverse the grab or release, then strike forward again to create space and try to confuse our opponent, as we cover our set up for Yop Cha Jirugi *(Side Piercing Kick)*.

As we chamber for the kick, we grab our opponents arm and pull them as we throw our arms back, this has the effect of pivoting their body (turning their knee side on) as well as keeping the focus of the attacker focused on the arms. We then use the kick to strike down onto our attackers knee joint or into their rib cage, whilst keeping hold of their arm.

Still holding onto our attackers arms, the focus is now on the injured knee joint as we land from the kick. We land in Kaunde Palmok Daebi Makgi *(Forearm Guarding Block)* ensuring we chamber to the outside of the attackers elbow joint, whilst gripping with our rear arm. The pulling back motion helps to ensure the arm is straight. We then drop forcefully

into the block, breaking our attackers elbow joint. Like the back fist break earlier, the focus should be on completing the block to ensure there is enough follow through to do the job.

The final move in this combination is Sonbadak Noollo Makgi *(Palm Pressing Block)*. This is often confusing as it is performed forward facing, with the palm blocks parallel to each other but at different heights. However, the preceding movements would have turned our opponent enough to apply the block as a joint break (or lock) as if you look at the pictures, the side kick chamber initiates a turn in our opponent, the side kick enforces it and the forearm guarding block further helps them on their way, as well as attacking the joint, leaving our opponent turned away with their arm angled to us (as opposed to straight out, fist forward).

If the last movement didn't break the joint we have a follow up. We drop our arms and perform Sonbadak Noollo Makgi *(Palm Pressing Block)* against the joint, with one palm going downwards and the other upwards, either side of the joint to break it. You will notice how one block attacks from a sideways on direction and the other from an up/down direction, ensuring one way or the other, the joint is broken.

Next we have:

- **Kaunde Palmok Daebi Makgi** *(Forearm Guarding Block)*
- **Sonbadak Noollo Makgi** *(Palm Pressing Block)*
- **Kyockja Jirugi** *(Angle Punch)*
- **Sang Bandalson Digutja Makgi** [54] *(Twin Arc Hand Stick Block)*

Again, we get the chance to perform the same application on the opposite side or we can use this application as an alternative. Due to the fact that it needs the final angle punch to ensure we meet the M.O. this is the best place to practice, though it could of course be utilized with the same preceding combination. Kyockja Jirugi and the fact that it goes past the centre line leads me to believe its not a punch as its main application, as most punches in the Ch'ang Hon pattern are aligned to the centre.

Our left arm is grabbed (its more likely to be our highest hand from the proceeding movement as that is more in the line of sight), again we

---

[54] This block is often termed a number of different ways. For a complete summary, refer to the alternative applications section, p230.

perform Kaunde Palmok Daebi Makgi *(Forearm Guarding Block)* in the same way as before except instead of going for the elbow joint, we use the front arm to lock into rear of the shoulder joint, using the fist as a grip if needed, to control our adversary.

From there we utilize Sonbadak Noollo Makgi *(Palm Pressing Block),* the chambering motion means we drop the front hand and raise the rear and this compliments the lock. The front arm keeps our assailant in the lock position by pushing on the shoulder blade, whilst our other hand brings our assailant's arm up, keeping it straight. We then change the hand positions like in the pattern and push our opponents arm down again, using our front arm to bend their elbow to ensure the arm goes up behind their back.

From here we slip our front arm out and turn into Kyockja Jirugi *(Angle Punch)* and choke our opponent (this is the reason it goes beyond the centre line; to ensure the arm is across the neck for the choke). Our reaction arm keeps hold of theirs ensuring they cannot escape before using Sang Bandalson Digutja Makgi *(Twin Arc Hand Stick Block)* to discard our opponent once they have been choked out (or before if need be).

Of course, though the pattern draws our reaction hand to our hip, if we have a struggling opponent we can simply cup our hands and make the choke stronger.

We complete the pattern by again using:

- **Sang Bandalson Digutja Makgi** *(Twin Arc Hand Stick Block)*

We can use the second Sang Bandalson Digutja Makgi *(Twin Arc Hand Stick Block)* as simple strike to complete the pattern. We turn and dodge a strike by dropping low into L-Stance, whilst striking to our attackers throat and groin simultaneously, or we can strike to the eyes or groin (as shown in the second picture) or use the lower hand to grab and pull the testicles.

The original application of Sang Bandalson Digutja Makgi *(Twin Arc Hand Stick Block)* is shown in the **Alternative Applications** section, as due to advances in weaponry it is less relevant today, but interesting nonetheless, as many still remain confused or feel it's to block a stick due to the change in the name of this application, it also fits the MO well.

Alternative Applications To Joong-Gun tul

Alternative Application to movements 1,2,3 and 1 :

- **Sonkal Dung Kaunde Makgi**

  (Reverse Knife-hand Middle Block)

- **Najunde Ap Cha Busigi**

  (Low Section Front Snap Kick)

- **Sonbadak Ollyo Makgi**

  (Palm Upward Block)

- **Sonkal Dung Kaunde Makgi** *(Reverse Knife-hand Middle Block)*

As the students arm is grabbed, he performs a quick succession of striking techniques to soften his opponent.

First high under the attackers arm pit to the pressure points located there, then he kicks low, to the attackers shin or groin.

These strikes will relax the attackers grip enough for the student to release and grab onto the attackers arm, before using the circular motion of Sonbadak Ollyo Makgi *(Palm Upward Block)* to take the attackers grabbing arm behind him. Even if the student doesn't catch hold of the attackers arm, the circular motion can slip through the gap between the attackers torso and arm, before turning back to perform Sonkal Dung Kaunde Makgi *(Reverse Knife-hand Middle Block)* to ensure the arm is locked.

Alternative Application to movement 8 or 10:

- **Wi Palkup Taeragi** *(Upward Elbow Strike)*

Wi Palkup Taeragi can be used to stop a leg grab (commonly termed a *'shoot'* technique).

As the attacker dives forward towards the students legs (specifically the thighs) in order to grab and unbalance him, we intercept by moving forward and performing Wi Palkup Taeragi.

The technique will check our opponent on the shoulders with a painful strike, stopping the take down in mid flow.

There isn't a need to aim for one shoulder or another, just aim central as it is in the pattern, as even if the elbow strikes the head or more likely the face of the attacker, it has a natural tendency to slip to one side or the other due to the roundness of the head and either shoulder will stop the take down.

The more committed the attacker is, the faster he will go and the more impact he will create when he meets with the students elbow.

Alternative Application to movement 24, 25 and 26:

- **Kaunde Ap Joomok Jirugi**

   (Middle Fore Fist Punch)

   in **Niunja Sogi** *(L Stance)*

- **Yop Cha Jirugi** *(Side Piercing Kick)*

- **Kaunde Palmok Daebi Makgi**

   (Forearm Guarding Block)

If the students lead arm is grabbed, he can use that as an anchor point to perform a scissor takedown.

The student side kicks past the opponent and instead of stepping back down again, he jumps with the support leg up behind the attacker (lower than his other leg) whilst simultaneously twisting his body (maintaining hold of the attackers original grab). This forces the opponents equilibrium to change rapidly and forces him off balance and he falls over backwards.

This technique should be performed at high speed. The following Palmok Daebi Makgi *(Forearm Guarding Block)* is used to finish the opponent by striking him with the side of the lead fist.

The rear hand of Palmok Daebi Makgi *(Forearm Guarding Block)* can also be used to maintain balance whilst in the air, as if gripped we finish with the opponents arm locked across the students body, leaving him open wide for the counter attack.

Alternative Application to movement 27 or 29:

- **Sonbadak Noollo Makgi** *(Palm Pressing Block)*

The standard explanation of this block is that of simultaneously blocking a kick and a punch. However, this is very unlikely to happen, but an attacker may throw one or the other, either a kick (or knee) or a punch (or similar technique) and Sonbadak Noollo Makgi *(Palm Pressing Block)* can be used as a quick response to these types of attack – just not at the same time.

When one of the palms are used in a blocking application, the other arm works on the action/reaction principle, accentuating the block with more force, this combination also enables concentration of the chest muscles adding further power to which ever hand is blocking. This power is enough to even stop a knee or break the arm if hit at the correct point (the elbow).

Alternative Application to movement 30:

- **Kyockja Jirugi** *(Angle Punch)*
- **Sang Bandalson Digutja Makgi**

  (Twin Arc Hand Stick Block)

Kyockja Jirugi *(Angle Punch)* is a decent technique to use against a mid level clothing grab. As the student is grabbed, he pivots and performs Kyockja Jirugi *(Angle Punch)*. The sudden rotation forces the attackers grip off with the chest and side torso. The student is then in a great position to follow up with a side elbow strike or to use the next movement in the pattern.

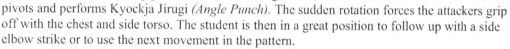
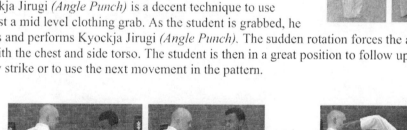

Alternative Application to movement 30:

- **Kyockja Jirugi** *(Angle Punch)*
- **Sang Bandalson Digutja Makgi**

  (Twin Arc Hand Stick Block)

Similar to the clothing grab above, Kyockja Jirugi can also be used if the arm is grabbed. The student pivots and angles the arm as he does so, which makes it extremely hard for the attacker to hold on. The release should of course immediately be followed up with a counter strike like Twin Arc Hand or Back Fist (as shown here). For a *'cross-grab'*, simply use the front elbow application shown in Yul-Gok tul.

Alternative Application to movement 30 :

- **Kyockja Jirugi** *(Angle Punch)*

Angle punch can be used as a standard strike at close distance. In this example, the student is grabbed in a front bear hug, but has his hands free.

The student simply uses the punch in a similar fashion to a hooking punch of a boxer.

Alternative Application to movement 30 and 31:

- **Kyockja Jirugi** *(Angle Punch)*
- **Sang Bandalson Digutja Makgi**

  (Twin Arc Hand Stick Block)

Kyockja Jirugi can also be used as a close range throwing technique. As the student grapples close to his opponent he loops his arm around his opponents neck and twists into the technique. This violent motion has the effect of throwing the opponent, which can be further augmented with Sang Bandalson Digutja Makgi *(Twin Arc Hand Stick Block)* to ensure his opponent is thrown completely.

Alternative Application to movement 30 :

- **Kyockja Jirugi** *(Angle Punch)*

The fact that the students arm in the technique of Kyockja Jirugi extends past the centre line means it can also be used as a holding technique, to shield yourself from a second attacker, by using the first attacker as the shield.

Ideally the first attacker should have been taken out first so they don't struggle, but the student could also use choking to minimize

this and can use the shield as a bargaining tool or hostage in this way. The fist is used to grip onto the shield. If the second attacker strikes, he will hit his companion! When escape becomes viable, use the U-Shape Block to throw your *shield* into the opponent to create a gap.

Alternative Application to movement 31 or 32:

- **Sang Bandalson Digutja Makgi** (*Twin Arc Hand Stick Block*)

With a slight adaptation, Sang Bandalson Digutja Makgi (and the movement between the two) can be used to facilitate a release from a side head lock.

As the attacker grabs onto the student, Sang Bandalson Digutja Makgi *(Twin Arc Hand Stick Block)* is deployed with the top hand going above the attackers head and gripping onto his hair or if bald, into his eyes. Straight away the student should violently yank the attackers head backwards whilst simultaneously using the lower hand to scoop the attackers leg upwards. The whole block used in a circular motion, lifting the attacker off the ground and throwing him backwards. The sudden surprise from this attack will usually be enough to release the head lock, though if not, the student would land on top of the attacker and immediately strike with the elbow until the attacker is unconscious.

Alternative Application to movement 31 or 32:

- **Sang Bandalson Digutja Makgi** (*Twin Arc Hand Stick Block*)

As mentioned in the text, this block is often termed by a number of names. These are:

1. U Shape Block - *Mongdung' I Makgi*
2. Twin Arc Hand U Shape Block - *Sang Bandalson Mongdung' I Makgi*
3. Twin Arc Hand Stick Block - *Sang Bandalson Digutja Makgi*
4. or simply Stick Block - *Digutja Makgi*

   The above includes the most commonly translated version of each, whether correct or not.

The term *'stick block'* and the change from military to civilian teaching of Taekwon-do (which possibly saw the change of terms from *Mongdung'I* to *Digutja*) leads to a lot of confusions of this (and similar) techniques. First of all *'Digutja'* doesn't mean stick at all, it actually refers to a shape in the Korean alphabet; a 'ㄷ' shape. *'Mongdung' I'* means baton, club or stick (hence why I personally prefer the term *'Digutja'*. So it actually means 'ㄷ' shaped block.

For further reference *Sang* means twin, *Ban* means half, *Dal* means moon and *Son* means hand. Any arc shape in Korean is refered to as *'half-moon'* shape, so altogether *'Sang Bandalson Digutja Makgi'* means *'Twin Half Moon Hand Block'* or *'Twin Arc Hand Block'*.

Many are incorrectly taught that this technique is to grab a stick or pole from an adversary, but the original application was not to grab a stick, but to grab a rifle, held in a guard position, where the butt of the gun is held on the palm of the hand. More advanced applications, like those in Po-Eun teach to grab the gun and counter attack with it, but this version simply grabs hold of the weapon and pulls it back. The application uses the skin between the thumb and forefinger, meaning that when grabbed, the hands automatically seal round the gun forming a grip.

In the application pictures we have substituted a simple 22 air rifle in replacement of a standard, army issue rifle of the era. Bear in mind that during the Korean War, South Korean soldiers would have possibly used American rifles and the North Koreans would have used Russian or Japanese rifles, which were both much longer in length and had the possibility of a bayonet attached.

Springfield M1 Garand Rifle (US), available during the Korean War

Japanese Rifle available during the Korean War

Modern 22 Air Rifle

'Minds are like parachutes...they only function when open'

CHAPTER 16

Toi-Gye tul

the training and contingency pattern

퇴 계 틀

Toi-Gye is the pseudonym (penname) of the noted scholar Yi Hwang (16th century A.D.), an authority on neo-Confucianism.

The 37 movements of the pattern refer to his birthplace on 37 degrees latitude, and the diagram represents scholar.

Toi-Gye has 37 Movements

Toi-Gye tul - *Step by Step*

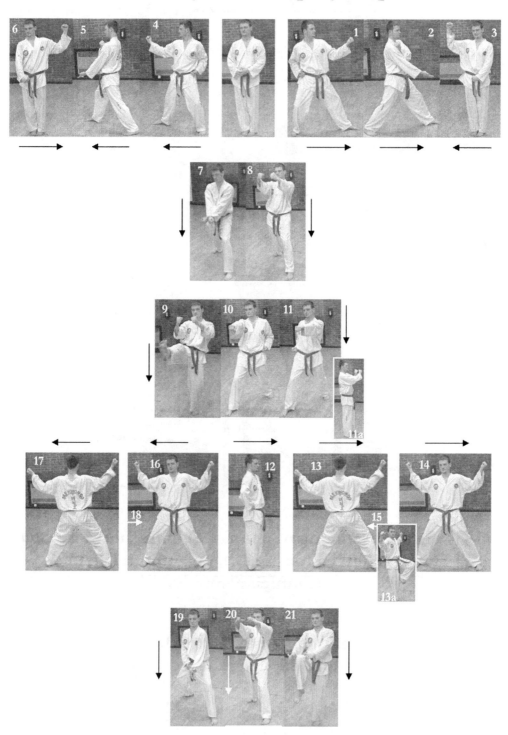

Joined photos indicate a combination with no step

A gap between pictures indicates a step

Photos are for reference and clarity.

The arrows (➤) show the correct direction in relation to the start position.

Toi-Gye tul - *Introduction*

Toi-Gye is the second of the senior coloured belt patterns. It is introduced at 3rd kup (blue belt) and as such the combinations and applications increase again slightly in skill level to reflect the grade of the student.

Like the previous pattern Toi-Gye starts from the ready posture Moa Junbi Sogi 'B' (Closed Ready Stance 'B') and just like in other patterns, I cannot find a direct relation between the ready posture and the pattern interpretation.

Toi-Gye has 37 movements, and the reason usually given for this is Toi-Gye's birthplace on 37 degrees latitude. However, as a latitude line runs all the way around the earth, this could in theory be anywhere along that line, as there is no longitude measurement given to give a correct coordinate, plus it is well known (and thus documented) that Toi-Gye was born in On'gye-ri (now Tosan) in the province of Gyeongsang, making this explanation of the 37 movements within the pattern seem even more odd!

However, if we look a little closer, we see that Yi-Hwang, whose penname was Toi-Gye, was born in the province of Gyeongsang in 1501. At the age of 33 he passed the provincial civil service preliminary examination with the highest of honours, an exam only usually passed by the older generations, so led him to be regarded highly by his contemporaries. Yi-Hwang continued his scholarly pursuits whilst in office, changing positions within the government (29 times in total) as he did until he passed away at the age of 70 in 1570. For 37 years he was recognised and held in the highest esteem, perhaps this is a better reason that Toi-Gye has 37 movements?

A court document written by Yi Hwang, 1550s

Text written by Yi Hwang

Yi-Hwang acquired the penname Toi-Gye during his youth. Toi-Gye means *'returning stream'*. Toi-Gye significantly influenced neo-Confucianism with his school of thought, which was based on the philosophy of *'Li'* and *'Chi'*, similar in concept to that of body and soul and a possible reason why this pattern denotes many double type movements, like the low block and back fist strike (movements 3 and 6), the infamous 'W block' and forearm pushing block amongst others. Toi-Gyes thoughts were that *'Li'* and *'Chi'* did not co-exist equally but rather the *'Chi'* supported the *'Li'* with the *'Li'* being the predominant component – think of the double movements contained in the patterns and the similarities with this train of thought when they appear, with one arm dominant and the other in a more supporting role.

Toi-Gyes concepts proved very popular and gained support from both other scholars and government officials alike, so much so that in 1557 he became head of a shrine in the province where he was born. Though a shrine, it was also similar to a private school and meeting place for scholars and was called Tosan Sowon. It enjoyed (as did Toi-Gye) a prosperity due to Yi-Hwangs political connections and the fact that it had royal patronage due to it being a shrine to a Confucian sage.

Upon his death, Toi-Gye was promoted to the highest ministerial rank having served four different kings throughout his lifetime of public service. His mortuary tablet is housed in a Confucian shrine, as well as in the shrine of King Sonjo whilst his students continue his teachings and the academy remains a centre for the study of Toi-Gye, with memorial services in his honour being held twice a year.

Tosan Sowon

Toi-Gye contains many movements or combinations that are new to the student, possibly the most discussed being San Makgi or 'W' block (also known as mountain block) or more precisely why there are six of them – all is revealed in this chapter.

Many of the double movements are seen as movements against two opponents at once, but, although this is one of the senior coloured belt patterns, I sincerely doubt the student is skilled enough to fend off two attackers at the same time, plus of course the timing of the two opponents attacking would have to be in sync totally so that any double movement can be utilized properly. However, though its doubtful that the movements are actually against multiple opponents, the *double* aspect does play a major part in Toi-Gye's make-up.

As I studied this pattern in-depth, I came to realize that many of the combinations and in fact many of the single movements have in fact a double intention, a fail safe or contingency application if you will, so that if one movement doesn't work, there is a back up movement in place. This seems to be the case as well with single movements that make up parts of the whole combination of the application – these movements I have called 'two pronged' movements.

Toi-Gye takes a different direction than the other patterns taught up to this point with its infusion of military training exercises and techniques, some of which are now defunct and have often caused considerable confusion in the past because of this. The *'jump'* and its actual reason for being are explored with the most taught application tried, tested and discounted as being unrealistic with minimal chance of success if applied as taught. Instead it has been researched for its original application, with a more practical solution offered as well as its original military relevance with regards to Taekwon-do.

As a note, the opening sequence of techniques in Toi-Gye tul have changed. These days, following the 'upset fingertip thrust' a low block and back fist combination is taught, originally the back fist was a side front block, which though now different, is actually not that different, especially in regards to the techniques original (pre-Taekwon-do) application.

Applications from Toi-Gye tul

Toi-Gye starts from the ready posture **Moa Junbi Sogi 'B'** (*Closed Ready Stance B*)

We turn to the left and perform:

- **Kaunde An Palmok Makgi**
  (*Inner Forearm Block*)

- **Dwijibun Sonkut Tulgi**
  (*Upset Fingertip Thrust*)

- **Dung Joomok / Najunde**
  Bakat Palmok Makgi (*Back Fist / Low Section Block Combination*)

From the ready posture (*Moa Junbi Sogi 'B'*) our arm is grabbed. We immediately turn to deal with the grab, turning into L-Stance (*Niunja Sogi*) to keep our head back from an attack, whilst simultaneously using Kaunde An Palmok Makgi (*Inner Forearm Block*) to try and twist out of the grip and clear a path for our counter strike.

From here we shift our footing into Gunnon Sogi (*Walking Stance*) whilst striking with Dwijibun Sonkut Tulgi (*Upset Fingertip Thrust*). We use Dwijibun Sonkut Tulgi to strike down under the testicles, grab them and pull back and upwards (into the position of the back fist)

whilst a split second later striking them with Najunde Bakat Palmok Makgi *(Low Section Block)* – enough to put any soldier out of action for a while!

If we lose our grip, we simply strike the groin with a hammer fist. We use the original blocking hand to grab onto our opponent and pull them in as we strike. As a natural response for a male, when an attack heads towards that sensitive region is to pull back – this would of course make our attack ineffective, so instead, we pull them close enough so their vision of that region is covered, thus allowing our intended grab to reach its target and take effect.

The Najunde Bakat Palmok Makgi in this application is a two pronged movement (three pronged if you count the hammer fist). It can be used to enhance and accentuate the actual counter-attack by striking the testicles as they are pulled or, as may be the case, to help remove the attackers grip from the students arm which is a more than likely scenario if the testicles are grabbed. We do this by either striking directly to the attackers arms or pulling it along our own arm to push their hands off as we pull the gripped arm in the opposite direction (the back fist).

We turn to our right and perform:

- **Kaunde An Palmok Makgi**

  (Inner Forearm Block)

- **Dwijibun Sonkut Tulgi**

  (Upset Fingertip Thrust)

- **Dung Joomok / Najunde Bakat Palmok Makgi**

  (Back Fist / Low Section Block Combination)

The next combination of movements see us repeat the movements just practiced, allowing to either practice on both sides or use a different application. For this combination we look at the standard application taught (for the first two movements at least)

From our previous position we are grabbed from the side, either by a single handed grip or a side choke. We utilize Kaunde An Palmok Makgi *(Inner Forearm Block)* to strike against either the carotid artery (shown here), bicep, triceps or ideally, as we are pulling back our shoulders into the L-Stance, the elbow joint itself. This is attained by using the reaction hand to grab our opponents arm and pull it straight as we drop into the L-Stance whilst striking the straightened joint. The actual chamber for Kaunde An Palmok Makgi *(Inner Forearm Block)* can be used to strike at the grab and remove it if desired.

After counter attacking our opponent, we use Dwijibun Sonkut Tulgi *(Upset Fingertip Thrust)* to strike to the pressure point on top of the pubic bone (which I'm told is not only very painful but also makes the opponent wet themselves if struck correctly), using the original blocking hand to grab onto our opponent and pull them in as we strike. This has the effect of not only covering the strike, but increasing its power and penetration.

As mentioned, a usual response to an attack around the groin area is naturally to grab at the striking hand/arm, so we use the third set of movements by pulling our right arm high into Dung Joomok (Back Fist) which has the effect of pulling our opponents arms up and out the way, allowing us to re-enforce our attack by using Najunde Bakat Palmok Makgi *(Low Section Block)*, by striking with a side fist to our opponents groin. This co-incidentally allows us to pull free from the grip as the pain hits home once again. We could of course use Najunde Bakat Palmok Makgi as in the previous combination to help forcibly remove the attackers hands from our arm.

The back fist could, in theory be used against a second attacker or even as a strike in a grab like a bear hug, though it is highly unlikely.

Following this we use:

- **Kyocha Joomok Noollo Makgi**

  (X Fist Pressing Block)

- **Sang Sewo Jirugi**

  (Twin Vertical Punch)

- **Ap cha Busigi** *(Front Snap kick)*

- **Doo Jirugi** *(Double Punch)*

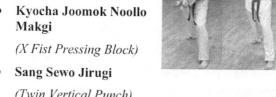

From our forward facing position, we are grabbed and attacked by our opponents knee. A close range knee strike is a powerful and fast attack and this movement is taught to have minimal or no twist in it at all, we simply drop straight into the block. By not twisting, we use maximum speed and by dropping forward into Gunnon Sogi *(Walking Stance)* we create power and stability to use that power whilst intercepting the powerful knee strike.

Again, we have a two-pronged movement depending on how successful our application is. Here we use Sang Sewo Jirugi *(Twin Vertical Punch)* to throw our opponent backwards.

After intercepting the knee strike, we grab the leg either side, pull upwards as per in the pattern and thrust forwards as we perform Sang Sewo Jirugi, effectively throwing our opponent backwards. By pulling up before thrusting forward we are hoping to flip them back, instead of simply pushing them backwards, so they strike their head on the floor. Pulling up slightly also makes it much harder for the attacker to maintain balance and consequently, easier for the student to throw them back.

As they try to recover, we finish them off (or simply try to stop them getting back up) with Ap

Cha Busigi *(Front Snap kick)*, in this case to the throat but any target is viable and finally if needed, by breaking their neck using Doo Jirugi *(Double Punch)* as detailed previously in other patterns, and they drop lifelessly to the floor.

The two pronged movement to Sewo Jirugi *(Twin Vertical Punch)* as you may have guessed is, if we lose our grip, or they escape from the grab, we simply follow through with the Twin Vertical Punch, and follow up with the Front Snap kick, but to the mid-section rather than the head and finish with the neck break or two punches if desired.

Next we turn and perform:

- **Sang Yop Palkup Tulgi** *(Twin Side Elbow Thrust)*
- **San Makgi** *(W Block)*

Someone once told me that General Choi said that this movement is not a Twin Side Elbow Thrust but is *'just performed and looks like'* a Twin Side Elbow Thrust. With that in mind, the fact that the actual performance of this technique has changed and what I am going to tell you about San Makgi *(W Block)* next, it *seems* that this movement is a preparatory movement for the first of the six San Makgi's we perform.

San Makgi *(W Block)* is also the subject of an eternal debate as to the applications of the block, however, none of the San Makgi's found in Toi-Gye were originally intended to have a primary application in blocking (though I intend to show you many secondary applications to San Makgi). In fact, San Makgi is simply an exercise put in place to develop two vital components, strength and torque.

The strength element is the reason there are six San Makgi's in a row rather than one. The arms are kept up at shoulder height over a prolonged period, which helps to increase strength in the arms and shoulders, ideal for soldiers with heavy packs, who carry heavy weapons and also serves to increase power in blocking or striking, after all, bigger or stronger muscles with speed equal more power.

The second element is torque of the waist, this two increases power and it teaches us how to twist into techniques and add an element of extra power using one of the largest groups of muscles in our body, the stomach muscles. The twist into each of these blocks should be used in the following way; we turn at our waist and use our stomach (and back muscles) to torque our arms around into place. Torque is again practiced later on in Toi-Gye, plus you may notice that we further utilize torque in the next pattern, Hwa-Rang, particularly for the two turning kicks and some of the other techniques in the pattern.

The stamping motion of each block is there to ground us and force us to drop our weight down (another element to increasing power). We turn into Annun Sogi *(Sitting Stance)* so we are forced to use our waist/stomach muscles to control the movement, rather than allowing us to stop our momentum by stepping into a forward type stance like Gunnon Sogi *(Walking Stance)* and using our front leg to stop us. All in all it isolates a specific muscle group and forces us to train them – if we perform each technique properly!

That said, both Sang Yop Palkup Tulgi *(Twin Side Elbow Thrust)* and San Makgi *(W Block)* have useful applications which can be taught and utilized.

First of all, Sang Yop Palkup Tulgi *(Twin Side Elbow Thrust)* as I mentioned previously, has been taught in two specific ways over time. The difference is in how the arms are brought to the hips. The application shown here uses the motion of the arms crossing the centre of the body on their way to the hips.

As a recap, we are using:

- **Sang Yop Palkup Tulgi** *(Twin Side Elbow Thrust)*
- **San Makgi** *(W Block)*

We use this combination of techniques as a release from a bear hug.

The student is grabbed in a bear hug from the rear. Reacting immediately the student tries to turn as they raise their arms in preparation for Sang Yop Palkup Tulgi *(Twin Side Elbow Thrust)*.

The twisting round helps to unbalance the opponent (even if we do not get a successful turn) and the raising of the arms to loosen their bear hug. As both are performed together the opponent has to concentrate on the grip as he is force to try to keep his balance and the grip at the same time, resulting in neither being as strong as they might be.

From here the student performs Sang Yop Palkup Tulgi *(Twin Side Elbow Thrust)* to further ensure a release. As the students fists pass the opponents grip, he strikes to the back of their hand with either or both hands, using the middle joints of his fingers against the small bones and pressure points of the opponents hands. This is very painful and causes a reactionary release, which is further enhanced by using San Makgi *(W Block)* to throw the opponents arms from around us as we twist out of the bear hug.

Next we pivot into our second:

- **San Makgi** *(W Block)*

Here we use San Makgi to demonstrate a foot stamp to the small bones in the opponents foot. A technique coming from the days when soft shoes were predominant but still a viable technique to know in this day and age.

The student simply pivots round and raises their foot to around knee height, forming a foot

sword so they can attack with the blade of the foot. They stamp downwards onto their opponents foot, just below the ankle, dropping all their weight down into the sitting stance.

This is a very painful technique, originally designed to crush the small bones that make up the foot, after all, a man who cannot stand cannot fight! Even with modern footwear it is still a very painful technique if performed correctly.

Next we pivot into our third:

- **San Makgi** *(W Block)*

Here the student demonstrates a slight variation on the previous technique by chambering in the same way but using the blade of the foot to attack the shin.

Simply strike at the top and rip the blade of the foot down along the shin bone as he tries to finish the technique and land in sitting stance – again, very painful and especially good if you are wearing shoes because of the harder rims.

Next we pivot into our fourth:

- **San Makgi** *(W Block)*

This time we use the chambering motion of the technique (the legs) to facilitate a sweep and finish with a stamp.

When our opponent is in close, we pivot so we are past their leg and attempt to chamber. By doing so we catch the back of

their leg or foot, pulling them off balance and sweep them to the floor.

The arm motion compliments the sweeping motion by pulling our opponent off balance (so they can't launch an attack) and also in the direction of the sweep, making it easier to achieve. Finishing the technique by stamping back down to ground, hitting whatever target is available, which depending on how they fell could be their knee, groin or head or any other viable target area.

Next we pivot into our fifth:

- **San Makgi** *(W Block)*

The students arm is grabbed across their body. The student pivots 180 degrees into San Makgi ensuring they travel around to the outside of their opponents grabbing arm. In doing so, the grabbed arm is pulled backwards which helps to lock out the opponents elbow joint and the free arm travels in at speed to perform a locking or breaking motion. The striking arm can either hit the triceps for a painful pressure point strike, then lock or directly strike onto the elbow joint to cause an arm break or simply strike the back of the skull.

We pivot into our sixth and final:

- **San Makgi** *(W Block)*

We utilize the final San Makgi in the series as an adaptation of the last application but turning to the inside of our opponent, striking and tripping him.

As the student is grabbed, he pivots round pulling his captured hand free or simply opening up his opponent whilst striking with the opposite arm to the jaw or carotid artery on the neck.

The leg is retracted so it can travel past the opponent and extended behind our opponents leg as we strike, causing the strike to induce a trip.

Next we move from San Makgi into:

- **Doo Palmok Najunde Mirro Makgi** (Double Forearm Low Section Pushing Block)
- **Mori Japgi** (Head Grab)
- **Moorup Chagi** (Knee Kick)
- **Kaunde Sonkal Daebi Makgi** (Knife-hand Guarding Block)

Here, we find a similar application to one we had earlier, that again we could use against a kick but we will use it in a similar vein as before – from a choke.

As the attacker grabs us around the throat, we drop down into Niunja Sogi (L Stance) whilst simultaneously chambering and performing Doo Palmok Najunde Mirro Makgi (Double Forearm Low Section Pushing Block). This releases the pressure to our throat by pushing between the attackers hands whilst at the same time bringing us closer to our point of attack.

We use Doo Palmok Najunde Mirro Makgi *(Double Forearm Low Section Pushing Block)* to scoop underneath the attackers lead leg and quickly utilize the next part of the application – the head grab.

Like before, the consecutive motion of these movements means that we hook under the attackers leg and forcibly pull it upwards, then throw the attacker backwards and we can follow up with a knee strike to the head of our downed attacker if need be.

Often, the attacker will simply be thrown backwards by the force of our upwards and outwards motion, however, we can utilize the open hands to aid our attackers flight back to earth in the form of a push. Changing from L-Stance into Walking Stance allows us to propel all our force forward so the attacker flies back with speed and force.

Again, the two-pronged motion comes into effect. If we don't manage to bring their leg high enough to throw them back or if the leg slips off mid manoeuvre whilst they are unbalanced, we grab onto them around the head *(Mori Japgi)* and simply knee them in the groin, abdomen or head, pulling them onto our knee before they regain their footing.

With their head lowered it is easy to use Kaunde Sonkal Daebi Makgi *(Knife-hand Guarding Block)* to grab the head and wrench the neck to finish them off — hence the 180 degree turn, though we can also utilize this in the next combination of applications.

We follow on with:

- **Ap Cha Busigi** *(Front Snap Kick)*
- **Open Sonkut Tulgi** *(Flat Fingertip Thrust)*

As we turn we are grabbed, either one handed in preparation for a strike or with both hands in a choke, which we will use here to demonstrate the application. The immediate threat is to our air supply so we use Ap Cha Busigi *(Front Snap Kick)* to immediately kick them in the shin which creates two responses:

1. It causes immediate pain to our opponent causing them to react and release pressure from the grab

2. The pain takes the focus away from high section (their grab, but most importantly our throat and their high defences)

We immediately follow the front snap kick with Open Sonkut Tulgi *(Flat Fingertip Thrust)* as a strike to the throat. Most merit the use of this technique to the eyes, which of course is a valid target. However, fingertip techniques are meant to be used against soft targets and even though the eyes are soft, they are surrounded by bone, meaning a mis-targeted shot may render our counter strike less effective, or even, ineffective altogether. It may actually injure the students fingertips. The throat however, has the benefit of being surrounded by soft tissue meaning that if we mis-target, we don't injure ourselves and if we hit on target we strike the larynx maybe even crushing it. Even if slightly misjudged, the strike has a funny way of still making its way to the larynx but at a sideward angle (try it lightly on yourself to see) plus, if they turn their head to avoid the strike, we still have the neck arteries to hit but if going for the eyes and they do the same, we again strike only bone!

Like before we *could* use Kaunde Sonkal Daebi Makgi *(Knife-hand Guarding Block)* in order to crank the neck.

We follow on with:

- **Kaunde Sonkal Daebi Makgi**
  (Knife-hand Guarding Block)

- **Ap Cha Busigi** *(Front Snap Kick)*

- **Open Sonkut Tulgi**
  (Flat Fingertip Thrust)

- **Dung Joomok Nopunde Taeragi with Najunde Makgi**
  (Backfist High Strike with Low Block)

Again, we practice the same combination on the opposite side, but this time we will use **Kaunde Sonkal Daebi Makgi** *(Knife-hand Guarding Block)* as we have previously to firstly cover against an incoming strike by using the chambering motion to strike our opponents attacking arm, hitting pressure points on the bicep and forearm as well and following on with a knife-hand strike to the carotid artery in the neck.

However, by doing this, if we don't succeed in taking our attacker out, their focus is again high, meaning another high blow from us may be blocked. We resolve this by kicking low, either the shin or simply straight up into the groin (as we are liable to be pretty close and a shin kick may miss as we probably can't see the target properly). We follow up again with Open Sonkut Tulgi *(Flat Fingertip Thrust)* as we attempt to strike the throat (or eyes) – but our attack is foiled and our arm is grabbed instead. Again, we have a back-up to this.

The next movement is often taught as a double block/strike application. For example, as you block one attacker at the front, you strike a second attacker at the rear. This is highly unlikely as the targeting of both techniques would have to be absolutely spot on, further more, the timing of such an attack is highly improbable to have both attackers in the correct position at the same time. That said, the sliding back into L-Stance with a low block is a decent defensive technique on its own as is a back fist to the rear, but again, on its own. I believe in combination they represent a release technique similar to the low block release shown in Chon-Ji.

As mentioned above, we have tried to strike to the throat with Open Sonkut Tulgi *(Flat Fingertip Thrust),* however, this time our strike is caught. In order to effect a release, we pull back our extended arm, in this instance our right arm, and utilize all our body weight to do so by stepping back a stance – this pulls our attackers arm out in front of us but on its own may not effect a release from a strong grip. So, as we pull back our right arm, we strike the attackers arm with our left forearm either to their forearm (radial nerve) or their bicep and this, combined with the twisting motion as our right arm pulls back, secures the release.

Should the front kick have the desired effect Open Sonkut Tulgi *(Flat Fingertip Thrust)* can be used in an alternative way to pull the opponent into the floor, which is detailed in the **alternative applications** section.

We follow on with:

- **Kyocha Sogi, Kyocha Joomok Noollo Makgi** *(X-Fist Pressing Block in X Stance)*

- **Doo Palmok Makgi** *(Double Forearm Block)*

And combinations of:

- **Najunde Sonkal Daebi Makgi** *(Low Section Knife-hand Guarding Block)*
- **An Palmok Dollimyo Makgi** *(Inner Forearm Circular Block)*

From the released position (using the application we performed previously), we are now in limbo. A situation has occurred where a flurry of techniques have been used, but we haven't taken out our attacker sufficiently and to move forward again means we could end up in the same situation as before. This is where Kyocha Joomok Noollo Makgi *(X-Fist Pressing Block)* comes in!

Of course, the next set of combinations can be used separately from the previous set and really go to show just how in-depth Toi-Gye goes into *'Double Entendre'* or *'two pronged'* applications as it actually offers us alternative endings following the jump into X-stance.

Kyocha Sogi, Kyocha Joomok Noollo Makgi *(X-Fist Pressing Block in X Stance)* was a hard nut to crack as most students are taught it's a jump over a pole where they land and then block a front kick, but if you haven't tried this then trust me when I say its an almost impossible application to do and therefore highly improbable as an application. After some in-depth research and discussions on this technique with both my instructor Mr Bryan as well as my friend Yi, Yun Wook as to the merits or demerits of the applications, I have come to a conclusion as to what this application was originally intended for, but as you will see, it is now defunct and so has been relegated to the **alternative applications** section as it is relative only from a historical point of view as part of the *'military make up'* of Taekwon-do.

As well as the above, during my research for this book I read about how, in an old Shotokan kata, this technique was used to actually jump past opponents; the following technique after this (in Shotokan) left the student turned and facing the attackers rear. However, the Taekwon-do version works with different dynamics. Firstly, we are taught that the jump into Kyocha Sogi *(X Stance)* is performed at an angle, rather than directly forward. Secondly, after landing, unlike the Shotokan variation, we then move into a position that is facing away from the attacker. However, the original technique offers a valuable insight into what this application can be used for, which is similar, but not the same as the original variant. That said, after thinking about this combination for a while, I came to the conclusion I mentioned above, which is that of alternative finishing techniques based on similar principles.

However, I also believe that the three Dollimyo Makgi's *(Circular Blocks)* in succession are another training exercise and are actually a follow on from the earlier San Makgi's *(W Block's)* and the training exercise they provided as their primary purpose. Although Dollimyo Makgi does have secondary applications as well, their main function (in this pattern) is to train the waist, and how to use torque by use of the waist, but this time it is via a smaller motion as there are no steps between, just a pivot. Its kind of like how a beginner is taught to chamber really far back to provide power to the blocks but by black belt everything is coming together enough (hip twist, muscle tension, technique etc) to produce the same amount of power with less chambering. Basically, San Makgi is learning to use torque via large motions and Dollimyo Makgi is learning to use torque with minimal motion.

Onto the applications themselves…

Going back to how we finished previously (so it flows with the pattern – though its not essential); we have tried and failed to finish our attacker with the previous techniques and their applications. We were grabbed, but escaped and have moved back from our attacker and its time to make a last ditched effort to gain the upper hand. On this particular attacker, kicks haven't worked, strikes haven't worked and blocks as strikes haven't worked either so what do we use? The answer is – our whole body!

As we launch ourselves into the air to land in **Kyocha Sogi,** performing **Kyocha Joomok Noollo Makgi** *(X-Fist Pressing Block in X Stance)* we are taught to jump high, at an angle, and land diagonal to where we started. Usually the explanation to this is simply being told to land there to ensure we finish on the start position (which we do). However, I believe this *'direction indicator'*, like its Shotokan predecessor, offers a valuable insight into how we are meant to perform this application. It is not simply a high jump, but a jump up and past our opponent, the *'direction indicator'* telling us to jump not only past but also behind our opponent (as much as possible) as obviously we cannot go through them directly. We are taught to land in Kyocha Sogi *(X Stance)*; with Kyocha Sogi being a wind up position to aid power, via torque, to the finishing applications in this combination.

As we jump up, we grab onto our attackers shoulder with Kyocha Joomok (X-Fist), fly past (keeping a tight grip – hence the fists) to land beyond and slightly behind our opponent, dropping down as we land, yanking our opponent backwards. The students arms are crossed in case of a missed grip, so there is still  something to help carry him forward rather than falling straight down. This photo sequence is laid out from right to left to show how the jump pulls the opponent backwards.

Providing all goes well, we will have landed with our opponent way off balance and falling backwards where we can proceed with any of the next techniques.

The final techniques of this pattern offer four variants of direction following our landing:

1. **Continuous** in the direction we jumped into Doo Palmok Makgi *(Double Forearm Block)*

2. **Turning to our right** into Najunde Sonkal Daebi Makgi *(Low Section Knife-hand Guarding Block)*

3. **Turning to our left** into Najunde Sonkal Daebi Makgi *(Low Section Knife-hand Guarding Block)*

4. **Or turning back** on ourselves using An Palmok Dollimyo Makgi *(Inner Forearm Circular Block)*

Why the four directions? Well, its impossible to accurately guess how an opponent would fall following our jump, grab and pull application from the previous technique, so the student is offered follow up techniques in all four directions.

If when the student lands the opponent has just lost balance, but not fallen over, the power generated by untwisting from X-Stance and the backwards momentum of the opponent, is enough to throw the opponent forcefully back. This is achieved by grabbing onto the attackers shoulder and closest arm (or hooking under it) and performing Doo Palmok Makgi, with devastating effect, as you can see in the pictures.

If, when he lands, the student has managed to off-balance the opponent enough to topple him backwards (so he's on his backside) he grabs onto his head and unwinds from X-Stance *(Kyocha Sogi)* using Doo Palmok Makgi *(Double Forearm Block)* to break the opponents neck.

This works just as well if the attacker tries to stabilize himself by dropping down onto one knee or a similar positioned height. The student can grab both the hair and the jaw and step forward into the Doo Palmok Makgi *(Double Forearm Block)*, yanking our opponents head up and back sharply to break the neck.

If the above action didn't finish the opponent or if they twisted around as they went down, Doo Palmok Makgi *(Double Forearm Block)* can be used to simply throw them forward into the ground, face first, but this doesn't fit with the M.O. as this would not break his neck or incapacitate the attacker to such a degree he couldn't get up and attack again (though we could of course simply kick him when down!).

Consequently, if when the student lands and the opponent has stumbled backwards but managed to twist round somewhat, the student can perform the throwing technique, as detailed in Yul-Gok, by grabbing onto our opponent and performing a shoulder throw. This can be further enhanced by following this up with Najunde Sonkal Daebi Makgi *(Low Section Knife-hand Guarding Block)* by grabbing onto the opponents head and twisting sharply round to break his neck if needed – which is detailed later in this chapter.

Or, if when the student lands, the opponent has tried to counter falling over by twisting and dropping down, the student can use the follow up movements of Najunde Sonkal Daebi Makgi *(Low Section Knife-hand Guarding Block) and* An Palmok Dollimyo Makgi *(Inner Forearm Circular Block)* to finish the opponent.

The student grabs around the opponents head, ensuring the head is between both hands. He pivots and in doing so performs an L-Stance which supports the opponents back and doesn't allow it to continue round (to alleviate the neck break) as the student performs Najunde Sonkal Daebi Makgi *(Low Section Knife-hand Guarding Block)* which forces the neck beyond its capacity for rotation and thus breaks it. This has a back up technique which is detailed a bit later.

If the student lands and his opponent has shifted side on but is still in an upstanding position, the student can unwind from Kyocha Sogi *(X-Stance)* and try to throw them forward using Doo Palmok Makgi or even perform a different type of throwing technique using *Najunde Sonkal Daebi Makgi*, either by grabbing on to our opponent, or more likely grabbing around their waist (similar to how the fingertip thrust hip throw throw from Won-Hyo worked – as this is a knife-hand application) and throwing our opponent. This techniques drives the attacker towards the floor, meaning the aim is not to just simply throw our opponent, but drive them head first into the ground.

This combination is further finished, should the opponent try to get back up, by performing Dollimyo Makgi *(Circular Block)* as a neck break or choke. As the opponent tries to get up, the student strikes the side of the head with the first portion of the block, immediately dropping down (the first part of the knee spring) aiming to choke the opponent, whilst grabbing onto the hair with the reaction hand and wrapping the blocking arm under and around the opponents neck. The knee spring is completed, as is the block, which enables the student to firstly apply force to the choke and make the choke easier to perform by pulling the opponents neck up (and thus elongating it, exposing the larynx) whilst the reaction hand pulls the opponents head in the opposite direction. If trying to break or damage the opponents neck, the block is performed more continuously with the first strike of the block turning the opponents head and the rest of the block ensuring it continues round. The final yank of the block outward ensures the break or choke is complete.

Alternatively, we could simply use the hair grab and yank as shown in Yul-Gok tuls applications.

Of course we have the same application in the opposite direction so we can perform this application no matter what way the opponent has turned, again having Dollimyo Makgi (*Circular Block*) as a follow up if required to completely finish the opponent.

The bottom line is, for this series of applications, both Doo Palmok Makgi (*Double Forearm Block*) and Najunde Sonkal Daebi Makgi (*Low Section Knife-hand Guarding Block*) are used to grab and throw our opponent into the floor or to directly try to finish. Dollimyo Makgi (*Circular Block*) is there as a back up to finish them and they all gain their power using torque by uncoiling from Kyocha Sogi (*X Stance*) as we would land close to the opponent.

The options we have for follow ups depends on either our preference or more likely, the position we landed in. All four main angles are covered, all are deployed to finish our opponent by throwing them off balance while we then follow up – as a natural instinct when off balanced is to regain it, which means their guards are dropped momentarily, enabling the follow ups.

The landing part of the block also contains a two-pronged application. The first as described above and the second, if our attacker manages to withdraw or retain some balance whilst we are in the air, as we land we strike with Kyocha Joomok Noollo Makgi *(X-Fist Pressing Block)*. It maybe the case that we only managed to off-balance our opponent a bit and this may leave his leg exposed, meaning we land on the knee joint or thigh with our block, trying to damage their leg.

If we toppled them right over, we have used the chambering motion of the block to grab to their shoulders and we finish them by trying to target directly across this throat, in a guillotine motion, dropping low into Kyocha Sogi *(X Stance)* to enhance our technique and crush their neck.

Of course, there are many variables to how they will fall so we can also use the pressing block on any available targets, even if just against the chest as the force of it coming down will be considerable.

Even if we were not spot on with our strike to the neck (i.e. the attacker is not taken out totally), we can use Doo Palmok Makgi *(Double Forearm Block)* to break the opponents neck or throw the opponent as detailed previously. We can even use Najunde Sonkal Daebi Makgi *(Low Section Knife-hand Guarding Block)* as a softening technique (or as a straight strike) before going in for the finish with Dollimyo Makgi *(Circular Block)* to break the neck or go straight for the choke.

Of course, this is just an example of how one movement compliments the next and the applications can be used in shorter combinations or even by themselves and all these options are available to the student who is well versed in them. The way they are presented here is to show how they can be used in the actual training of the pattern, movement by movement, as well as some actual applications for the movements themselves.

The pattern leaves us with two un-associated Dollimyo Makgi's and a punch.

Toi-Gye finishes with:

- **An Palmok Dollimyo Makgi**

  (Inner Forearm Circular Block)

- **An Palmok Dollimyo Makgi**

  (Inner Forearm Circular Block)

- **Ap Joomok Jirugi** *(Fore Fist Punch)*

Here, we use the first An Palmok Dollimyo Makgi *(Inner Forearm Circular Block)* which is with our right arm to grab hold of our opponents arm and swing it round, pulling at the shoulder, throwing our opponents equilibrium off as the block circles around. Upon the peak of the first block, the second block is employed. The student pivots and drops, to allow the block to travel under the attackers arm that he has hold of, circles round, and strikes at the joint. Leaving the block in place, he then steps forward into Annun Sogi (Sitting Stance) whilst retaining grip on the attackers arm, locking her arm, or accentuating the elbow break and effectively throwing the opponent back.

Alternative Applications To Toi-Gye tul

Alternative Application to movement 12 and 13:

- **Sang Yop Palkup Tulgi** *(Twin Side Elbow Thrust)*
- **San Makgi** *(W Block)*

Sang Yop Palkup Tulgi can be used to transform a grab into an armlock and is an application taken from when belt grabs were used in standard training.

As the belt is grabbed (this could be the students trousers or a clothing grab at waist height), the student performs Sang Yop Palkup Tulgi, including the pivot, exactly the same as in the pattern. This can be used to simply release a grip by attacking the elbow joint but here we use it to make an arm lock. The hands move across to secure the opponents grip so they cannot escape and the student pivots round, locking their arm against his own elbow.

Following the lock, the student then pivots into **San Makgi** *(W Block)* and utilizes one of the applications shown in the main applications section whilst maintaining a grip on the attackers arm. The further twisting on the block pulls the attacker round and off balance further allowing the student an opportunity to sweep the attackers leg, strike to the attackers foot or knee or (as shown in these pictures) use San Makgi to strike to the triceps (or elbow or back of opponents head).

Alternative Application to movement 18 and 19:

- **San Makgi** *(W Block)*
- **Doo Palmok Najunde Mirro Makgi**

  (Double Forearm Low Section Pushing Block)

If these two motions are reversed, i.e. the Low Section Pushing Block is performed, followed by the W block, they can be used to pick up and carry or throw an opponent using what is commonly termed a *'fireman's lift'* or similar. The student drops down so the lead arm of Doo Palmok Najunde Mirro Makgi hooks the opponents legs, then the student goes into San Makgi, lifting his opponent onto and across his own shoulders. From here, the attacker can be flung, unceremoniously to the ground, head first!

Alternative Application to movement s 13, 14, 15, 16, 17 or 18:

- **San Makgi** *(W Block)*

For this application to San Makgi we use mainly the arm motion of the block to secure an armlock.

As our opponent attempts to grab us around the neck and take us down into a side choke, we use the turning motion of the block and quickly pivot and lock our attackers arm between our neck and our raised arm. The lock comes on at the triceps in order to lock the arm straight.

If we apply it at the shoulder, the lock is not so secure as our attacker may be able to wriggle free. We take our attacker down to the floor by continuing in the same direction whilst pivoting in a downward spiral.

Alternative Application to movement 26, 27, 28 and 29:

- **Ap Cha Busigi** *(Front Snap Kick)*

- **Open Sonkut Tulgi**

    (Flat Fingertip Thrust)

- **Dung Joomok Nopunde Taeragi with Najunde Makgi**

    (Back fist High Strike with Low Block)

- **Kyocha Sogi** *(X Stance – Jump)*

Should the front kick have the desired effect (remember, soldiers wore heavy boots), Open Sonkut Tulgi *(Flat Fingertip Thrust)* is used to enhance the application by grabbing our opponent head and pulling them forwards.

A usual reaction to a low section front kick, whether to the shin or groin, is for the attacker to bend at the waist or try to move their struck leg backwards, away from the pain. Open Sonkut Tulgi *(Flat Fingertip Thrust)* simply utilizes this reaction, helping them on their way to the floor, face first, by grabbing above the head, either holding on to the hair (which is preferable) or simply pulling back and down, whilst using the low block to enhance the technique further and strike the back or the head or neck in the same direction.

Even the jump into the X-Stance can be used to move the student away from the attacker as he hits the floor as this possibly wouldn't finish the attacker and would leave the student vulnerable for a leg grab.

Alternative Application to movements 29, 30, 31 or 32:

- **Kyocha Sogi, Kyocha Joomok Noollo Makgi** *(X-Fist Pressing Block in X Stance)*
- **Doo Palmok Makgi** *(Double Forearm Block)*
- **Najunde Sonkal Daebi Makgi** *(Low Section Knife-hand Guarding Block)*
- **An Palmok Dollimyo Makgi** *(Inner Forearm Circular Block)*

As mentioned in the main chapter, the original application to this combination may now be defunct, but warrants discussion as it provides an insight into the make-up of Taekwon-do as a military art.

After discussions and research, certain points about the technique seemed to fit together to form the overall conclusion that Kyocha Sogi, Kyocha Joomok Noollo Makgi *(X-Fist Pressing Block in X Stance)* is an anti-rifle technique. In Joong-Gun the student would have been taught Digutja Makgi *(Stick or U Shape Block)* as a means for grabbing a rifle held in a guard position, Toi-Gye takes things a step further and counters against a rifle (and bayonet) pointed at you from your side front.

As the student is guarded with the pointed rifle, it is a case of jumping up high to avoid either a shot or the bayonet. The direction of the jump is at an angle towards the rifleman and the X-Stance, like in Yul-Gok, is the actual block, as well as the X-Fist Pressing Block. If the soldier steps back, the student needs to be close enough to employ the technique and relieve the soldier of his weapon hence the reason for the angled jump – it takes you out of a direct line of fire, as well as avoiding the bayonet if swung (as we are closer in, we would get hit with the gun, rather than the bayonet) and allows for the soldier moving backwards if startled.

The student attempts to actually land on the gun itself, hence why we turn in the air. The X-Stance pushes the bayonet end of the gun down and the X-Fist attacks the weapon close to the soldiers grip, forcing him to drop the weapon. If he does move back, we have the X-Fist Pressing Block as a back up.

After the student has relieved the soldier of his weapon, he continues straight on as shown in the main application and uses Doo Palmok Makgi *(Double Forearm Block)* to throw the opponent away from the weapon, leaving him sprawled on the floor giving the student more than enough time to pick up the gun and shoot the aggressor or stab him with the bayonet.

Alternative Application to movements 31/32 or 33/34:

- **Najunde Sonkal Daebi Makgi**

  (Low Section Knife-hand Guarding Block)

- **An Palmok Dollimyo Makgi**

  (Inner Forearm Circular Block)

Using Najunde Sonkal Daebi Makgi the student is able to take an opponent into a headlock (perhaps as they try a tackle or front bear hug), before proceeding to use the choke application as shown in the main chapter to break or crank the neck using Dollimyo Makgi.

The student uses the attackers momentum as he wraps his double knife-hands around the opponents head as he attempts a tackle, bringing the arms into the low block position, leaving the opponent in a vulnerable position for the follow up choke or neck crank using Dollimyo Makgi.

Alternative Application to movement 29:

- **Kyocha Sogi, Kyocha Joomok Noollo Makgi**

  (X-Fist Pressing Block in X Stance)

The jump into Kyocha Sogi can also be used to train jumping knee strikes. Because of the twist in the air, either knee can be utilized depending on which the student feels most comfortable with, with the added advantage of stability provided by the chambering motion of the X-Fist Pressing Block. Upon striking and landing, the follow ups can be the same as detailed in the main applications section

Alternative Application to movements 35 and 36:

- **An Palmok Dollimyo Makgi** *(Inner Forearm Circular Block)*

An Palmok Dollimyo Makgi is ideal to use as a finger lock. If the attacker were to try and push you or even if they were just waving their hand about in front of you whilst shouting and hollering in a threatening manner, the student would grab onto the opponents hand and proceed with performing Dollimyo Makgi. Pulling the attackers hand down, then looping round to form the lock.

Alternative Application to movements 35 and 36:

- **An Palmok Dollimyo Makgi** *(Inner Forearm Circular Block)*

Dollimyo Makgi can also be utilized straight away as a choke either as a follow on from the jump or on its own.

From the previous jump, if the opponent is facing the student with their head down slightly, Dollimyo Makgi's main blocking arm strikes the side of the jaw and loops around the opponents neck, whilst the reaction arm keeps the head down as well as ensuring the strike doesn't simply send it off in another direction. He then proceeds by wrapping the arm in a circular motion around the neck, whilst pulling the head up to expose the neck - utilizing the knee spring to do so, as this helps the choke do its work more easily as explained earlier. The student should try to complete the blocking motion to ensure a successful choke.

From the rear side, where the opponent has been pulled and bends close to student as he lands, the same motion is used. Strike the jaw to stun the opponent, whilst the reaction hand keeps the head downwards and re-enforces the strike. Wrap the blocking arm around the neck, raise up using the knee spring as you try to complete the block, choking the opponent.

The stance is mainly used for stability and either arm can be used to perform the choke. If its more practical to use the opposite arm, for example the opponent is across you slightly, then simply wrap the blocking arm straight around whilst pushing down with the reaction arm and again - force the block to make the choke.

'The greatest undeveloped territory in the world lies under your hat'

CHAPTER 17

In Conclusion

'*There will come a time when you believe everything is finished.*
That will be the beginning'

- Louis L'Amour

In the previous chapters I have listed the who, the why, the where and the 'how to', so all that's left is for the astute student or instructor to implement the applications shown in this book. Special attention needs to be paid particularly to Chapter 5 (Utilizing Applications), as without following these guidelines, it will not matter how many different applications you know, how well you can demonstrate them to unresisting students or training partners, the actual transition of knowledge to realization will be lost if you do not train them effectively.

Quick Recap

To reflect back on the emphasis of each pattern, we *can* utilize each in the main for specific purposes and focus:

- **Saju Jirugi** – *first steps, basic introduction using the hips for power and Taekwon-do mechanics of twisting into blocks*
- **Saju Makgi** – *as with Saju Jirugi, as well as basic blocking tools of knife-hand and forearm*
- **Chon-Ji** – *basics of power generation via rotation, forward and backward force as well as hip twist*
- **Dan-Gun** – *for attacking the neck and head*
- **Do-San** – *to release from grabs*
- **Won-Hyo** – *for close quarter fighting*
- **Yul-Gok** – *for grabbing and holding our opponents*
- **Joong-Gun** – *for attacking the elbow joints*
- **Toi-Gye** – *for more advanced training and contingency techniques*

Of course, with all the other applications listed, these do not have to be adhered to, but they are possibly the strengths of each pattern and so gives a common purpose within the techniques and applications that the student is able to focus on and with a common train of thought, when practicing alone or solo, the applications to each pattern becomes easier to remember and thus visualize.

Repetitio Est Mater Studiorum

'Repetition is the Mother of Learning Techniques'

In the old days of Karate, students focused on a single Kata and practiced it over and over again. Not for a few months between grading's, but for years, day in, day out. In the Korean military, the drill instructors did precisely that, drilling the soldiers (the students) over and over again, hours at a time, day after day after day, certainly not for 10 minutes, twice a week! Techniques became second nature, and its that, combined with knowing what a technique is for, what it can really do and what it is actually is capable of, mixed with training them realistically that will enable the student of Taekwon-do to gain benefit from their patterns training, once again making them an essential part of the system we are learning.

Muscle memory and knowledge of the application is half the endeavour here, but an important one none the less. Those that dislike patterns will tell you that solo training is of no use as there are no resisting opponents. But muscle memory is very important when trying to use a technique, not just one contained within a pattern, but any technique, especially under duress!

As an example, here is a little story I read concerning muscle memory, by Mike Thue, a 3rd Dan in Shorin Ryu:

> *In my office we have a door security keypad, with a mechanical punch code that changes every three months or so. (I'd tell you the code but I'd have to kill you). The bathrooms, however, are out in the hall. To use the restroom, you need to exit our suite. So I am in and out at least several times a day depending on caloric intake.*
>
> *I had totally habituated the old door code, and could enter it "on auto pilot", without thinking about it. The trouble is, the code just changed last week.*
>
> *Several things were immediately noticeable. The first couple of days, I would automatically try and enter the old code first, without realizing it. I also noticed that my "finger dexterity" with the new code sequence was significantly lower, even when I was concentrating on it. Then after a couple of days standing in the hall, I began to consciously walk up to the door and remind myself of the new code. I am still doing that, but it is quickly fading into my subconscious and I am fast 'retooling' myself. I expect to be back on autopilot inside another week or so. At half a dozen times a day (I drink a lot of coffee), that's a total of about 90 reps over three weeks. Finally, I also realized that I could not remember the old code from TWO changes back. It was mysteriously gone.*

What this story shows is how doing something, anything, over and over, becomes ingrained. Apply that to practicing patterns and the same applies. You'll notice the bit about forgetting the old key codes and the same applies to those that rush to grade, concentrating solely on their newest pattern in order to perfect it ready to achieve that new belt – but in doing this, they relegate old patterns as *lower grade stuff*, which is a bad concept. I often tell my students that once they pass their grade, say for example 6th kup to 5th kup (Green belt), that Won-Hyo tul is no longer a 6th kup pattern, but simply one of the patterns they must practice alongside all their other patterns, it is no less important than the one they are learning and no more important to those they have learnt before. Chon-Ji, Dan-Gun, Do-San and Won-Hyo are now all equal in status and should be practiced as such!

'Repetitio Est Mater Studiorum' comes from a Latin proverb and means *'Repetition is the Mother of Learning Techniques'*. Training a pattern over and over is not in vain, it is not a waste of time and effort, it is the way to make your patterns have real meaning, for them to become ingrained into your muscle memory so when you need to use the techniques contained within them, you don't have to think about them, you just use them. By continual pattern training, with visualization and with intelligence we work the techniques into our muscle memory until they become second nature. When under duress and our fine motor skills do not work as well (a consequence of stress and adrenaline), our gross muscle skills kick in, so we can implement a

technique, without thinking, without hesitation and use it to perform what is required without thinking about the finer details – they simply work!

Exercitatio Est Mater Studiorum

'Drilling is the Mother of Training Techniques'

As mentioned previously, knowing and training your patterns is only half the story, it is essential to practice the applications on semi-resisting and resisting partners to appreciate them fully or to weed out the applications you feel are not suitable or workable for you personally. There are many drills one can think up to train applications with a partner, and ways of drilling applications are mentioned in Chapter 5. *'Exercitatio Est Mater Studiorum'* means *'Drilling is the Mother of Training Techniques'* – one compliments the other, and without either, much less benefits are obtained from their training. Those that do not like patterns co-incidentally still train drills, they still do part of the same training they just do not realize it or will not acknowledge it. A consequence I've seen of this is that the technical ability can be lacking in those that feel that training only with a resisting partner is the *'only way'* to do it! Without a certain degree of technical ability, it simply makes it even harder to apply an application, in fact, if you think about it, it's a catch 22!

The Acid Test

'One may explain water but the mouth will not become wet' - Takuan

The real acid test is to apply an application against a fully resisting opponent and the secret to that is surprise! Of course all the training mentioned previously, the correct knowledge etc. are vitally important and make the technique work quickly and effortlessly, but without an element of surprise it makes things remarkably difficult.

Whilst taking photographs for this book a couple of interesting things happened which go someway to back up how important the element of surprise is:

I had been thinking about which applications to use as a cover for the book, one set in particular seemed ideal and I was convinced these were the ones we would use. Consequently I had been going over and over the applications in my head to ensure that when we shot the photos it would all flow well, without any errors. Errors or untidiness are not a problem when executing applications, as self defence is neither clean or tidy but they were important for a book cover, after all, whose going to buy a book with a sloppy looking application on the cover – its not exactly the best advert for its contents! Anyway, for a few days I had been mulling these applications over in my head and running through them, on my own, but visualizing an opponent, ready for the shoot.

We were due to shoot the photos after I had finished my seniors class on a Saturday. During the seniors class, one of my 1st kups (red belt/black tag) asked me to spar with him which I did. It was just a fun spar as we were drawing near to the end of class. It wasn't anything special, just competition type sparring. But during this spar, the 1st kup grabbed my arm and I kicked into patterns mode. From that point (him grabbing my arm) I was able to execute three pattern techniques and perform their applications with hardly any resistance due to the fact he didn't realise what was happening to him - until it was too late! The applications saw the student go from grabbing me, to nullifying his punch with the other hand (by pulling my guard down) to him being placed in an armlock and ending up in a choke position with me behind him, still in control of his arm and it all happened in the blink of an eye! They worked for 3 reasons:

1. I used the element of surprise

2. I knew the pattern techniques inside out having done the pattern hundred of times, so I could perform them without hardly any thought

3. I had drilled them, in my mind and with semi-resisting opponents

The actual techniques and applications I used that day are shown on pages 221 to 222. We didn't use them in the end for the cover, but decided to keep them in the book to highlight applications in action (see page 59).

On a separate occasion David was shooting some photos for the book. The student demonstrating the actual technique and application for some reason, couldn't grasp the concept. To be fair he hadn't done much application work as he was a junior grade (6th kup), but it was a simple application to demonstrate. Even though David explained the concept and the student was told to simply perform the technique as it was in the pattern, he still altered it so he achieved a similar result but via a much harder and more effort intensive way. The application is shown on page 151 and is a way of using Chookyo Makgi (Rising Block) to force an opponent off you. After seeing that he wasn't grasping the concept, I put a question to him; what was the point of him practicing a technique over and over again in one way, only to alter it when you use it and make considerably more effort for yourself? He tried again, but still wasn't quite grasping the concept so I said I would demonstrate it on him. I asked him to grab hold of me and upon doing so performed the application as intended. As he didn't have a grasp totally on how the application was meant to work, he couldn't comprehend the effect of it, so couldn't prepare himself suitably. In essence, he was caught with surprise as well, despite knowing what I was going to do, what I was trying to achieve and how I was going to do it.

As he grabbed hold of me, he was physically and mentally prepared for me to respond, he dug deep by dropping his weight down and held me tightly. I performed the application and even I was surprised at how well it worked and the effect it had, as was everyone else that was watching at that point. The student not only release his tight grip on me when I applied the technique, he literally flew up and backwards about 8 feet (that's backwards, not upwards!), narrowly missing the back wall and only just managing to keep his footing thanks to one of the other students dashing forward to protect him (and his head) from colliding with the brick wall behind.

Like before, the application worked with the element of surprise, even though the student was mentally and physically prepared to accept the technique performed against him, he knew the technique, he knew what it was supposed to do and even knew it was coming – but it still worked exceptionally as due to his inexperience he overlooked the fact that not only did the technique push out horizontally, it also rose diagonally, pushing him up and back at the same time, something which he didn't expect. His natural instinct to regain balance kicked in and he let go of his grip but he couldn't maintain his footing due to the technique and by then it was all over. In a real situation I would have rushed forward and finished it straight away.

A simple example you can try with you fellow students to highlight this important point is:

Tell one of them you are going to pick them up and they must resist. Firstly by just dropping their weight and secondly, if your brave enough, allowing them to slap you a bit and struggle. You'll see how hard things can be without the element of surprise.

A few weeks later, when they are chatting to someone else and their attention is away from you, move quietly behind them and quickly try to pick them up and you'll see how effective the element of surprise is!

Unless your opponent knows the techniques and applications of your patterns pretty well, the techniques actually contain an element of surprise in themselves, within the techniques (with their applications). This coupled with speed increases that element making it hard to effect a counter to them. People can have quick flinch type responses to striking as a natural ability and can be conditioned by varying means to instinctively block or parry such blows. Think of how many play fights you've had as a child, how many boxing matches or movies have stimulated you to bob and weave your head etc. But many pattern applications are not seemingly natural, they are conditioned and trained responses and as such, unknown outside of those that train, making a conditioned response to them difficult, if they are applied without thought and the element of surprise is utilized.

Manual Bashers

'Given enough time, any man may master the physical. With enough knowledge, any man may become wise. It is the true warrior who can master both....and surpass the result' - Tien T'ai

Apart from those that dislike patterns training altogether or those that don't wish to move beyond the *'patterns are for balance'* or *'patterns are our historical link'* mentality, there are those that refuse to deviate from the Taekwon-do manuals written by General Choi at all. The problem here is that in part, the Ch'ang Hon patterns of ITF Taekwon-do are well documented, possibly more so than any other art and this is where the problem lies. They are well documented in part, but not in whole, as discussed in Chapter 1 of this book, but some instructors refuse to accept there could be flaws, or that the pre-described applications do not make sense. They will only teach and follow what is written in the encyclopedia's word for word, even if what they teach is in detriment to the student and could in fact place them in grave danger should they try to use the technique for real! Worse still is that some use quoting the manuals to hide a real lack of ability, after all, studying, remembering and then regurgitating text from a book isn't really that difficult to do, if so inclined, whereas training to a high standard in all areas, maintaining those standards as well as imparting those standard onto students is sizably more difficult.

As an instructor, like many, I chose Taekwon-do because it suited me, because I enjoy it and because I can see the many benefits it can offer to others, but though I love Taekwon-do, my foremost concern as an instructor is for (and always has been) my students and their abilities, skills and effectiveness and due to this, I refuse to teach things that I know simply wont work. I will tell them what the manuals interpretation of the technique is and I will also tell them why I feel a different application is better suited to the technique. The point to remember is that General Choi was only human, he did some great things and should remain highly respected for what he achieved in his lifetime, but no one is flawless if they are human; not you, not I and not General Choi I'm afraid, despite what some like to believe. His books contain many details about the patterns, but lack many as well, they contain some good applications and some not so good ones, in essence they are a technical library but no library carries every book ever written and it is okay to supplement the Encyclopedias with other sources, such as this book.

In actual fact, as I've also mentioned in Chapter one, the encyclopedias shouldn't be over looked with regards to applications, I simply feel that instructors and students shouldn't be stuck in a hole, trying to use applications that are clearly unworkable or even ones that are workable by some, but do not work for that particular individual. By combining the two (the applications shown in the Encyclopedia of Taekwon-do and the applications shown in this book) the student, at a minimum has a choice of two applications to chose from, and in some cases five or six – simply discard the ones you don't like or feel wouldn't work for you and use the ones that do! That said, I stand by my work and believe that if they are trained correctly, any of the applications in this book are applicable to anyone and workable by anyone, as the only weakness with regards to them is how you train them and how much you train them, thus providing the guidelines are followed and adhered to, I see no reason why you cannot adopt them, train them and use them if needed!

To Evolve We Must De-Evolve

'History is not a simple record of the past. It is a critique of the present and a warning for the future' - Quan Tzu

I mentioned in the introduction about how Taekwon-do has developed into a more sport related art or a more pastime related art rather than a martial art and there's no reason why it cannot remain both, but for it to retain its martial element I feel it is heading in the wrong direction.

Taekwon-do has always been referred to as an *'evolving'* art, but it has evolved so much in so many areas that the original art as founded, is only just linked to today's art in many schools by a few kicking techniques, the movement in the patterns and some Korean terminology. The sport and pastime aspects have taken over.

But what do I actually mean when I say *'To evolve, Taekwon-do needs to de-evolve?'*. Well its simple really: elements and practices within the art need to be reinstated or taught properly on the road to black belt and beyond!

For example,

- The throwing techniques that are rarely taught should be instituted as standard training, they are part of the original Ch'ang Hon Taekwon-do.

- Take down techniques, either by throws, trips or sweeping should also be taught as standard training as again, they are part of the original Ch'ang Hon Taekwon-do.

- Many schools do not place any focus on vital point striking, but it is an important part of Taekwon-do, so should be part of all students study.

- The same applies to basic pressure point knowledge, which is rarely taught, a basic appreciation of pressure points should be introduced somewhere along the students curriculum.

- The way sparring is only performed as *'sport'* based, or as most term it *'competition sparring'* should take second place to *'traditional sparring'*, which allows attacks to all parts of the body, both above and below the waist, as well as sweeping and throwing techniques.

- Consideration should be given to the over performance of the *new* sine wave (see appendix X), and how it effects techniques with regards to their realism in self defence. It needn't be eradicated, as it was always there, just not over-emphasised so much and only used where appropriate.

- The 'over the top' emphasis of technical ability over technique in patterns is detrimental to the use of patterns as a tool of self defence. Yes, solo training should emphasis technique, but as covered in this book, this is only the first stage. A student simply cannot utilize applications if they have to perform 100% correctly – as nothing in self defence is perfect and a distinction should be made.

- With this book there is no need for the lack of proper application knowledge when teaching patterns. Many instructors simply teach the moves with no insights into how or why they work or even what they are for. This book addresses that issue with realistic pattern applications, as well as the original historical applications – so instructors really have no excuse not to ensure their students are fully informed!

- The changing of pattern techniques to look nice at tournaments is a cause for concern and could be very detrimental to the use of pattern in relation to self defence. It will slowly but surely becomes the norm, until the original techniques are forgotten and thus the original applications can no longer be performed.

- The way 1 step is performed now-a-days by many schools simply does nothing to train the student in the reason it was originally intended. 1 step is often taught in such a way that it lacks any realism at all with the attacking student performing the whole attack before the defending student responds. 1 step should be training 'reaction' and thus a more reactive response to attacks should be reinstituted. No waiting, simply kihap and attack! The defending student either avoids or blocks or gets hit – it really is that simple!

- These days grading's are seen as a rite of passage, with many students working on the incorrect assumption that the minimum times listed in the manuals or via Taekwon-do schools for both kup and dan grades, are the waiting times before grading's. However, in order to absorb, rather than simply duplicate techniques or patterns, a student needs to remain at a grade until they 'become' that grade – this often takes a fair while longer than the minimum stated times!

- Taekwon-do training is continually becoming watered down to make it more amenable to the general public, more so the lazy ones I'm sad to say. A black belt in Taekwon-do should mean hard work all the way, this is the only way to make a martial art system viable. Too many schools water down their syllabus, or lower the requirements needed to pass a grade meaning the end result is a watered down student.

- The devaluation of the black belt has been happening for many years now, in many cases simply to boost an associations black belt numbers. Unfortunately, the politics of martial arts means associations lower the criteria for the achievement of dan grades and thus the whole system is watered down.

- The lack of associated skills required to attain a dan grade[55] in many schools these days is shocking. Though I don't expect all schools to agree or demand what is required at Rayners Lane Academy to attain a black belt, students often get by with poor levels in even the basic areas of pattern performance and sparring, still pass even if they don't break and often require no more than that to gain a black belt. The long and short of this is Dan grades knowing less and less.

- Similar to the above is the deregulating of the destruction elements at grading's. Destruction has always been a major part of Taekwon-do and some schools allow multiple attempts or simply discard it altogether if the student cannot break at all. A black belt should break to a stationary target within the first few attempts period and a 16 stone guy shouldn't be allowed to break with stepping side kicks that use his weight rather than technique. All this takes away the emphasis of what the destruction element was originally intended for.

The effect of all this is lamentable as its not the students fault. On far too many occasions I have had students from other schools turn up to train along side mine, which is great, after all we are all in the same family but the short cuts and low standards instructors are prepared to give and accept soon becomes apparent and the poor student is left wondering about the worth of their grade. For example, there have been black belts proud of their achievements and status, made to look like junior grades when sparring 4th kup students at the Academy, Senior coloured belt grades who cannot perform their lower grade patterns, let alone their current ones and many high grades with deep rooted technical flaws and that's said by someone (me) who doesn't go overboard on the technical aspects, though there are levels that all students can and should achieve at certain grades. Simply put, one is left to wonder just how these students were allowed to achieve the grade they wear with the level they are at – but I say again, this isn't the students fault – it's the instructors!

---

[55] See 'Dan Grade Requirements', p296

Taekwon-do has many facets within, too many schools concentrate on the sport element, leaving the discerning student with the impression that to be a good martial artists, one has to excel in tournaments, which is defiantly not the case. This is a disservice to the students you should be looking after the most, the ones who are not the natural athletes and will never excel in the sporting arena. A school that claims to teach Taekwon-do but ignores all the elements that make your average student better, whilst concentrating on the sporting elements isn't teaching Taekwon-do.

Sparring is just one element of Taekwon-do, as are patterns and all the other elements, they combine to make the whole, without all the parts, the jigsaw just isn't complete. Some are happy to make their own jigsaw out of just three pieces, with almost straight sides, but in reality each piece of the jigsaw is a jigsaw itself, all the little pieces, make the bigger pieces of the puzzle, before finally making the complete picture – this is true Taekwon-do!

If we want our art to maintain itself as a *martial* art, it must evolve, not on the levels of commercialism, though this area is not solely a problem in commercial schools, but any schools that skimp the in-depth teachings of Taekwon-do, where the focus is solely that of tournament champions, or the reasoning that it must be an enjoyable pastime for everyone – these areas are covered as a natural development of training. To maintain its integrity as a martial art, instructors, schools and associations alike need to re-include the areas mentioned in this section, in short to get the art back to what it was, the way it was meant to be - *to evolve it must de-evolve!*

Commercialism

'Fortune does not change men, it unmasks them' - Suzanne Necker

The term *'McDojang'* is heard more and more these days and its little wonder with some of the practices some schools use in the name of 'business'. I simply do not believe that these schools don't realize what they are doing or the things they have instituted in order to make students part with their money do not fall inline with the tenets of Taekwon-do. If what they offer is of value, these tactics wouldn't have to be used. Yes, run a professional school but adhere to the tenets you say at the beginning of every class, the second of which is integrity! Business as a rule is a cut-throat, money making world and I am deeply saddened that many instructors have reached this fork in the road and taken the easy path to profit, rather than the moral path which though it may be harder, can still achieve the same results, in fact better results, the off shoot of which unfortunately is less riches in a material sense but more in a sort of spiritual, moral sense and you can still manage the budget and put food on the table – I am living proof of this!

I am not against decent instructors making a living from their art, in fact I think it would be great if all the good instructors could do this, but unfortunately that is not the case as for every decent school, there are 5 *Mcdojangs* and 10 *belt factories*. The occasions of students coming from other schools to try our classes is proof that commercialism is destroying our arts. I say *'arts'* as its is not just the Taekwon-do schools but many of the arts, though the *'commercialism above standards'* is highly evident in many many schools and it is indeed a saddening offshoot of things once revered and respected! Too many students eventually venture outside their schools only to be left wondering about its credibility and their own training's worth – to me this is wrong as every instructor should be doing the best for our students. You would expect a doctor to do his best by his patients, a teacher to do his best by the students and so it should be with someone who professes to be a martial arts instructor!

Strong views perhaps, but you show me any pioneer or master of an art who trained for 30 minutes, a couple of times a week, or were allowed to take many of the short cuts modern instructors allow, on their way to black belt or master status. If you can list one, I can guarantee he would not stand up next to real pioneers and masters. This is not to claim the students of Rayners Lane Academy are superior to others, as there are many decent schools with great students out there, but when you look around, a simple comparison shows what happens when the commercial route is followed in detriment to all other areas – like standards!

Certainly the above isn't the case with every school, but it is becoming more and more common and strangely enough it seems to go hand in hand with the commercialism of martial arts that has been going on for the last decade or so, as more and more instructors start to make a living out of martial arts teaching. I am professional instructor myself, but there are things I wont compromise on and they are the technical ability, knowledge or standards of my students – they trust me and I aim to ensure that trust is kept for every single student that passes under me. Surely this should be the bottom line of all instructors?

Teaching at a professional level is indeed an evolution of martial arts, but the standards of what is given in return is often not a professional, for want of a better word, product, no matter how polished it may look – after all *'every thing that glitters is not always gold'*!

Fitness Work

'It is not the size of the dog in the fight, but the size of the fight in the dog'

For a student to become well versed in Taekwon-do, or any martial art in fact they need to train more than the odd class once a week. I have seen some schools even offer 30 minute classes and I am left wondering just what happens in these classes, as at Rayners Lane Academy classes often run for over 2 hours a time and the warm-up, fitness work and stretching can often take over an hour!

Some instructors I have heard claim that fitness training isn't actually martial arts and therefore should be the responsibility of the student outside of training, with training dedicated to martial arts training. Funnily enough, it is the same instructors that run 6 short classes per night, six times per week, packing students in and out like a factory conveyor belt – hence the term *'belt factory'*! However, everyone knows just how hard it is for students to motivate themselves outside of training to do anything, let alone pure fitness work. Sure, the dedicated student may do road work, bag work or run through their patterns a few times per week as extra, I use to and still do regularly, but these students are few and far between and most don't do anything unless they are actually at the dojang, being led by a capable instructor – the instructor is often their only motivation!

Even if they were taught brilliantly in their short classes, all these techniques are of no use if the student tires in a matter of seconds – and without fitness work, in a real situation with the adrenaline pumping this is destined to happen. Ask any pure Self Protection instructor and they will tell you the term often used as reason to their gruelling fitness session as *'Fit to Fight'* – a motto all students of the martial arts should adhere to!

One of the added benefits of continual hard fitness sessions, aside from building a healthy body is the development of a strong martial spirit and a strong spirit is essential to take that one extra step when the rest of your body is saying no! It may be that one day, it was this culmination of spirit training that ensures your student takes that one extra step that saved their life!

Training the spirit develops strong character and this character touches many areas of the students life without them even realizing it. It gives them the courage to try, when perhaps they wouldn't of before and if they try, perhaps they can achieve it – isn't that a fantastic thing! For those schools that talk of character development, this is the real deal and for those that don't, we achieve it this way anyway!

The Making Of A Black Belt

'It is good to have an end to journey towards, but it is the journey that matters in the end' - Ursula K. Le Guin

When a student walks into a dojang they have this vision in their head, perhaps attained through television or films, or from the legendary stories of the masters, recited by their friends or read in books but no matter where it comes from, it is still the same – the dream of mastery of a martial art and a *'Mcdojang'* instructor steals these dreams!

Parents bring their children to martial art classes for a myriad of reason, not least confidence and the same eventual dreams as the adults – maybe it's a parents wishful thinking, but there is no reason their children cannot grow up and mature into competent and capable martial artists. The problem is parents have no bench mark as they often start their children in the first martial art school they come across as they believe that *every* black belt is a master, *every* black belt is a great instructor and *every* black belt will guide and shape their child into a competent and capable martial artists – only someone who has been round the block or dared to venture further a field than their own school knows this isn't the case! My advice to parents these days, unfortunately, is to shop around and to do a lot of shopping!

I had a parent of a student call me once, saying she was unhappy with her present school as the instructor was charging more and more each time. He changed the uniforms every six months, forcing the students to buy the new ones and sold them equipment when they joined that they had never used! The final straw for this parent was the instructor trying to make her sign a new three year contract into the *'masters club'* for her son, who was six years old! Incidentally, this club costs £600 per year more than the *Black belt club*, which was £600 a year more than the non-black belt club members paid! I felt a little sorry for the parent, knowing she had been sold by the sales hype, so I invited her down to the school as she wanted and asked her what grade her son was – to which she replied he's a black belt! I was shocked, but nevertheless intrigued as to what qualities a six year old black belt would have. The parent was most concerned with her six year old retaining his grade and I had to bite my lip!

The parent turned up and this young black belt bounded into my class full of confidence, but as the class started the warm-up session he seemed concerned, looking around for his mother, eventually, before we had even finished this section he started to cry as he was completely out of his depth and this was just the warm up. After sobbing for a bit, he went to his mum for a cuddle and I asked her what he did to achieve his black belt, she said he had to do some combinations, punch some pads and show some kicks. I ask what patterns he learnt and she asked what was a pattern? Upon explaining, she said he hadn't learn any as it wasn't required for his age! Suffice to say, he never returned to my school. His former club had indeed given him something, they gave him a black belt he didn't earn, that didn't have any worth except to his parents pride (however misplaced it was), but worst of all they gave him bucket loads of false confidence that was taken away the minute he stepped out of that school into the real world of martial arts!

This is not an isolated case as many other parents have been sold similar things, with these unscrupulous instructors pandering to the parents and students ego's, by waving a black belt in front of them and letting them know just how achievable it is, as long as they pay the right price! Adults have been fooled in the same way as well, though they are more capable of handling the fact that they have been sold a dud and usually blame themselves for not doing their research properly in the first place and some, even if not all, are resolute about learning proper martial arts, so are content to start over. These students I hold in the highest regard, it is not an easy thing to admit and even harder to do – these students have the right spirit, one that can really take them where they want to go!

Students reasons for starting a martial art and then sticking with it can change over time and are varied, but *every* student, who attains the lofty rank of black belts wishes and hopes, at least initially, to be worthy of the grade after all *'the clothes maketh the man'* and so in Taekwon-do, *'the belt maketh the student'* so the worth of that belt needs to be maintained.

Once a black belt held much worth, simply because it was only obtainable with diligence and hard training. Now it is seen as obtainable by anyone, even with little effort, but more so as part of the schools ethos or part of their advertising campaign as long as they turn up and pay their money! A black belt should never be guaranteed, it is a celebration of blood, sweat and tears, of over coming many obstacles and a celebration of passing into the next phase of Taekwon-do training. The fork in a tough hard road that is meant to represent the wearer being *'Impervious to darkness and fear`* - a road that many are simply not capable of travelling (well actually they are, but it's a damn hard trek)! Its worth has been devalued.

Though some argue that Taekwon-do places a different emphasis on what a black belt means, as do some other arts, one only has to think back to when they began Taekwon-do and think what a black belt seemed to them, whether correct or not this is actually what it should mean (or at least pretty close to it). I sincerely doubt that any beginner has thought of a black belt grade as lacking in knowledge or skills, or not being able the perform *'black belty'* type things! I guess the essence is that in my mind at least, a black belt should have three attributes:

1. Knowledge in the areas related to the dan grade and skills at a certain level in applying that knowledge

2. A certain mental toughness fostered from many years of hard training

3. The ability to 'hang' with others of equal grade. By that I mean at all areas they should be roughly equal. There will always be students who can break more than others, or spar faster etc. But no black belt should look way out of their depth in any areas next to a fellow dan grade.

All three of these areas have been eroded over time, as clubs, instructors and associations give away black belts to one and all, claiming to make the black belt more accessible or simply ignoring what it originally represented to them, but its really an exercise of increasing numbers or not losing students income and the one who loses in the end, is actually the student who placed their faith and hope in you to begin with!

A black belts worth shouldn't be bought but should be affordable by all, affordable by way of hard work, sweat, tears and perhaps even a little blood on occasion – as these are the traits and trials of hard endeavours and nothing of any value comes easy. By making the road to black belt, a hard though not impossible journey, we can retain its value and its worth – though I feel it may be a little too late for that, but as Gandhi once said '*You must be the change you wish to see in the world*' so I for one will keep on keeping on!

Within Taekwon-do some feel that the black belt is simply a representation of someone who has a good grasp of the basics of our art and even though what actually represents the basics is debateable, some do not even seem to have done that in order to gain the right to wear the black belt around their waist. But even then, saying it simply represents the basics doesn't relate to the meaning of black belt in Taekwon-do, which says the wearer should be '*impervious to darkness and fear*' – how many six year olds feel like that? In my mind, simply having a grasp of the basics doesn't correlate to being impervious to darkness and fear, which takes me back to the aforementioned 3 attributes that should make a black belt! And that to me is just the minimum requirements in my mind, to me there is more to be a black belt than just that, but that's a whole new discussion!

The Future

'If we don't change direction soon, we'll end up where we're going' - Professor Irwin Corey

It is my sincere hope that both students and instructors alike take onboard the training methods and applications detailed within this book and that they become part of their regular training along side the normal or standard type of pattern practice. By doing this, the patterns aspects of Taekwon-do not only gain a fresh lease of life but also become much more of a relevant training tool which means Taekwon-do as an art regains one of its most vital components to the level that it should be – Patterns and their relevance to self defence.

In fact, if I may be so bold as to go one step further, it is also my sincere hope that the heads of the various Taekwon-do Associations and Federations incorporate the training and knowledge of these pattern applications into their core syllabus, allowing instructors and students to use and learn the patterns in even more depth than was previously possible, allowing the student to make the connection between *Patterns* and *Hosinsol*!

I would hope that every association head wants to better their association, their students and their training methods and this book is the means by which to do so. I am not just referring to the smaller associations, but the large ones as well – the International ones, as I'm sure, like me, they love Taekwon-do and want it to be recognized for what it should be, not a sport, not a pastime, but the fearsome Korean martial art it once was.

*'No combat ready Unit has ever passed inspection.
No inspection ready Unit has ever passed combat'*

END NOTES

'Glory is temporary.
Wisdom lasts forever.
Train for a deeper understanding of yourself'

Ch'ang Hon Taekwon-do Hae Sul: Volume 2 and 3

Ch'ang Hon Taekwon-do Hae Sul: Volume 2 is in the works and is being written as this first volume is going through the publishing process. Obviously, I have spent many years training and practicing the patterns detailed in this book, a study which was invaluable when writing Volume 1. Volume 2 will carry on where this book left off and will concentrate on the patterns from Hwa-Rang tul onwards and perhaps in the future, there will even be a volume 3 but that is many years, if not decades away, as to write such a book requires much in-depth study as Volume 3 will include patterns close to and beyond my present grade.

Your Thoughts Are Welcome

Though this book is in print, it is not beyond revision which will inevitably happen in the future. As a valued reader, I hope you enjoyed this book and as such would welcome your feedback on it. I am only human and as such am open to error and welcome the chance to correct any errors. I may have missed an important application which should be detailed and if this is the case, they could be corrected and/or included in future revisions. You may feel that a part of the book may be factually incorrect and needs amending even though I have endeavoured to triple check all the facts contained within it – all these can be included, corrected, or updated in future revisions.

You can email the author directly at: **instructor@raynerslanetkd.com**

The Ch'ang Hon Taekwon-do Hae Sul Forum

To further enhance discussion on this book, the issues it addresses, the Ch'ang Hon tuls, pattern applications and training, the author has set up a private forum, specifically for the readers of this book.

The forum allows readers to give feedback on this book, discuss specific chapters or sections, discuss the applications in the book and even to add something that may find its way into future revisions or volume 2 or 3. The forum is not a general Taekwon-do or Martial Arts discussion forum but is specifically designed around the topics in this book and to further enhance the readerships views and knowledge. If you enjoyed the book, I feel you may enjoy participating n the forum as well. As the author I personally invite you to the *'Ch'ang Hon Taekwon-do Hae Sul Forum'* and hope that you take the time to register and post on it because your views, irrespective of your grade, are valuable.

The forum address is: **www.changhonhaesul.proboards99.com**

This is a private forum for readers of this book and as such you will need to register. When you do, please use your full name as we wish to keep this forum as friendly as possible and have found this is the best way of doing so.

To ensure and maintain the integrity of the forum, when you register and are approved you will receive an email telling you that your forum *'account'* is up and running. Upon receiving this, simply send a P.M. (personal message) via the forum to the forum administrator mentioning this section of the book and your profile will be updated further, revealing some forum sections that cannot been seen by the average user. These sections are just for you (and other readers of this book). I hope to see you there.

IAOMAS

International Alliance of Martial Art Schools

The 'International Alliance of Martial Art Schools' or IAOMAS as its fondly known, was founded on 12th September 2002, by the author, Stuart Anslow from England, David Melton from the United States of America and Tim Posynick from Canada and was first set up as a *'student support system'* to enable students of the martial arts to train, free of charge, wherever in the world they travel.

It is not principally a Taekwon-do organization, though there are many Taekwon-do Schools and instructors involved with it, both ITF and WTF based, more so, it's a collection of like-minded martial artists, martial art instructors and martial art students of every conceivable style and discipline, based around the world. It is a free, non-political organization that is available to all martial art schools and open minded instructors alike.

It has far outgrown its roots and offers much more on top of the *'student support system'* it was originally developed for thanks to the input of its members. It offers help and support to instructors and students to enhance their training and further both their own and their schools development, to discuss and gain advice on every conceivable facet of martial arts study and training, from technical and training issues to school management issues, as well as building many strong friendships.

It has full time school owners and instructors, part time instructors and students from white thru to black belt, many of whom are in constant contact with each other thanks to the setting up of the IAOMAS forum. All of whom converse on an equal level, with equal standing, with virtually all members leaving their titles, such as master, sensei, sifu, sabum etc. back in their place of training.

There are no restrictions on which style you train in, which governing body, federation or group you belong to (or don't as the case may be), as IAOMAS works with all martial artists, as long as they adhere to the basic principles which are IAOMAS core values – which are friendliness and helpfulness.

At the last count there were IAOMAS schools in 72 countries around the world and it is possibly the largest worldwide martial arts organization around today, on its last count it was fast approaching 700 schools worldwide – the odds are, if you do martial arts, then you know someone who is part of IAOMAS.

What's more, since its inception, it has been run and maintained free of charge by the support of members such as Colin Wee, who was responsible for setting up and maintaining the central directory of IAOMAS as a gift to the organization. There are many others too numerous to mention but who can often be found at the forum, who have made both large and small contributions to the running of IAOMAS or IAOMAS based projects, such as setting up, maintaining and running *'Country Sites'*, running the *'Honour Awards'*, translating IAOMAS sites into other languages or hosting IAOMAS seminars around the world. And its all because they believe in IAOMAS and what it stands for and represents.

Many friendships have been formed as a result of IAOMAS. The author has personally met, trained and even stayed with (and had stay) many of the IAOMAS instructors (and students) from both near and far, all of whom he has found to be genuine, salt of the earth, type people – as power mongers and control freaks simply do not join IAOMAS, as it is totally controlled by its member instructors in regards to its direction and development.

- To find out more about IAOMAS please visit: **www.iaomas.com**

- To visit the IAOMAS forum go to: **www.iaomas.org**

On the following pages are a few pictures of the author with some friends and fellow IAOMAS instructors from around the word, though he has met and trained with others, not all were captured on camera.

The author with Colin Wee (IAOMAS Australia) during his visit to England in August, 2003

The author with Heidi Hartmann and Axel Markner (IAOMAS Germany) during their visit to England in November, 2003

IAOMAS England instructors (left to right) Wayne Timlin (Thai Boxing), Robert Patton (Ryukyu Kobudo), Stuart Anslow and Michael Holden (Atemi Jitsu) - taken at the 1st IAOMAS UK Seminar in November 2003

The author with Fereidun Dariagard (IAOMAS Denmark) during one of his visits to England in February 2004

The author with Dave Melton (IAOMAS USA) during a visit to England in August, 2004

The author with Piotr Bernat (IAOMAS Poland) during a visit to England in November, 2004

The author with fellow instructors at the 2nd IAOMAS England Seminar in September, 2004 (left to right): Marc Jones, Andy Wright, Paul King, Alex Catterall, Oliver Van Overbeek, Stuart Anslow, Gary Hoptroff, Jason Davenport and Alan Cain

Dave Melton (USA), Tim White (USA) and Stuart Anslow (England) in
Washington DC, USA - October, 2005

The author with Gordon Slater, fellow Taekwon-do
instructor and IAOMAS England member, May 2003

The author with Kevin Pell at the Combat 'Hall Of
Fame' awards, October 2003

The author with Tim White (IAOMAS USA)
Virginia USA, October 2005

The author with Jamie Ward following the IAOMAS Seminar, 2003

IAOMAS students meet - Lyndsey Sainsbury
and Luke Pollard with the author. Ireland, 2004

The author with Andy Wright, Oliver Van-Overbeek and Alex Caterall at the IAOMAS Seminar, 2004

The author with IAOMAS Canada founder, Tim Posynick, May 2006

The author with Matthew Reid, Marc Jones and Emma Brown, May 2006

The author with Dave Melton, IAOMAS USA founder, August, 2004

The author with fellow instructors at the 3rd IAOMAS England Seminar in May, 2006 (left to right): Oliver Van Overbeek, Anthony Whittaker, Garth Barnard, Fereidun Dariagard, Stuart Anslow, Tim Posynick, Andy Wright, Malcolm Watson, Marc Jones, Tom Bryans and Emma Brown

Though I am lucky to have met and trained with a fair few IAOMAS instructors over the last few years and capture a few snap shots along the way, there are others I chat with on a regular basis, have competed with, or have met and/or trained with that I have not managed to capture on camera as yet, but still deserve a mention for the friendships we have had over the last few years.

My good friend Manuel Adrogue, IAOMAS Argentina

My good friend Chris Galea, IAOMAS Malta. 2002

My old sparring buddy and friend Elliott Walker

My good friend Glen Docke, IAOMAS Australia

Andrew Morrell, IAOMAS England

Philip Fox, IAOMAS Ireland, 2000 and 2004

Ray Pullman, IAOMAS Northern Ireland

Karl Webb, IAOMAS IAOMAS England

Many of the members have become close friends over the years even with the great distances between them – I consider a few of the members as very close friends indeed.

'A friend hears the song in my heart and sings it to me when my memory fails'

Rayners Lane Taekwon-do Academy

Rayners Lane Taekwon-do Academy was founded in April 1999 and has thrived ever since. The Academy adheres to the original ITF syllabus, though it has been expanded in order to develop students capabilities in all areas of self defence. The Academy teaches all the major aspects of Taekwon-do such as patterns, sparring and destruction but it also teaches areas that are sadly neglected in some schools. These areas include pattern interpretation, pattern application and self protection amongst others.

The path from 10th kup (white belt) to 1st degree (black belt) sees the students of Rayners Lane Academy learn and become capable in all ranges of fighting. From kicking, punching and striking, to sweeping and throwing, to wrist, arm and leg locks, to chokes, strangles and vertical grappling and although not part of the original syllabus - ground fighting techniques. This is coupled with a comprehensive modern Self Protection syllabus that runs along side the main grading syllabus.

Though its students train hard in all areas of Taekwon-do and not specifically for competition, they have done extremely well nonetheless and consistently bring home gold medals in every tournament they enter, the pinnacle of which was following in their own instructors footsteps in 2004, when 7 students became World Champions in their own right, two becoming double World Gold Medallists and many other students from the Academy placing in medal positions as well.

Though founded in 1999 it was nearly 7 years before a student completed the path from 10th kup to 1st degree black belt a the Academy.

In March 2006, three of the Academy's students gained their black belts, as well as the assistant instructor Mr Gautam gaining his 2nd degree after 5 years as a 1st degree. The grading was over 7 hours long for the six students taking part!

Further information on the Academy and the students, as well as hundreds of photos, video clips and articles can be found at the Academy's web site:
www.raynerslanetkd.com

Vikram Gautam, Tomasz Kubicki, Dev Patel and Parvez Sultan
upon receiving the results of their dan grading in March, 2006

Example requirements for 1st and 2nd degree grading at Rayners Lane

1st kups

Patterns

- Saju Makgi
- Saju Jirugi
- Chon-Ji tul
- Dan-Gun tul
- Do-San tul
- Won-Hyo tul
- Yul-Gok tul
- Joong-Gun tul
- Toi-Gye tul
- Hwa-Rang tul
- Choong-Moo tul

Sparring and Self Defence

- 3 Step Sparring
- 2 Step Sparring
- 1 Step Sparring (Traditional)
- 1 Step Sparring *with single attacks of any techniques, on any side*
- Relaxed 1 Step with knife (2 rounds)
- Hosinsul with frontal attacks (2 rounds)
- Hosinsul with rear attacks (2 rounds)
- Traditional Sparring** over 2 rounds
- Free sparring with knife attacks
  Padded Traditional Free Sparring over 2 rounds *(with more contact allowed)*
- Idale Matsogi (2 v 1 Sparring)
- Choke Sparring (a form of ground based sparring)

Destruction

- Twio Yop Cha Jirugi – 2 boards*** - both legs
- Fore Fist Punch - two boards
- Hand technique – weak side - 1 board***
- Non-measured break****
- Technical Break Demonstration

1st degrees

Patterns

- Kwang-Gae tul
- Ge-Baek tul
- Po-Eun tul
- Selection of coloured belt patterns*

Sparring and Self Defence

- 3 Step Sparring
- 2 Step Sparring
- 1 Step Sparring (Traditional)
- 1 Step Sparring *with single attacks of any techniques, on any side*
- Relaxed 1 Step with knife (2 rounds)
- Foot Sparring
- Hosinsul with frontal attacks (2 rounds)
- Hosinsul with rear attacks (2 rounds)
- Close Quarter Knife Defences *(front and rear)*
- Describe and demonstrate pressure point attacks
- Traditional Sparring** over 2 rounds
- Free sparring with knife attacks
- Padded Traditional Free Sparring over 2 rounds *(with more contact allowed)*
- Idale Matsogi (2 v 1 Sparring)
- Choke Sparring (a form of ground based sparring)

Destruction

- Twio Dollyo Chagi - head height - both legs
- Knife-hand Strike – 2 boards
- Hand technique – weak side - 1 board***
- Bandae Dollyo Chagi – 2 boards
- Non-measured break****
- Technical Break Demonstration

Notes: * chosen by examiners / ** meaning they can kick, strike, sweep, take down and throw / *** 2 boards is 1 black board and 1 cream board, whilst single board breaks are required through a black board / **** no measuring or distance taking, the student simply walks up to the holder and strikes, with a basic kicking technique chosen at random for each leg. 1 board for 1st kups, 2 boards for 1st dans

As well as the physical tests, students also undergo a comprehensive 'Pre-grading' and have to complete a written exam that takes about 2½ hours. Furthermore, 1st degrees and above have to give an *'in-class'* demonstration of applications to a pattern of their choice.

Though some may look at this list and baulk at the requirements, the simple fact is, when the student is allowed to grade it is because they are ready and they can perform all of the above to the required standards, as the focus at Rayners Lane is not 'belts' but 'knowledge' – that which is behind the belt! And this I believe is how it should be with all Taekwon-do. Believe it or not, with a few alterations and additions, this grading syllabus is based on the original Ch'ang Hon grading requirements for black belts.

Rayners Lane Taekwon-do Academy
26th April, 2006

Class photograph to commemorate completion of Volume 1

Back Row: **Omid Sekanderzada, Ladi Oshunniya, Juzer Karimjee, Vijay Sood, Sharad Nakarja, Fayaz Latifi, Tomasz Kubicki, Vikram Gautam, Stuart Anslow, Dev Patel, Parvez Sultan, Colin Avis, David Lane, Kanai Brand, Marek Handzel and Dennis Potipako**

3rd Row: **Abdi Yassin, Hiral Chohan, Priya Shah, Paaras Tank, Lloyd Lewis, Lyndsey Sainsbury, Sonal Lakhman, Saphaa Simab, Gill Nightingale, David Westmore, Amir Massoumian, Vikram Bakshi, Qadir Marikar, Simon Courtenage and Richard Simon**

2nd Row: **Alex O'Neill, Joseph O'Neill, Mustafa Adam, Abhijay Sood, Ben Clarke, Joe Lewis, Sapwat Simab, Masoud Hamed, Milad Hamed, Josh McCormack, Avinish Bakshi, Anjali Bakshi and Zuhayr Chagar**

Front Row: **Anay Lakhia, Haajira Maxxamad, Amrit Lohia, Nikhil Chande, Mustafa Maxxamad, Charlotte Fox, Umar Marikar, Yassin Adam and Toby Calnan**

Missing: **Farhad Ahmad, Hershal Shah, Kate Barry, Jammal Yassin, James Barker, Krishan Singhal, Adnan Said, Mustafa Said, Danny Brown, Salahadin Mohamed, Ayomide Odunaiya and Adeoluwa Tokuta**

Photo Album

On the next few pages are a few photographs from the authors history in Taekwon-do, many of which have never been made publicly available before.

Training at home. *Circa 1991*

The author dropping a downward kick. *Circa 1992*

The author competing as a red belt in the patterns divisions. *Circa 1993*

The author performing a demonstration with his instructor, David Bryan. *Circa 1993*

Representing Taekwon-do at a Kick Boxing event. *Circa 1993*

Performing at a demonstration.
Circa 1993

Representing Taekwon-do again in the Kick
Boxing ring. *Circa 1994*

David Bryan, VI – Performing at a demonstration.
Circa 1994

Twimyo Yop Cha Jirugi. *Circa 1994*

John O'Conner, David Bryan (the authors instructor) with the author. *Circa 1994*

John Pepper, one of the authors first
Taekwon-do instructors. *Circa 1993*

John O'Conner and Stuart Anslow after passing their 1st
degree exam. *Circa 1994*

John O'Conner and Stuart Anslow training as 1st degrees.
Circa 1994

The author performing Jump reverse Turning Kick.
Circa 1994

Derrick Clarke and Stuart Anslow. *Circa 1995*

The author competing at an Open tournament. *Circa 1995*

Ground kicks. *Circa 1995*

The author receiving a medal off Lau Gar legend, Neville *'the devil'* Wray. *Circa 1995*

John O'Conner, Stuart Anslow and Derrick Clarke, at an Open tournament. *Circa 1995*

The author competing at an Open tournament. *Circa 1995*

Flying Side Kick. *Circa 1995*

The author with Free Style Karate founder and legend, Alfie *'the animal'* Lewis. *Circa 1996*

Twimyo Doo Ap Cha Busigi. *Circa 1996*

Black Belt Sparring Divisions. *Circa 1996*

The author with Master Mahai, 8th dan , Korean Taekwon-do Association (KTA). *Circa 1999*

Destruction at the World Championships, *2000*

Grandmaster Hee Il Cho presents the author with his medal at the World Championships, *2000*

Fighting at the World Championships, *2000*

Fighting at the World Championships, *2000*

Grandmaster Hee Il Cho, 9th dan with the author, John O'Conner and Rayners Lane students Kate Barry, Lyndsey Sainsbury, Zoe and Toni Bennett. *2000*

Taken during a photo shoot for the magazine article *'Grappling For Kicks'*. *Circa 2000*

Early days at Rayners Lane Taekwon-do Acacdemy. Vikram Gautum (right) as a red belt. *Circa 2000*

Taken during a photo shoot for the magazine article *'Grappling For Kicks'*. *Circa 2000*

1st 'King of the Ring' title. *Circa 2001*

Chloe Anslow, aged 3, in dobok

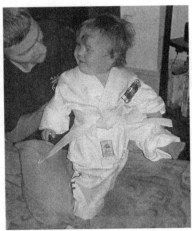

Logan Anslow, aged 1½ practising front kicks with his dad

Jorja Anslow, aged 1½, in dobok

The author performing flying side kick as part of a demonstration. *Circa 2001*

The author demonstrating pattern applications. *Circa 2001*

The author with Patrick McCarthy, VI
Taekwon-do Explosion 2002

Reverse Knife-hand Downward Strike through a stack of tiles. *Taekwon-do Explosion 2003*

The author (performing the kick) sparring at
Taekwon-do Explosion 2003

The author receiving his 'Hall of Fame 2003' award
from Combat magazine editor, Paul Clifton.

The author with Karate legend Unel Wellington.
Circa 2003

The author performing a scarf hold. *Circa 2003*

The author demonstrates Yop Cha Jirugi. *Circa 2003*

The author instructing choking
techniques to the class. *Circa 2003*

The author instructing throwing
techniques to the class. *Circa 2003*

The author on the 'floor to ceiling' ball. *Circa 2003*

Training at the top of St. Pauls Cathedral during a visit to London by Dave Melton, *2004*

The author teaching pattern applications at the IAOMAS Seminar, *2004*

Students of Rayners Lane Taekwon-do Academy with Grandmaster Hee Il Cho, at the World Championships, *2004*

Destruction at the World Championships, *2004*

The author performing a double flying side kick. *Circa 2005*

Students of Rayners Lane Taekwon-do-do Academy display their medal haul following the World Championships in 2004

The author with Mollie Samuals, 7 times world Karate Champion, *2005*

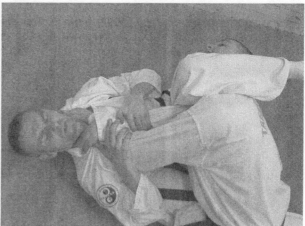

Groundwork - *Circa 2005*

The author performing on stage at the Youth Achievement Awards, *2005*

The author performing Jump Reverse Turning kick over his partners head at the East Coast Taekwondo Championships, Virginia USA – *October 2005*

The authors good friend, Lenny Ludlam,
who passed away in *November, 2005*

Reverse Downward knife-hand Strike at the East Coast
Taekwondo Championships, Virginia USA – *October 2005*

A *fun* armlock with
Master White, VIII - *2005*

Geared up to try WTF style
sparring, *2005*

WTF sparring with Dave Melton, *USA 2005*

'Rolling' with Dave Melton, *USA 2005*

Teaching Taekwon-do Applications at Jung Shin Hapkido Club.
May 2006

Rayners Lane students with Jose Maidana VII, ITF Argentina National Coach, *2005*

'Traditional Sparring (Padded), *2006*

The author after another 2 hour photo shoot (which always followed a class), *2006*

Having a laugh whilst explaining applications, *2006*

In full flow – *Taekwon-do Explosion, 2005*

Stuart and Gill at Stonehenge
May 2006

Appendix i
Taekwon-do Pattern Techniques
Cross Reference Guide

On the following pages I have provided a list[56] of all the techniques found in the coloured belt patterns, from Chon-Ji to Choong-Moo and including Saju Jirugi and Saju Makgi.

It can be used as a cross reference of techniques and denotes when they first appear and where else they appear. In the main, if the same technique is performed with a different stance it is not listed as a separate technique unless it changes the application considerably. Similar techniques, such as palm blocks for example, have been grouped together for easy reference.

There are four charts:

1. **Blocking Techniques** – all techniques described as blocks.

2. **Hand Techniques** – all strikes performed with the hands or elbow. Includes grabs and release techniques

3. **Kicking Techniques** – all techniques described as kicks

4. **Stances** – All stances are detailed where they first appear, though only less common stances are detailed by extra appearance. Walking Stance, L Stance and Sitting Stance are only detailed in the junior grade patterns as they appear in every pattern from then on.

Legend

- # denotes Ready Stance
- x1 / x2 etc denotes the number of appearances in the pattern
- *1 denotes where (which pattern) the technique first appears
- L/S, M/S, H/S denotes low, middle or high section

---

[56] These charts were compiled with the help of the Academy's Assistant Instructor, Vikram Gautam, II

Blocking Techniques

		Saju Jirugi	Saju Makgi	Chon-Ji	Dan-Gun	Do-San	Won-Hyo	Yul-Gok	Joong-Gun	Toi-Gye	Hwa-Rang	Choong-Moo
1	L/S Outer Forearm Block	x6		x4	x2					x3	2	2
2	L/S Knife-hand Block		x8*									
3	M/S Inner Forearm Block		x8*	x4				x2		x2		1
4	M/S Forearm Guarding Block						x2*		x2			1
5	M/S Knife-hand Guarding Block				x2*	x1	x3		x2	x2	x4	5
6	Twin Forearm Block				x2*		x4				x1	
7	H/S Wedging Block					x2*						
8	Outer Forearm Rising Block				x4*	x2						1
9	Circular Block						x2*			x4		
10	M/S Palm Hooking Block							x4*				
11	Twin Knife-hand Block							x2*				x1
12	H/S Outer Forearm Side Block					x4*		x2				
13	H/S Double Forearm Block							x2*	x2	x2		1
14	Reverse Knife-hand Middle Block								x2*			
15	Palm Upward Block								x2*			
16	Palm Pressing Block								x2*			
17	Palm Pushing Block										x1*	
18	Double Palm Upward Block											1
19	U-Shape Block								x2*			1
20	X Fist Rising Block								x1*			
21	X Fist Pressing block									2	x1	
22	X Knife-hand Checking Block											1
23	W Block									x6*		
24	L/S Knife-hand Guarding Block									x2*		
25	L/S Double Forearm Pushing Block									x1*		
26	Outer Forearm Inward Block											1

Hand Techniques

		Saju Jirugi	Saju Makgi	Chon-Ji	Dan-Gun	Do-San	Won-Hyo	Yul-Gok	Joong-Gun	Toi-Gye	Hwa-Rang	Choong-Moo
1	Obverse M/S Fore Fist Punch	x8*		x11				x3		x1	x4	
2	Double Punch					x2*		x4		x1	x1	
3	Reverse Mid Section Punch					x4*	x2	x2			x3	x1
4	Reverse H/S Punch								x2*			
5	H/S Fore Fist Punch				x8*							
6	Mid Punch in L Stance						x4*		x2			
7	Knife-hand Side Strike				x2*	x2					x1	
8	Inward Knife-hand Strike						x4*					x1
9	Straight Fingertip Thrust					x1*	x1	x2			x1	x1
10	Release Technique					x1*			x1			
11	Back Fist Strike					x2*	x2*	x1	x2	x3		x2
12	Front Elbow Strike							x2*				
13	Upward Elbow Strike								x2*			
14	Twin Vertical Fist								x1*	x1		
15	Twin Upset Punch								x1*			
16	Angle Punch								x1*			
17	Upset Fingertip Thrust									x2		x1
18	Twin Side Elbow Thrust									x1*		
19	Head Grab									x1*		x1
20	Flat Fingertip Thrust									x2*		x1
21	Upward Punch									x1*		
22	Side Punch (in L stance)									x1*		
23	Knife-hand Downward Strike									x1*		
24	Arm Grab									x1*		
25	Rear Elbow Strike/Thrust									x1*		
26	Dbl Mid/Low Section Block									x2*		
27	Reverse Knife-hand Strike											x1

- # denotes Ready Stance
- x1 / x2 etc denotes the number of appearances in the pattern
- *1 denotes where (which pattern) the technique first appears
- L/S, M/S, H/S denotes low, middle or high section

Kicking Techniques

		Saju Jirugi	Saju Makgi	Chon-Ji	Dan-Gun	Do-San	Won-Hyo	Yul-Gok	Joong-Gun	Toi-Gye	Hwa-Rang	Choong-Moo
1	Front Snap Kick					x2*	x2	x2	x2	x3		
2	Side Piercing Kick						x2*	x2	x2		x1	x3
3	Knee Kick									x1*		x1
4	Turning Kick										x2*	x2
5	Flying Side Kick											x1
6	Back Piercing Kick											x1

Stances

		Saju Jirugi	Saju Makgi	Chon-Ji	Dan-Gun	Do-San	Won-Hyo	Yul-Gok	Joong-Gun	Toi-Gye	Hwa-Rang	Choong-Moo
1	Parallel Ready Stance	#1*	#1*	#1	#1	#1		#1				#1
2	Closed Ready Stance 'A'						#1*					
3	Closed Ready Stance 'B'								#1*	#1*		
4	Closed Ready Stance 'C'										#1*	
5	Walking Stance	*	*									
6	L Stance			*	*							
7	Sitting Stance					x2*		x2				
8	Bending Ready Stance 'A'						x2*	x2				x1
9	X Stance							x1*		x1		
10	Fixed Stance						x4*				x1	x1
11	Rear Foot Stance								x2*			
12	Low Stance								x2*			
13	Closed Stance								x1*	x2	x1	
14	Vertical Stance										x1*	

Legend

- # denotes Ready Stance
- x1 / x2 etc denotes the number of appearances in the pattern
- *1 denotes where (which pattern) the technique first appears
- L/S, M/S, H/S denotes low, middle or high section

Appendix ii

Patterns/Kata Reference Guide

Below is a list of the 24 Ch'ang Hon patterns of Taekwon-do with reference to Shotokan Katas and at which grade they appear.

Grade	Ch'ang Hon Pattern	Shotokan Kata
10th Kup / Kyu	Saju Jirugi and Saju Makgi	Basics (Kihon Kata)*
9th Kup / Kyu	Chon-Ji	Heian Shodan[57]
8th Kup / Kyu	Dan-Gun	Heian Nidan[57]
7th Kup / Kyu	Do-San	Heian Sandan[57]
6th Kup / Kyu	Won-Hyo	Heian Yondan[57]
5th Kup / Kyu	Yul-Gok	Heian Godan[57]
4th Kup / Kyu	Joong-Gun	Tekki Shodan[57]
3rd Kup / Kyu	Toi-Gye	Bassai Dai[57]
2nd Kup / Kyu	Hwa-Rang	Jion[57] / Kanku Dai[57]
1st Kup / Kyu	Choong-Moo	Empi[57] / Hangetsu[57]
1st Degree / Dan	Ge-Baek, Po-Eun, Kwang-Gae	Bassai Sho / Jitte[57]
2nd Degree / Dan	Eui-Am, Choong-Jang, Juche**	Nijushiho / Kanku Sho / Tekki Nidan[57]
3rd Degree / Dan	Yoo-Sin, Sam-Il, Choi-Yong	See notes below

There is a kata called 'Taikyoku Shodan' that is considered very basic and is sometimes taught at 10th Kyu level.

**Juche replace pattern Kodang*

In Shotokan Karate, from 3rd Dan onwards the student learns all or most of the following kata: Chinte, Ji'on, Shochin, Unsu, Gojushiho Dai and/or Gojushiho Sho. There is also a Dan grade kata named 'Gangkaku'[38] which is not often taught and another called 'Meikyo' that is even less often taught. Some schools expect different kata learned at different grades, depending upon their Association.

As a further note, in Shotokan, 4th dans are usually graded via teaching experience and 5th dans and above are appointed by Associations, whereas in Taekwon-do a 4th degree must know Ul-Ji, Moon-Moo and Yong-Gae, a 5th degree must know Se-Jong and So San and a 6th degree must know the final pattern, Tong-Il. In Taekwon-do, 7th, 8th and 9th degree are the only honorary grades, appointed for dedication to the art.

---

[57] Kata learned by General Choi and detailed in his 1965 book "Taekwon-do" – see next appendix for further analysis

Appendix iii

Kata Analysis

General Choi learned and noted these katas in his 1965 book `Taekwon-do`

Kata Name	1965 Book Notes And Details
Hei-an	In the 1965 book, these are split into Hei-an I, Hei-an II up to Hei-an V – there are 5 Heian Katas in the original Shotokan
Bat-Sai	By cross referencing the 1965 book text with Shotokan pattern layouts, this is in reference to Bassai Dai (not Bassai Sho), as the number of movements and the text equal Bassai Dai.
En-Bi	It would seem this is in reference to the kata Empi. Though the 1965 book lists one less move than the kata layout I have, it would seem this is due to how sequential movements have been interpreted.
Ro-Hai	This was odd, as the kata Rohai is from the Wado-Ryu system of Karate. Upon further research I found that it is the same as the Shotokan kata Meikyo. However, in General Choi's book the movements listed for Ro-Hai match the Shotokan kata Gangaku, not Meikyo. Why, I do not know! Suffice to say, the Wado Ryu system of Karate was developed by Hironori Ohtsuka (1892-1982) and was a breakaway system from Shotokan, as Hironori Ohtsuka learnt direct from Funakoshi originally.
Kouh-Shang-Kouh	This is actually the kata Kanku-Dai (as opposed to Kanku-Sho). The movements (and number of moves) match exactly
Tet-Ki	This is divided in Tet-Ki I, Tet-Ki II and Tet-Ki III and refers to Tekki Nidan, Tekki Sandan and Tekki Shodan katas
Jit-Te	This is undoubtedly the kata Jitte, though the 1965 book lists only 24 movements and the kata layout I have lists 26, though it would seem this is again due to how sequential movements have been interpreted.
Han-Getsu	This is definitely the kata Hangetsu. The movements (and number of moves) match exactly
Ji-on	This is definitely Jion Kata, though the 1965 book lists one more move than the kata layout I have, it would seem this is due to how sequential movements have been interpreted.

Appendix iv
Pressure Point Reference

On the following pages are a list of vital points and pressure points referred to in this book. As mentioned, as I learned them specific names were not given, except perhaps an English type version like *'side of the neck'* for the carotid artery etc. I spoke to Pressure Point expert Prof. Rick Clark[58] about this and he termed it the *'Just Hit Here'* point of view and said that he rather likes the JHH (just hit here) point of view, as though Acupuncture can give you a way to talk about locations for the most part some of the point we use are not quite in line with those acupuncture points - so we have to say *'near Lung 5'* or similar.

It should be noted that the Korean equivalents are all noted in General Choi's 1965 book 'Taekwon-do' as vital points and that the TCM (Traditional Chinese Medicine) points are simply the closest referenced pressure point to the actual vital point target area, so may or may not have actually been the original point intended. The points are referenced in the book to two outline diagrams of the human body and are not all that clear so as to be totally specific to pinpoint an actual pressure point. I have also include the JHH (just hit here) points I was taught. I have included the ones that I would term *'pressure points'*, though Sensei Clark feels that there is no difference between vital points and pressure points and feels that no matter what you call them they are weak points that you attack, no matter the size or how generic they might be.

Sensei Clark demonstrating pressure point applications at Rayners Lane Academy, May 2003

Furthermore, this list is for reference only, the training or striking of pressure points should only be performed under proper supervision by an instructor with expertise in this area. Utmost restraint should be used at all times. When practicing, only apply 5 to 10% of power at all times. Never strike or manipulate two pressure points simultaneously as this can have very dangerous with potentially catastrophic effects. Be aware that over use of pressure points can have effects on the bodies natural condition. For example *'Lung'* pressure points can affect breathing and the respiratory system, *'Heart'* Pressure points speak for themselves etc. The bottom line is, do not touch what you do not know about! Certain points (such as Triple Warmer 23 - TW23 and Bladder 15 - B15) should never be struck at all!

Many thanks to Sensei Clark for looking over my charts, making a few amendments and adding the notes in the charts to make points easier to locate.

---

[58] Sensei Rick Clark is the founder of the Ao Denkou Jitsu fighting system and an expert in Pressure Points and their applications. He has trained in Ryukyu Kempo (8th Dan), Chung Do Kwan Taekwon-do (7th Dan), Ju-jitsu, Judo, Modern Arnis and Hapkido. http://www.ao-denkou-kai.org

Book Description	English	Korean	TCM
Temple	Temple	Kwanjanori	Triple Warmer 23
Side of neck	Carotid Artery	Moktongmaek	Small Intestine 16
Philtrum	Philtrum	Injung	Governing Vessel 23
Jaw #1	Jaw/Point of Chin	T'ŏk	Conceptor Vessel 24 would be the closeted one (but still its off just)
Jaw #2/3	Side of Jaw	T'ok	Side of Jaw: Spleen 5 Base of Jaw (the point just under the ear and by the jaw): Triple Warmer 17
Point on forearm, near elbow	Radial Nerve		Lung 5 or Lung 6
Point on forearm, near wrist	From the diagram in Gen Choi's book it's impossible to tell which point Gen. Choi is designating.	Sonmok	There are 3 points near the wrist Large Intestine 5, Triple Warmer 5/6, and Small Intestine 6 *The placement of the thumb gives a clue as to what meridian it would be. It would have to be Large Intestine (along the line of the thumb), Tripe Warmer (middle part of the arm), and Small Intestine (on the little finger side of the hand). I use a point just up from LI 5, about 1/2 inch and before you get to LI 6, and a point near SI 6*
Inside of Bicep		Point not shown in the book	Lung 3
Outside of Bicep		Point not shown in the book	Large Intestine 14
Armpit	Armpit	Kyŏdŭrang	Heart Meridian 1
Elbow Joint	Elbow Joint *This point appears to be located "in the posterior aspect of the cubital joint, in a depression between the olecronom of the ulna and tip of the medial epicondyle of the humerus" p. 134 "An outline of Chinese Acupuncture"* *The academy of traditional Chinese medicine, Foreign Languages Press: Peking (1975)*	P'almok Kwanjŏl	Small Intestine 8 *There are 6 different meridians on the arm - 3 on the inside of the arm and 3 on the outside (back of the arm) the lung is on the inside of the arm running along the radial bone. If you look at the chart you can see that the point is at the elbow on the outside (back) of the arm - because of the placement of the thumb. If the arm would have been turned the thumb would be in a different position and then I "might" have said it could be a Lung point. But because the thumb is turned and the placement of the "dot" I think it would be Small Intestine 8*

Book Description	English	Korean	TCM
Floating Ribs	Floating Ribs	Hyŏppok	(Most likely) Spleen 16
Groin	Groin	Nangsim	Not normally given a number or name in acupuncture
Testicles	Testicles		Not normally given a number or name in acupuncture.
Inside of thigh	Inside Thigh	Ch'ibu	Liver 9
Outside of Thigh	Outside Thigh	Point not shown in the book	Gall Bladder 31 or 32
Top of Foot	Instep	Palttŭng	Liver 3

As a final reference, in General Choi's 1965 book 'Taekwon-Do' (Daeha Publication Company: Seoul, Korea) on pages 34 and 35 he references 35 vital spots (Kupso), depicted by two outline figures of the human body, though he mentions 54 in regards to Taekwon-do. These points are listed in English and Korean. The complete list of 35 is as follows:

No	English	Korean	No	English	Korean
1	Skull	Taesinum	19	Inner Thighs	Ch'ibu
2	Bridge of Nose	Migan	20	Shins	Kyŏnggol
3	Eyelid	Angŏm	21	Insteps	Palttŭng
4	Eyes	Anbu	22	Temple	Kwanjanori
5	Philtrum	Injung	23	Ear Points	Huibu
6	Neck Artery	Moktongmaek	24	Jaw	Polttagwi
7	Point of Chin	T'ŏk	25	Upper Neck	Witmok
8	Clavicle	Soegol Sang'wa	26	Upper Back	Kyŏn Kap
9	Adam's Apple	Kyŏlhu	27	Armpits	Kyŏdŭrang
10	Windpipe	Sumt'ong	28	Small Back	Kyŏng Ch'u
11	Chest	Kasŭm	29	Kidney	K'ongp'at
12	Wrist	Sonmok	30	Inner Wrist	Ansonmok
13	Solar Plexus	Myŏngch'i	31	Coccyx	Mijŏbu
14	Ribs	Chŏnggwŏng	32	Hollow of Knee	Ogŭm
15	Elbow Joints	P'almok Kwangjŏl	33	Leg Joint	Murŭp Kwanjŏl
16	Floating Ribs	Hyŏppok	34	Calf	Changttanji
17	Abdomen	Habokpu	35	Heel Achilles	Twitch'uk Yukchŏm
18	Groin	Nangsim			

What is *Ki*?

(In general terms)

By Yi, Yun Wook, IV

Ki in Japanese. *Gi* in Korean, *Chi* (or *qi*) in Chinese comes from different pronunciation of reading the Chinese character: 氣 meaning space surrounding you or air. The Chinese character for *ki* roughly translates as "air" or "the surrounding air around us in space", it also translates to "energy" as well. Western culture, often translates "*ki*" to "energy force" as used in Steven Spielberg's Star Wars. (To lessen the confusion of interchanging the terms *ki*, *gi*, *chi*, or *qi*, the term "*ki*" will be used throughout this article).

Ki is life energy that flows in your body and other living creatures (and sometimes in elements like metal which can conduct your *ki*). This life energy, *ki* can come into your body, stay in your body, and also be transferred from your body. The *ki* is harnessed from the foods you eat, from the energy source in the air around you, and from living things including other people. Once harnessed, it flows into your body via "large channels" and through a network of smaller branching channels to every part of the body.

It is a force that maintains and protects your body physically and spiritually (not the religious spiritualism, but more like *l 'esprit de corps*-the readiness in the mind). In simple words, *ki* is the force behind life.

Do we know it?

In the East, there is a nonchalant attitude about *ki*: So it exists, it is always there, we use it, we live it, what's the big deal? The Eastern thought is that everything is interconnected, man and nature *ki* is natural, therefore *ki* is always a part of us.

Chinese, Japanese, Koreans, and other Asian cultures take *ki* as part of daily life. For instance, in Korean the following expressions are used in everyday conversations:

"*ki gah mahk hyuh*" used when faced with unreasonable situations or when totally astounded. This translates as, i.e." you are disrupting my *ki* and incapacitating me".

"*ki reul joo gyuh*" used when faced with complete suppression of doing something. This translates into "you are killing my *ki* energy flow completely, denying my *raison d' être*".

"*ki gah sahl aht dah*" used upon hearing a very surprising good news or when recovered from a mishap or illness. It means "my *ki* has been revived".

Other similar expressions also exist in Chinese and Japanese.

In contrast, in the West, man and nature are separate. This separation concept is probably why *ki* remains as an Asian mystique in the Western culture.

Can you see it?

Few people, either with training or no training have heightened senses of *ki*. They can see auras (purportedly equal to *ki* energy levels) around the head or bodies of people and their own *ki*. Or when they hold a weapon such as a spear, staff, or a sword, the aura extends out to the weapon. The resulting power from *ki* is supposedly visible by the physical power often found in martial arts demonstrations. But this is not scientifically proven.

Can you feel it?

Some people deem *ki* as the "sixth sense", but people who practice *ki* claim that you can physically experience *ki* in many ways. One way to feel to is close your eyes, and have someone's hand come near your ear. You will sense it without the person actually touching your ear. That is your *ki* sensing. When properly "tuned", one can heighten the sensitivity and feel someone in a distance or sense the surroundings without visual contact. Some feel the *ki* of other living entities and when in close vicinity, the emotions as well. Others claim to feel the emotions of others by touch alone without seeing the facial expressions. Countless swordsmen stories in China, Japan, and Korea talk about the hero swordsman detecting bad *ki* of would be assassins in an open field or closed taverns.

How is it used in martial arts?

There is an internal *ki* and an external *ki*. Internal *ki* maintains yourself and your body with *dan june* (an area below your belly button) as the body centre. External *ki* is passing your internal *ki* others to increase other's energy level similar to jump starting a weak car battery. Healing is achieved through "reception points" throughout the human body. These are points where your *ki* connects to the person receiving your *ki*. The points are called by various names: Acupuncture points; acupressure points; acupoints; pressure points; points of the meridian, *kyusho,* etc. These are the points in the pathways of the *ki* in your body directly connected to the body's major life channels which includes the organs and your consciousness.

Depending on your transferring level of your *ki* and your mind set, you can inflict pain or permanently damage to a person through these points. Trained martial artists will use this knowledge to immobilize the opponent by applying *ki* to a single or multiple points. Or even sense the opponent's intent and moves before he or she attacks.

Does understanding of ki come to you?

I can only talk from my personal experience. It has been only in the past 3-5 years after 30+ years of training TKD. There have been many breathing exercises and *ki* exercises in TKD I was taught many years ago. Then one day, I began to sense the *ki* when executing my movements. I began to sense the "power" by combining certain postures and movement along with a certain mindset. I cannot describe this verbally, it is something you feel with your consciousness.

For me, I began to see "auras" around human bodies as faint contour outlines. I started rubbing my eyes in disbelief the first time. The sizes of "auras" varied by people, regardless of their body size. Some were surrounded by larger auras than others, and some did not have any.

When sparring I could feel more *ki* in my body both in absorbing attacks and executing techniques. When I came in physical contact (even with the slightest touch of finger) with people having larger contour lines around their body, I could feel their energy and sometimes their emotions. When driving underneath a tree with my car windows closed I could feel the "fluttering breeze". Initially, I thought I was losing my sanity. Only after talking to old GMs and Chinese *ki* masters, I realized it was *ki*. I had developed the awareness of *ki* as a self-discovery. It was there all along. But I am still fine tuning and learning. There is so much more to learn.

Final note: The dangers of learning *ki* in seminars

Asian masters disapprove of teaching *ki* to students with a miniscule knowledge of *ki*. Teaching others for profit with few hour seminars, tapes, and DVDs. It takes more than one day to understand what is going on and continuous learning throughout your life is a must. Teaching and finding a profit source with something you barely understand is not the beginnings of teaching positive *ki* either. By all means, seminars would be beneficial as the starting point in understanding *ki*.

True Chinese *qigong* (*ki*) masters when handing down their techniques have an agreement with their students not to use or teach *ki* techniques for profit. Teaching "*ki*" for profit is very frowned upon, and viewed as the "sincerity of *ki*" being lost from the "profiteer". This is also one aspect of why *ki* has its mystique. Real *ki* masters rarely reveal themselves or blow their horn.

Modern day instructors may teach the superficial aspects of *ki* (where to strikes are effective) with exorbitant seminar fees for profit. But they would not be able to tell you what the Chinese characters for each point means and how they are related to each other. Understanding Chinese interprets each of the 300+ points and leads to broader understanding of the points. The legacy of *ki* can only be found only in the understanding of the Chinese characters of each pressure point, and how they connect to the flow of *ki*. The Chinese character names of each acupressure points indicate not only what each points do to the overall flow, but the function of the pressure points. The etymology of the Chinese character and names are the key to the true understanding of *ki* and its interconnection to the whole picture of *ki*. True individual with total understanding of the ki always try to harness the good *ki*. People who really know *ki*, will not teach it for profit. In order to understand *ki*, one needs to understand the whole picture of the source, application, harnessing, and the level of the *ki* of the person doing the controlled strikes or healing. The sincerity of the individual doing *ki* also matters.

Many students after learning some aspect of "*ki*" in quick fix courses will start boasting off to others or use it unwisely to intimidate others. Egos and "*ki*" have been always at odds with each other. Egos + *ki* is not a good combination. There is also a very fine line between ego and profit. I am only pointing out fallacies of learning bad *ki*. If one were to pursue further into understanding *ki*, that is another matter.

What is ignored in "ki" seminars.

It may be vague, but there is more to *ki*. What is most important is the overall understanding. What makes one or two day seminars teaching about *ki* starting with the wrong foot. It is more like being teaching how to become a good football player in few hours to some people who have not experienced games. Few techniques might work, but it does not provide the whole aspect of the football. You have to attain a certain workout experience with your own body before you can apply the tips and the techniques. You also have to understand the meanings in Chinese for each acupressure point explains the function, location, and the effect of the strike. You have to continue learning.

Appendix vi

Patterns: *Telling it like it is!*
The Sine Wave

By Stuart Anslow III

Published in Taekwon-do and Korean Martial Arts Magazine, March 2001[59]

Recently I attended an event that showed me a mass of `sine wave` patterns on display, which in turn prompted me to write this article.

Many students simply don't understand the relevance of pattern practice, either why they do it, their purpose or what techniques are for! General Choi stated in his manual, under the section `Essential Information` with regards to patterns, that:

> **7. Students should know the purpose of each movement.**
> **8. Students should perform each movement with realism.**

This article is not to discuss individual techniques contained within patterns (no 7), although a few might be highlighted within the context of this article, but to hopefully enlighten a few students as to `why we practice patterns`! However, the total, overall practice of patterns falls with no.8: Students should perform each movement with realism, and thus their pattern which of course contains 'each movement'!

In this new era of three main ITF groups and many more independent Chang-Hon Taekwon-do schools there are now three main variations on the ITF tuls (when I refer to ITF I am not referring to any organisation, but to the style of Taekwon-do, i.e. Ch'ang-hon, which is mostly referred to as 'ITF style' whether correct or not)

These three main variations can be seen as:

1. Very old, almost Karate type performance – emphasising lots of hip twist, off-turned shoulders and no knee-spring or sine-wave motions

2. Original, emphasising both hip twist and knee spring, but not sine-wave per se.

3. New, emphasising little or no hip twist or knee spring and lots of sine wave (as it is now taught!)

First though, let me clear up why I refer to the above as very old, original and new.

---

[59] Though the article remains exactly how it was first published, the pictures have been re-shot for this book

I refer to very old as '*very old*' as I feel these patterns were stylised whilst Taekwon-do was still finding its identity and thus retain a lot of Karate influences (which isn't a bad thing by the way), but in Taekwon-do terms they are old, the foundation you may say, but still needed further examination, study and development.

I refer to original, as '*original*', as they were <u>refined</u> versions of the '*very old*', utilising hip twist still, but also using knee-spring etc. Movements were now more fluid and students were expected to retain a rhythmic motion in their pattern performance. This is where I believe Taekwon-do found its true identity!

I refer to new as new as contrary to what many believe, the sine-wave has only been 'forcefully' pushed within Taekwon-do in the last 5 years or so (maybe less than that), maybe more so in other countries but not in the UK. So sine-wave patterns are a relatively new way of performance.

So which way should you practice? Well this is a question that only instructors can answer, as for a student you have to follow your instructor, or as an instructor you have to follow your association and what they say they want!

When I or my students have spoken to other students from other schools about pattern practice you often hear students say that patterns practice is for balance, poise, body shifting, smoothness, to develop rhythmic motion, to allow one to practice dangerous techniques without causing injury etc,

Whilst all of the above may be true; they are all benefits of practicing patterns, they are not the foremost reason for pattern practice; they are extra beneficiaries of pattern practice.

In Volume 1 of General Choi's encyclopaedia, under the section headed '*Patterns*' (p154), General Choi states '*Patterns are various fundamental movements, most of which represent either attack or defence techniques, set to a fixed or logical sequence*'. He further goes on to mention the other benefits of practicing patterns i.e. Balance, poise etc. So it should be noted that before the extra benefits, it is stated that patterns represent self defence techniques, set out logically to aid the students practice

If we look at the above statement and take no.8 of the 'Essential Information' on patterns, that we should practice with realism, then these few facts come into view:

1. To be realistic a technique needs to be fast, a slow technique simply will not work in 99% of cases (including blocks and strikes)
2. To be realistic a technique needs to be targeted (preferably to a vital or pressure point)
3. To be realistic a technique needs to be powerful
4. To be realistic a technique needs to be instinctive (especially in relation to blocking)

So now we get into the controversial area of the sine-wave. As a note of interest sine-wave was introduced at a seminar in Derby by the General in 1983, but it was mentioned and not so forcefully pushed as it is now. So in reality it has been around in ITF Taekwon-do for over 20 years, but my instructor, nor his, nor I were told to perform patterns how they are performed now with the sine-wave, but more on this later.

In the manual three waves (of motion/of movement) are given equal space; sine wave, horizontal wave and saw tooth wave[60] (when was the last time you practiced this?). The horizontal wave is a straight line movement; the saw tooth wave is a straight up and down movement and the sine wave is represented as a slight up and down motion on a curve, which flows smoothly from one stance to the next, as in the diagram A below (vol. 4, p.203)

diagram 1

So you would basically raise your body slightly when you move forward and drop as you step into the stance. It is a smooth transition from one technique/stance to the next. But, I have seen the sine-wave that is so heavily performed today by dropping first, then raising up, the finally following the final (longer) curve, down into the technique, making what students are calling sine-wave looking something like this (although I'm no artist):

diagram 2

Now compare that to the above version (diagram 2)! It looks far from being a smooth flow! In fact it is more like the saw tooth wave than the sine wave as General Choi described, It should also be noted that General Choi said on the same page that "posture A (the sine wave) is the only motion used in Taekwon-do". It should further be noted that General Choi said "*once the movement is in motion it is not stopped*" which is why, after seeing the article I found out that Adam Porter, a current ITF Instructor feels most peoples sine wave is wrong and is more akin to the saw tooth wave! This ITF instructor further states "*General Choi has taken his variation of this idea and labelled it 'sine wave.' But he did not come up with this type of movement. I actually tell my students this and the ones who train with other ITF instructors always suffer apoplexy!*", he also goes onto say "*Examples of similar ideas to sine wave are in wing chun, Ed Parkers kenpo (he has his own term for it 'the marriage of gravity') and of course people like DSI are talking about 'the wave form' as a 'player to the game.' If you get a chance to check out the much advertised martial arts and fitness video 'power punching' the theory put forward is also a similar idea to the sine wave.*"! All good food for thought!

---

[60] See appendium

Correct motion using the sine wave, as originally put forth by General Choi, as in diagram 1

There are more points to note here:

As I said previously, sine-wave was not 'pushed' until recent years, however, a slight dropping of body weight into techniques has been. This is not the same as the 'bobbing' motion (as it has been described) that is so overly emphasised in sine-wave based patterns now-a-days.

Further more, if you look at good original pattern practitioners/original masters you will notice a slight drop into techniques anyway, a natural motion that develops through training, whether emphasised or not, which is more in-line with the original sine-wave concept introduced in 1983.

I think instructors are over-emphasising the actual motion so as to emphasise the sine-wave element itself as a new thing, but we were dropping into movements naturally anyway, performing similar or the same as in diagram 1 and always have been.

However, if you look at the second diagram, you will notice the first drop, then a raise and finally a drop! How can all these movements help techniques with speed? Remember, for a technique to be effective it has to have speed! (Power=mass x speed). And what purpose does the first dropping motion serve, if indeed, and this is debatable, sine wave does add more power than hip twists? In fact, any dropping motion adds power as it utilizes both body weight of the practitioner and gravity, and as I said above, this is naturally gained through training.

In Taekwon-Do by Gen. Choi Hong Hi 1972. Published by ITF and 533 pages. On page 29. it says "*The formula we can use to calculate the power of any technique is:* "

$P = 1/2 \, mv^{**}2$ (what I am trying to show here is "v square")

P= Power
1/2 = constant
m = mass
v = velocity or speed

"*This equation clearly reveals why developing speed is the most important factor in developing power: For example, if the mass in increased by a factor of three (with the speed kept constant)*" *then the power is also increased by the factor of three. But if the speed is increased by a factor of three (with mass kept constant) then the power is increase by a factor of nine.*" The sine wave (diagram 2), is in fact counter-productive in developing speed!

If we go back to diagram 1, I feel this has always been practiced to certain degrees before the sine-wave, by name, was thrust into the spot light but never referred to as sine-wave. Thus, making the 'new' sine-wave seem like a different concept to original motion, which is now pushed as a different way of movement (diagram 2), so instructors are teaching something different from what they learnt or originally did, when in fact they should be teaching the same! And it is not a natural movement. Rising up as you shift forward and dropping back down is natural, as the legs straighten and bend that way, dropping, rising and dropping again is unnatural and when students try to emulate that, the results are far from good in relation to helping make patterns applicable to self defence.

Another major point to note is that General Choi said that when moving forward the shoulders should be half facing, this goes in line with the natural motion of walking, where the hips sway, thus creating another natural motion, the hip twist. Try stepping the length of a walking stance (1 and ½ shoulder widths), with your shoulders half facing and hips full facing, it is very uncomfortable and feels very unnatural!

Why remove hip twist from natural motions, i.e. moving forward into a basic punch. Surely for ultimate speed and power, the slight natural dropping motion as described above, coupled with hip twist is required. Both added together create this! In his article on the *'Theory Of Power'*, which is found in all versions of the encyclopaedia, under the sub-section *'Mass'* General Choi stated *'No doubt the maximum body weight is applied with the motion of turning the hip.'*

Also, the sine wave was meant to replace the hip twist, but hip twist adds power and when you can do a proper hip twist, long pre-postured blocking techniques are not required any more, as the power comes from the hip, thus increasing speed of defence and effectiveness, how can the 'new' sine wave motion be shortened in time, with training!

Apparently, the knee spring is no longer emphasized or has been removed completely in favour of sine-wave (diagram b), but in the same sub-section from the *'Theory Of Power'* General Choi also stated *'Another way of increasing body weight is the utilization of a springing action of the knee joint. This is achieved by slightly raising the hip at the beginning of the motion and lowering the hip at the moment of impact to drop the body weight into the motion'*, something I was taught from the very beginning. Never was I taught that the head must remain at the same height like in many Karate kata's, a slight raise and drop has always been taught, but I never learnt the sine-wave as it is being shown now (fig. 2), never was I taught drop, then raise, then drop again! General Choi also stated in the sub-section *'Equilibrium'* that *'Flexibility and knee spring are also important in maintaining balance for both a quick attack and instant recovery.'*

There are other differences between the `original` and `new` type patterns. Certain techniques have been altered and in my opinion not necessarily for the better, but that's another article.

As an instructor, it is my job to ensure my students benefit from training in the best way possible. It is not the chief instructor's job or any grading panel, but the instructor's responsibility. The problems arise when what is deemed in the best interests of the students is not the same as what is required to pass a grading. Thus effectively forcing instructors to teach something that may not actually be in the student's best interests.

This was highlighted recently when my students entered a tournament, which was run by a group that emphasis the sine-wave (when referring to sine wave I am referring to figure 2). Now I've no problem with what you or anyone else wants to practice, sine-wave (A or B, 1 or 2) or not, but it was billed as an 'open' tournament, so all three types of pattern performance should have been taken into account, but unfortunately it wasn't. My students performed their patterns with power, fluidity and grace as they had been taught; techniques looked effective, as they are meant to be, because they are effective, as they are taught that way! But each one went out 1st round as they did not do the sine-wave. When I mentioned this to someone they stated this truth *"in order to win anything, you have to perform their way!"*, but to do that would be for me personally to teach in a way that I do not feel is beneficial to the students and thus cannot do. It should also be noted that those same students (with the exception of 2) went on to win the gold medal in each of their sparring divisions!

So, if you take into account that what you teach should be what is most beneficial to the student, which style of patterns (tuls) should you teach? Most instructors have a choice between 'original' or 'new' types! (Except of course if you've only been training 5 years or so!). Of course, anyone who knows the relationship between Tul and Ilbo Matsogi (Patterns and One-Step Sparring) will realise that by the time sine-wave B is performed you would certainly have been struck, even with a basic obverse punch!

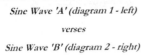

Sine Wave 'A' (diagram 1 - left)

verses

Sine Wave 'B' (diagram 2 - right)

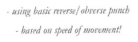

- using basic reverse/obverse punch

- based on speed of movement!

When thinking about this consider also the following:

The '*original*' patterns were the same patterns taught to the Korean military. The same army that was renowned for its effective techniques during the Vietnam War, so much so, they were hardly attacked at all.

The '*original*' patterns are the same patterns that all of the original masters and 1st instructors of General Choi taught (those that stayed with him through their development that is). These were the pioneers that spread the art around the world!

Even Grandmaster Ki Ha Rhee was referred to as 'too Karate' as he didn't perform as in diagram B at one of the Generals last UK seminars and Grandmaster Rhee was considered General Choi's number one student and is held in very high regard by probably all Taekwon-do instructors in the UK for his power and techniques, if he can't (or doesn't want to) get it right, what hope is there for the rest of us! Besides which, Grandmaster Rhee is a great role model for all Taekwon-do students!

Example of speed aspects using:
Sine Wave B (diagram 2): left
Horizontal Wave - middle
Sine Wave A (diagram 1) - right
in L Stance with an outward Knife-hand Strike

Those that are 'pro' sine-wave, inclusive to all other ways of thinking often state that "*They do sine-wave and they are in the organisation (formerly) headed by the founder, so there way is Taekwon-do and all others are not*". To this I recall someone replying, "*That's incorrect, we learnt the patterns as first passed on by the founder General Choi, the original patterns, you are now learning are a modified version*" Food for thought! Although, if you've read this article properly you may have realised you were actually performing sine-wave, even if you never realised it!

Others feel it was a political move to gain some of those that left the ITF Organisation back into it by saying that if they were not learning patterns with sine-wave, they cannot be practising or teaching Taekwon-do! Which is of course ridiculous? Unfortunately, politics and `student's best interests` do not often go hand in hand! And again, they were probably already were performing it how the General originally showed it!

Although I obviously speak via my own training in this article, with my own observations, I wanted a rounded view point from other respected Taekwon-do stylists, both within the ITF as an organisation and out side of it and they had this to say,

Adam Porter, an ITF instructor I know had this to say (as well as what is mentioned above) after reading this article: "*In all these arguments though it's worth pointing out you will always be able to find two people of equal size, each using different methods, one of whom will be able to display more power than the other.*" Which I feel is a fair point!

Another instructor I know, whom is native Korean and has trained under no less than four of General Choi's original, 1st generation pioneering instructors, had this to say:

"*The sine wave is not accepted by all factions of ITF stylists. It came somewhere around the 90s. It is a recent thing. Not accepted by all Grandmasters.* "

He also said "*Taekwon-do is different from Karate (especially ITF TKD). General Choi found all techniques have much more power if you accelerate faster upon initial acceleration. That is how the kicks and other movements are so powerful and fast and deadly in true Taekwon-do. For example, virtually all movements in the original ITF Taekwon-do techniques have added acceleration. After twisting your body or hips (1st acceleration) your hand or foot techniques speeds up more (2nd acceleration on top of your 1st acceleration) to give more power not found in most other martial arts. Sine wave principle is another version of that. A bit of sine wave was always there even in the old TKD techniques, except this time in my opinion; they went a bit too far and it got over exaggerated.*"

Hwa-Rangs Upward Punch

Yoo-Sins Reverse Trap/Punch

Another well respected ITF instructor from Argentina had this to say on reading the article "*I cannot agree more on everything you have written. Excellent. Extraordinary. I have additional reasons against the exaggerated modern sine wave: It is not compatible with the application of certain techniques which are supposed to be delivered upward (i.e., Hwa-Rang and Ge-Baek's under punches) or almost horizontally*

Kwang-Gaes Upset Punch

(like Yoo-Sins's direct reverse punches where the opposite hand is over the punching upper-arm trapping the opponent's attack while going for the armpit/ribcage). Furthermore, the exaggeration has lead to make up an unrealistic rhythm that prevents combinations. One thing is to know we are not Karate, but let's keep the good things of our ancestors!!!

In summary, I don't recall anyone, especially General Choi saying *"hold on, I got it wrong"* and changing the Diagram/method from A to B!

So what is right and what is wrong? Neither really if you feel it works for you (but there's a long way between *feel* and *real*), although I certainly have my preference, but the old adage of '**If it ain't broke, don't fix it**' certainly springs to mind!

Patterns: *Telling it like it is!*
The Sine Wave - Appendium

Sine Wave A, often termed 'Natural Motion'

Sine Wave B (Over emphasized version)

Horizontal Wave

Saw Tooth Wave

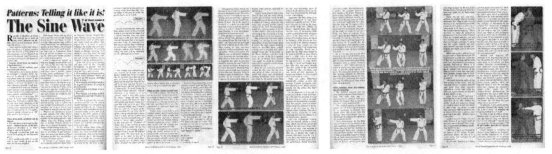

Sine Wave Article – First published in Taekwon-do and Korean Martial Arts Magazine, March 2001

Appendix vii

The Battle of Tra Binh Dong

Reprinted by permission of the *Marine Corps Gazette*

In early February 1967, North Vietnamese Army (NVA) commanders took advantage of the truce following the Tet holiday to begin preparations for a major attack. The 2d NVA Division infiltrated into the coastal lowlands of the Quang Ngai Province. Using elephants to transport 120mm mortars, the division assembled a regimental-sized force composed of two battalions from the 1st and 21st Regiments and a battalion of Viet Cong guerrillas in order to attack the city of Quang Ngai and the U.S. Marine base at Chu Lai. Built at the direction of LtGen Victor H. Krulak, Commanding General, Fleet Marine Forces Pacific, the base was a critical aviation and logistics center that supported operations across the I Corps tactical zone. The airbase was home to nine fixed-wing squadrons assigned to Marine Aviation Group 12 (MAG–12) and MAG–13, the 1st Service and 9th Engineer Support Battalions, and the 1st Hospital Company.

The 2d ROK Marine Brigade had been assigned a tactical area of operations within the Chu Lai region since August 1966. Although the Blue Dragons were not under the command of III Marine Amphibious Force (III MAF), Korean and American Marines coordinated their actions in defense of the base. The Blue Dragon Brigade was organized around three infantry battalions supported by a composite (105mm and 155mm) artillery battalion, heavy mortar company, an aviation detachment, and headquarters, service, medical, and security companies.

The 3d Battalion's 11th Company was assigned near the village of Tra Binh Dong. Capt Jung Kyung Jin, a graduate of the Korean Naval Academy's 15th Class (1961), commanded 294 Marines positioned in a clearing atop a small hill on the outskirts of the village. Within the 300-by 200-meter heart-shaped perimeter, the Marines built trenches connecting their fighting positions, mortar pits, and command posts. Barbed wire and claymore mines surrounded the trenches, and heavy and light machineguns were interspersed throughout the perimeter. Capt Jung's company was reinforced with a section of 4.2-inch mortars, a communications detachment, and supported by the brigade's 105mm and 155mm artillery batteries.

On 14 February 1967, at approximately 2320, an enemy force approached the company's perimeter from the west. A Marine in the observation post detected the movement and reported back to the 3d Platoon. Capt Jung quickly placed the company on alert. He waited until the platoon-sized unit closed to within 5 meters of the company's perimeter before ordering his Marines to fire. Flares lit up the sky, revealing one corpse tangled in the wire and the remaining Vietnamese withdrawing to the tree line. Believing that the objective of this attack was to test the Marines' defense, Capt Jung immediately prepared his company for the larger attack that would surely follow, assigning additional Marines to the listening posts, reapportioning ammunition, checking crew-served weapons, and reviewing fire support plans. Using the call sign "Seoul," Capt Jung ordered his platoon commanders to remain vigilant throughout the night.

At 0410, approximately 2,400 North Vietnamese soldiers began their attack on the 11th Company with an intense barrage of mortar and recoilless rifle fire. One battalion advanced from the southeast, blowing whistles, beating drums, and screaming "Tai Han ra di, ra di" (come out

Koreans) as they advanced on the 1st Platoon's position. Two minutes later, two more battalions attacked from the north to the 3d Platoon's sector. The Marines immediately responded with rifle and machinegun fire. Under attack from two directions, Capt Jung ordered the weapons platoon commander to direct fires from the company's mortars and provide a situation report to the battalion commander, while telling the forward observer to begin coordinating artillery support from the brigade's 105mm and 155mm batteries. Clad in a running shirt under his flak jacket, Capt Jung moved about the company's perimeter, assessing the situation and encouraging his Marines. Despite the intensity of direct and indirect fire weapons and claymore mines, the North Vietnamese continued to advance upon the company's position, attacking in human waves.

Rearmed and reequipped, the third wave of the assault attacked the 3d Platoon's position and destroyed the protective wire with Bangalore torpedoes. Led by soldiers armed with rocket propelled grenades and flamethrowers, the North Vietnamese attempted to infiltrate a platoon into the breach at approximately 0422. SSgt Bae Jang Choon's 1st Squad bore the brunt of the assault. Despite a serious wound to his right shoulder, SSgt Bae refused to abandon his position, ordering his Marines to stand their ground and prepare for hand-to-hand combat. The fighting shifted from rifles to grenades as North Vietnamese commanders continued to push soldiers into the breach. Entrenching tools, pix axes, and fists became the Marines' weapons when the North Vietnamese entered the trenches.

In the face of an overwhelming and relentless enemy, the actions of the squad were characterized by tenacity and selflessness. PFC Kim Myoug Deok killed 10 enemy soldiers with his automatic rifle as they crawled toward his position. Despite serious injuries received from hand-to-hand combat, Sgt Lee Hak Won took handgrenades in both hands, waited for the enemy to draw near, and detonated the grenades in a suicide attack that killed himself and four Vietnamese soldiers. PFC Lee Young Bok, who was the only member of the squad not to have been killed or injured at this point, lured the enemy toward his position, disappeared into a spider hole, then released several grenades as the soldiers entered the trench, temporarily obstructing the attack.

In the 1st Platoon sector, the North Vietnamese set up a mortar firing point that was now firing upon the company command post. 2dLt Shin Won Bae, 1st Platoon commander, immediately assembled an assault force to destroy the mortar position, located behind a group of rocks approximately 100 meters in front of his platoon's position. Ordering his squad leaders to provide covering fire, 2dLt Shin and his platoon sergeant, GySgt Kim Yong Kil, led a fire team toward the rocks amidst constant enemy fire. When they closed to within 20 meters of the objective, GySgt Kim threw two handgrenades toward the hidden enemy. At the instant the grenades exploded, the Marines moved forward, repeating this tactic until they reached the rocks. Twenty dead soldiers surrounded the three menacing tubes, which the Marines quickly seized and withdrew to the platoon's position.

On the other side of the perimeter, the entire 3d Platoon was engaged in hand-to-hand combat as they fought to hold their position against the Vietnamese attack. Discovering two soldiers attempting to take the Marines' 60mm mortars from the mortar pit, PFC Lee Ki On struck both in the face with the butt of his pistol, recovered the mortars, then killed the pair with a handgrenade. As two Marines fought enemy soldiers within the confines of the 4.2-inch mortar pit, a North Vietnamese armed with a flamethrower advanced on the pit, spewing flames. PFCs

Kim Bo Hyun and Yung Sang Yul dashed toward the enemy under cover of friendly fire, attacked the flamethrower with grenades in a spectacular explosion, and seized one light machinegun.

The North Vietnamese attempted the same tactic against the 1st Platoon, sending soldiers armed with two flamethrowers into the breach in the platoon's lines. 2dLt Shin and SSgt Oh Sung Hwan dashed toward the flames. Firing machineguns and throwing handgrenades, the two Marines killed the soldiers, seized the Soviet-made flamethrowers, and rallied the platoon to restore the perimeter.

Two hours into the attack, the Marines faced a grave situation. The North Vietnamese continued to attack from two directions, had breached the perimeter at both points of attack, and now held approximately one-third of the company's position. Believing that his position might be overrun, Capt Jung considered calling for a napalm strike on his own position from U.S. Marine Corps aircraft on station. However, the thick fog and rain made visibility so poor that even this desperate measure was not an option. More significantly, the ferocity of the enemy attack began to falter in the face of the desperate resistance by the 3d Platoon Marines. Capt Jung ordered the 2d Platoon commander to provide one squad to 3d Platoon to assist them in their fight.

At 0630 1stLt Kim Se Chang, the forward observer attached to the company, determined the likely location of the regimental command post and began directing fires from the brigade's 105mm howitzers against it. The Blue Dragon artillerymen responded with devastating fires that soon crippled the enemy's ability to direct the attack. His assistant, SSgt Kim Hyun Chul, refused to take the binoculars from his eyes despite intense small arms fire as he scanned the trees in search of the enemy's mortars. Locating the enemy 61mm, 81mm, and 120mm mortars, he reported their locations to his lieutenant who quickly passed them along to the fire direction center. The Marine artillery quickly overwhelmed the enemy mortars.

Isolated from their commander and lacking fire support, the North Vietnamese attack began to falter as casualties rapidly mounted. Capt Jung then made what would be the critical decision of the battle—assembling a squad-sized counterattack force from the 1st and 2d Platoons and ordering it into the breach to isolate the North Vietnamese soldiers within the perimeter. 1stLt Kim Ki Hong, the weapons platoon commander, volunteered to lead the Marines in a daring and courageous counterattack. As the 3d Platoon Marines and North Vietnamese soldiers engaged in hand-to-hand combat in the trenches immediately below the company's observation post, 1stLt Kim led his squad in a double envelopment of the North Vietnamese within the perimeter beginning at 0652. The lieutenant quickly killed five enemy soldiers with his pistol and began pushing the enemy back into the breach. Encouraged and emboldened by the attack, SSgt Kim Son Kwan, the 3d Platoon platoon sergeant, led his Marines in joining the assault, shouting and using whatever weapon was available to strike the enemy. With the North Vietnamese surrounded by the assault force, it was the Koreans turn to shout "ra di, ra di." The North Vietnamese refused calls to surrender and continued a desperate resistance, only to be shot to death by the Marines.

The soldiers who managed to escape the Marines linked up with North Vietnamese support units. In order to lure the company-sized force toward the Marine position, at 0724 Capt Jung ordered the 3d Platoon to destroy its bunkers and withdraw to the company observation post. 1st and 2d

Platoons were directed to envelop the attackers on order. Sensing victory, the North Vietnamese again began to beat gongs as they advanced upon the company for a final time. When they closed to within 80 meters, Capt Jung ordered his Marines to fire and began coordinating fires from the brigade's heavy mortar company. Shortly thereafter, the skies cleared and four U.S. Marine Corps A–4 Skyhawks repeatedly attacked the remaining Vietnamese force. Helicopters followed the attack aircraft and cut their path of retreat.

At 0800, 16 helicopters carrying the 6th Company, 2d Battalion arrived from the Blue Dragon Brigade headquarters. Advancing outward from the protective wire, the Marine reinforcements began clearing operations. The fleeing North Vietnamese left the bodies of 243 soldiers behind. An additional 60 soldiers were presumed to have been killed. As a testament to the ferocity of the battle, over 100 North Vietnamese corpses lay within the company's perimeter, and 140 bodies lay next to the protective wire. One of the two prisoners captured during the fighting was a North Vietnamese battalion commander. The company also captured 3 flamethrowers, 5 antitank rocket launchers, 2 machineguns, 28 rifles, 100 pieces of dynamite, and over 6,000 rounds of ammunition. The 11th Company lost 15 Marines during the fighting, and 33 were injured. Following the defeat, the North Vietnamese abandoned plans for subsequent attacks against the Chu Lai airbase and the city of Quang Ngai.

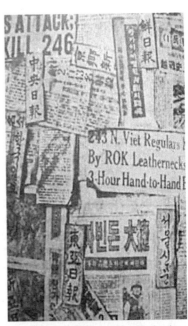

News of the battle traveled throughout the country and world. The commanding generals of III MAF and 2d ROK Marine Brigade went to Tra Binh Dong and met with the 11th Company Marines the morning of the battle. They were quickly followed by the commanders of I Corps, ROK Forces Vietnam, and the U.S. Military Assistance Command Vietnam. After being briefed on the battle, President Park Chung Hee directed that all enlisted Marines in the 11th Company be promoted one rank, the first unit-wide promotion since the Korean War. He also dispatched the Prime Minister, Defense Minister, and Marine Commandant to Vietnam. Defense Minister Kim Sung Eun—the most storied Marine commander of the Korean War, commander of the only other unit to be promoted en masse, and former Commandant—promoted the Marines on behalf of the President.

Newspaper headlines about the battle. All major Korean and English language papers, including the Chosun Ilbo, Dong-A Ilbo, Seoul Shinmun, Korea Herald, and Pacific Stars and Stripes, gave front page cover to accounts of the battle.

The Korean Government awarded more decorations for the battle of Tra Binh Dong than any other action of the Vietnam War. Capt Jung and 2dLt Shin received the Taeguk Medal, Korea's equivalent of the Medal of Honor; the Korean Government awarded the medal only 11 times during the war, and Tra Binh Dong was the only battle for which the medal was awarded to two individuals. GySgt Kim and SSgt Bae received the Ulchi Medal, Korea's second highest award for valor; the Chung Mu Medal, the third highest military decoration, was awarded to 11 Marines. The 11th Company received the U.S. and ROK Presidential Unit Citations in recognition of their "effective teamwork, aggressive fighting spirit and many individual acts of heroism."

Accounts of the battle were carried in media throughout the world. *The New York Times* reported the battle as the "South Korean's greatest victory in their 15 months in South Vietnam."[61] Following a briefing to foreign journalists, the phrase "Myth-Making Marines" began to appear in the press, continuing the legacy of the "Ghost-Catching Marines" and "Invincible Marines" of the Korean War.

---

[61] *'Koreans Kill 242 in Vietnam Clash'*, The New York Times, 16 February 1967

Bibliography

Abernethy, Iain, *Karate's Grappling Methods*. Neth Publishing, 1st edition

Clarke, Rick, *Pressure Point Fighting*. Tuttle Publishing, 2001

Clayton, Bruce.D, *Shotokan's Secret*. Ohara Publications, 2005

Cho, Hee Il, *The Complete Tae Kwon Do Hyung: Vol 1*. Master Cho, 1984

Choi, Hong Hi, *Taekwon-do*. Deaha Publication Company, 1965

Choi, Hong Hi, *Encyclopaedia Of Taekwon-do*. ITF, 1993

Choi, Hong Hi, *Taekwon-do And I: Vol 1*. ITF

Durand, LtCol James F, *"The Battle of Tra Binh Dong and the Korean Origins of the U.S. Marine Corps Martial Arts Program"*. Marine Corps Gazette

Hartman, Ron, *"Taekwondo Tutor"*. http://www.tkdtutor.com

He,Young, Kimm, Dr. *"Hong Hi – A Tae Kwon –Do History lesson"*. Taekwondo Times Magazine, January, 2000

Heron, Maria, *"Interview with General Choi Hong Hi, Founder of Taekwon-do"*. The Times, 1999

McCarthy, Patrick, *Ancient Okinawan Martial Arts: Korryu Uchinadi: Vol 2*. Tuttle Publishing , 1999

Oyama, Masutatsu, *Mas Oyama's Essential Karate*. Sterling Publishing Company, 1978

Prinz von Hohenzollern, Carl, *Meine Erlebnisse Wahrend Des Russisch-Japanischen Krieges, 1904-1905*. Berlin : Ernst Siegfried Mittler und Sohn, 1912

Thompson, Geoff, *Dead or Alive*. Summersdale Publishers, 1997

Thompson, Geoff, *Real Self Defence*. Summersdale Publishers, 1993

Webb, Karl, *"Taekwon-do Linage Tree"*. http://www.cska.co.uk

Wee, Colin, *Fighting Heaven and Earth*. Draft version of the manuscript, 2004

Author Unknown, *"Excerpt from an enemy directive (VietCong)"*. Seized July 22, 1966 (Published by Time Magazine, 24 February, 1967)

Author Unknown, *"A Savage Week"*. Time Magazine, 24 February, 1967

Author Unknown, *"Koreans Kill 242 in Vietnam Clash"*. The New York Times, 16 February 1967

Author's Unknown, Various *"Interviews With General Choi, Hong Hi"*. Combat Magazine, 1970's, 1980's, 1990's

Author Unknown, *"Biography of Grand Master Kong, Young Il, 9th Dan"*.
http://www.ictf.info/biographies.html

Authors Unknown, *"Dosan Online Memorial"*. http://www.ahnchangho.or.kr

Anslow, Stuart. "*Patterns: Are We Missing The Point*". Taekwon-do and Korean Martial Arts Magazine, March 2001

Anslow, Stuart. *"Grappling For Kicks"*. Taekwon-do and Korean Martial Arts Magazine, August 2001

Anslow, Stuart. *"An Interview with Grandmaster Kong Young Il."* Taekwon-do and Korean Arts Magazine, November 2004

Notes

Lightning Source UK Ltd.
Milton Keynes UK
UKOW020903070312

188389UK00011B/1/P